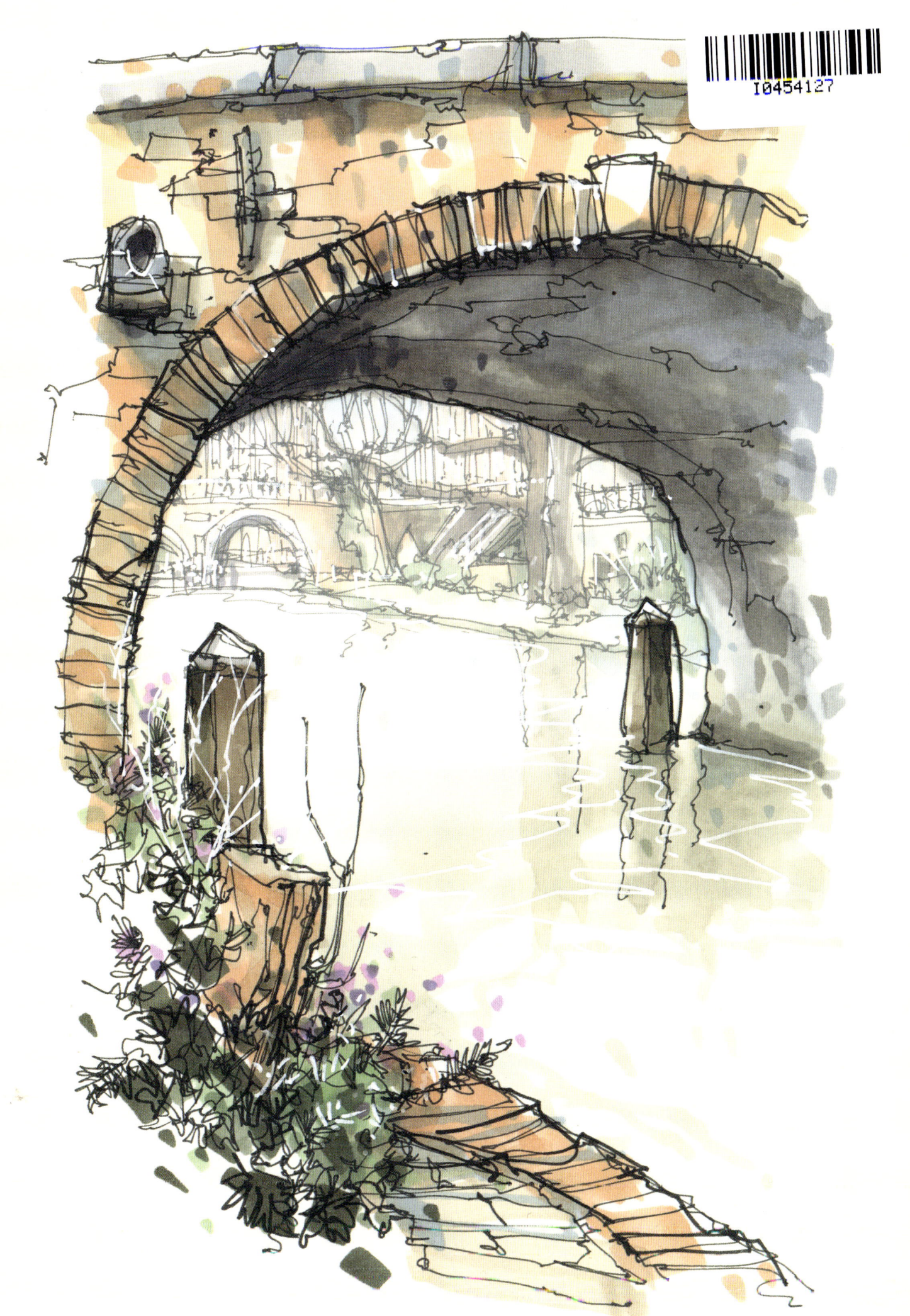

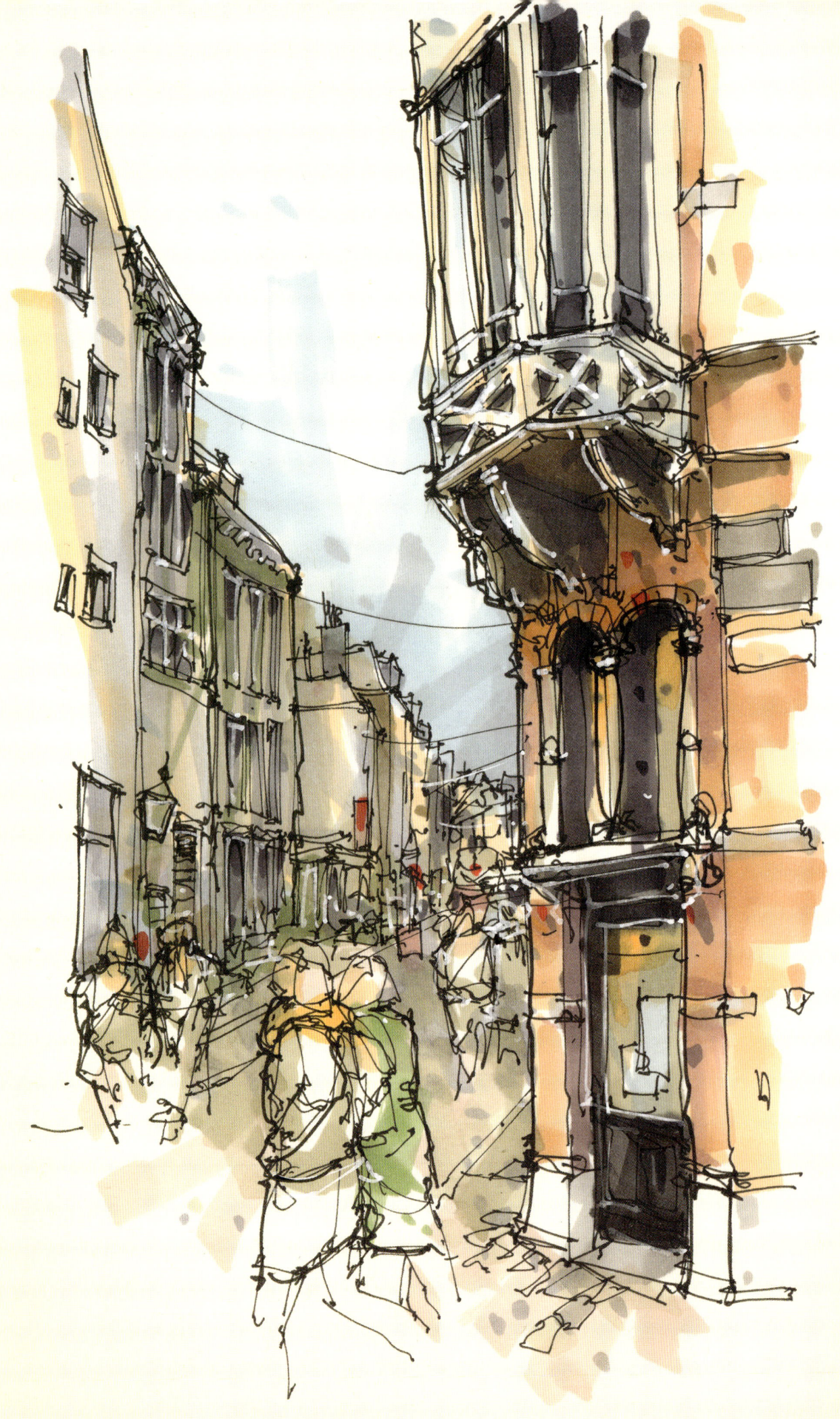

HOUSESKETCHING

Learn to Create
Energetic and Expressive
Architectural Drawings

Albert Kiefer

Housesketcher

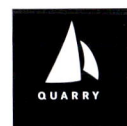

Quarto.com

© 2024 Quarto Publishing Group USA Inc.
Text, Photos, Illustrations © 2024 Albert Kiefer

First Published in 2024 by Quarry Books,
an imprint of The Quarto Group,
100 Cummings Center, Suite 265-D,
Beverly, MA 01915, USA
T (978) 282-9590   F (978) 283-2742

EEA Representation, WTS Tax d.o.o.,
Žanova ulica 3, 4000 Kranj, Slovenia.
www.wts-tax.si

Quarry Books titles are also available at discount for retail, wholesale, promotional, and bulk purchase. For details, contact the Special Sales Manager by email at specialsales@quarto.com or by mail at The Quarto Group, Attn: Special Sales Manager, 100 Cummings Center, Suite 265-D, Beverly, MA 01915, USA.

10 9 8 7 6 5

ISBN: 978-0-7603-8910-2

Digital edition published in 2024
eISBN: 978-0-7603-8911-9

Library of Congress Cataloging-in-Publication Data

Names: Kiefer, Albert (Artist), author.
Title: Housesketching : learn to create energetic and
    expressive architectural drawings / Albert Kiefer,
    Housesketcher.
Description: Beverly, MA : Quarry, 2024. | Includes
    index. | Identifiers: LCCN 2024010063 (print) |
    LCCN 2024010064 (ebook) | ISBN 9780760389102
    (paperback) | ISBN 9780760389119 (ebook)
Subjects: LCSH: Buildings in art. | Architecture in
    art. | Drawing—Technique.
Classification: LCC NC825.B8 K54 2024 (print) |
    LCC NC825.B8 (ebook) | DDC 743/.84—dc23/
    eng/20240325
LC record available at
    https://lccn.loc.gov/2024010063
LC ebook record available at
    https://lccn.loc.gov/2024010064

Cover Images: Albert Kiefer
Design and Page Layout: Laura Shaw Design

Printed in Guangdong, China TT102025

TO ALL THE SILENT AND TIMID ONES,
YOU MATTER!

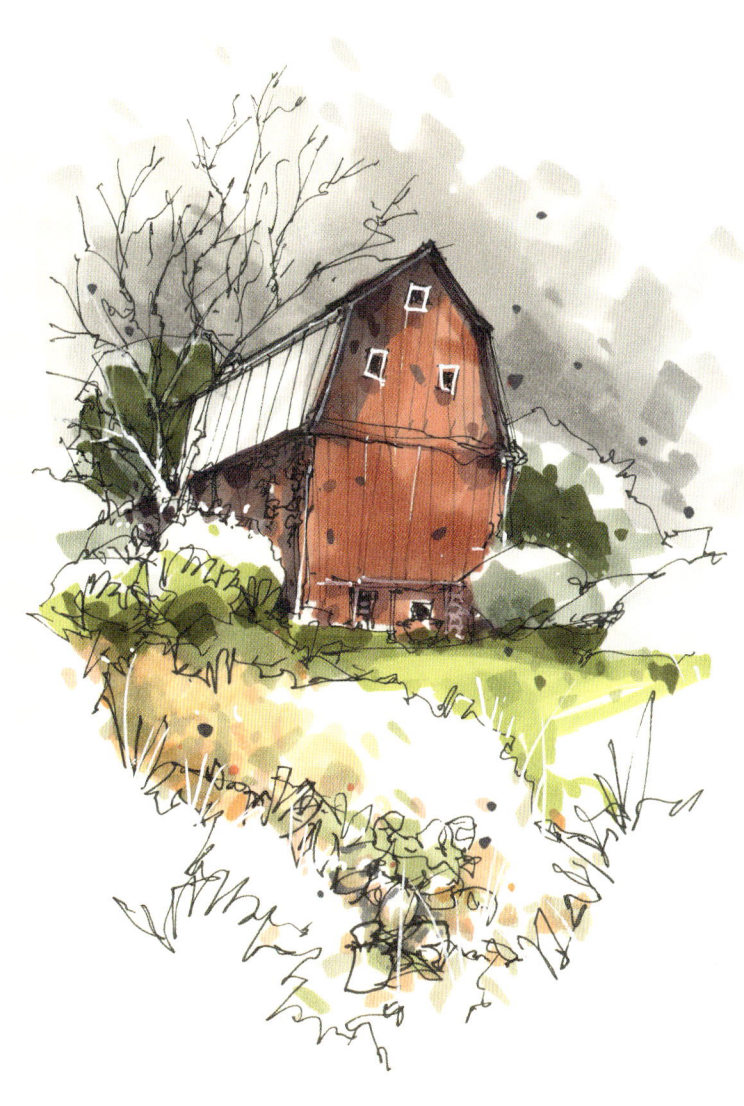

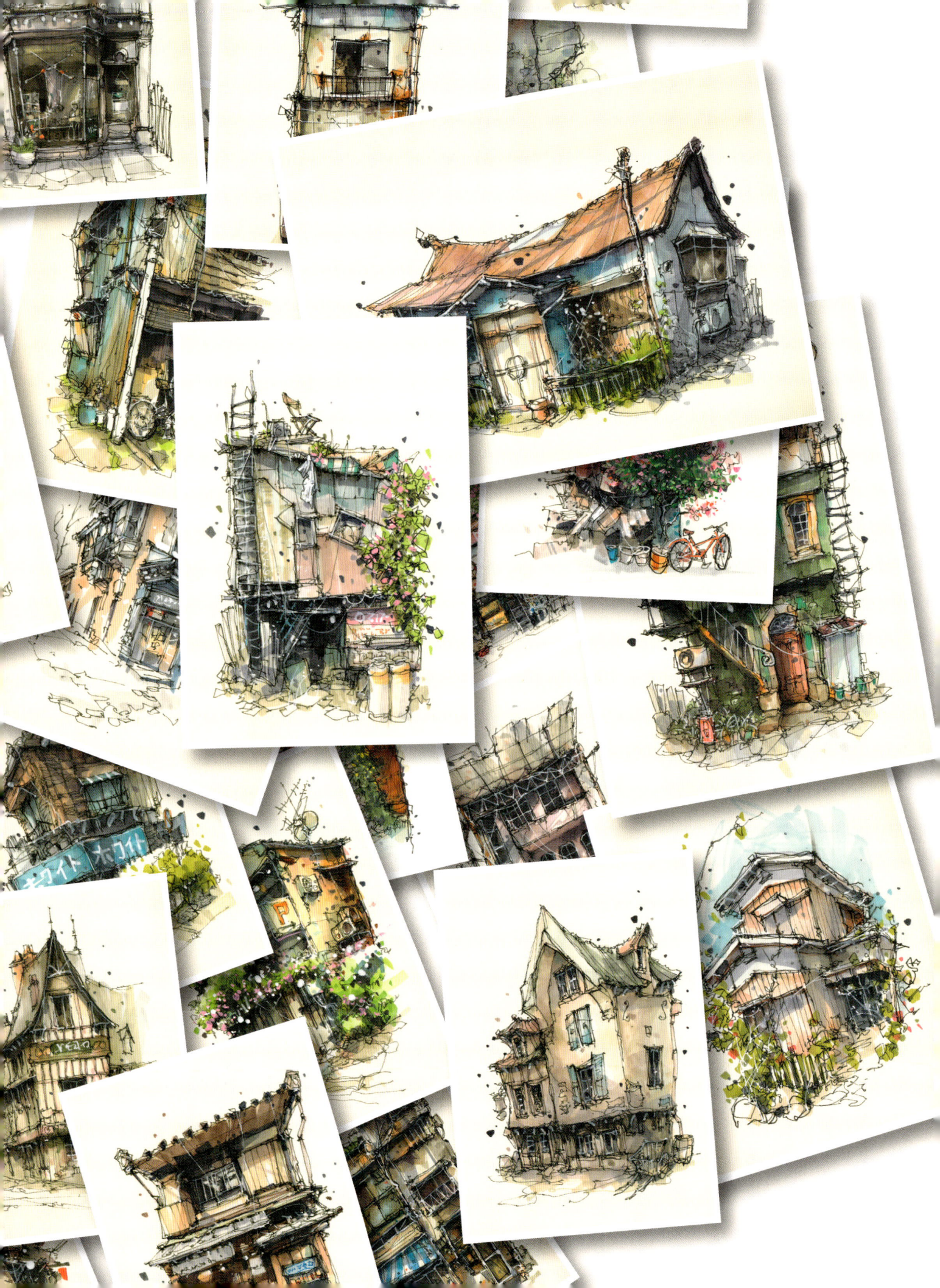

CONTENTS

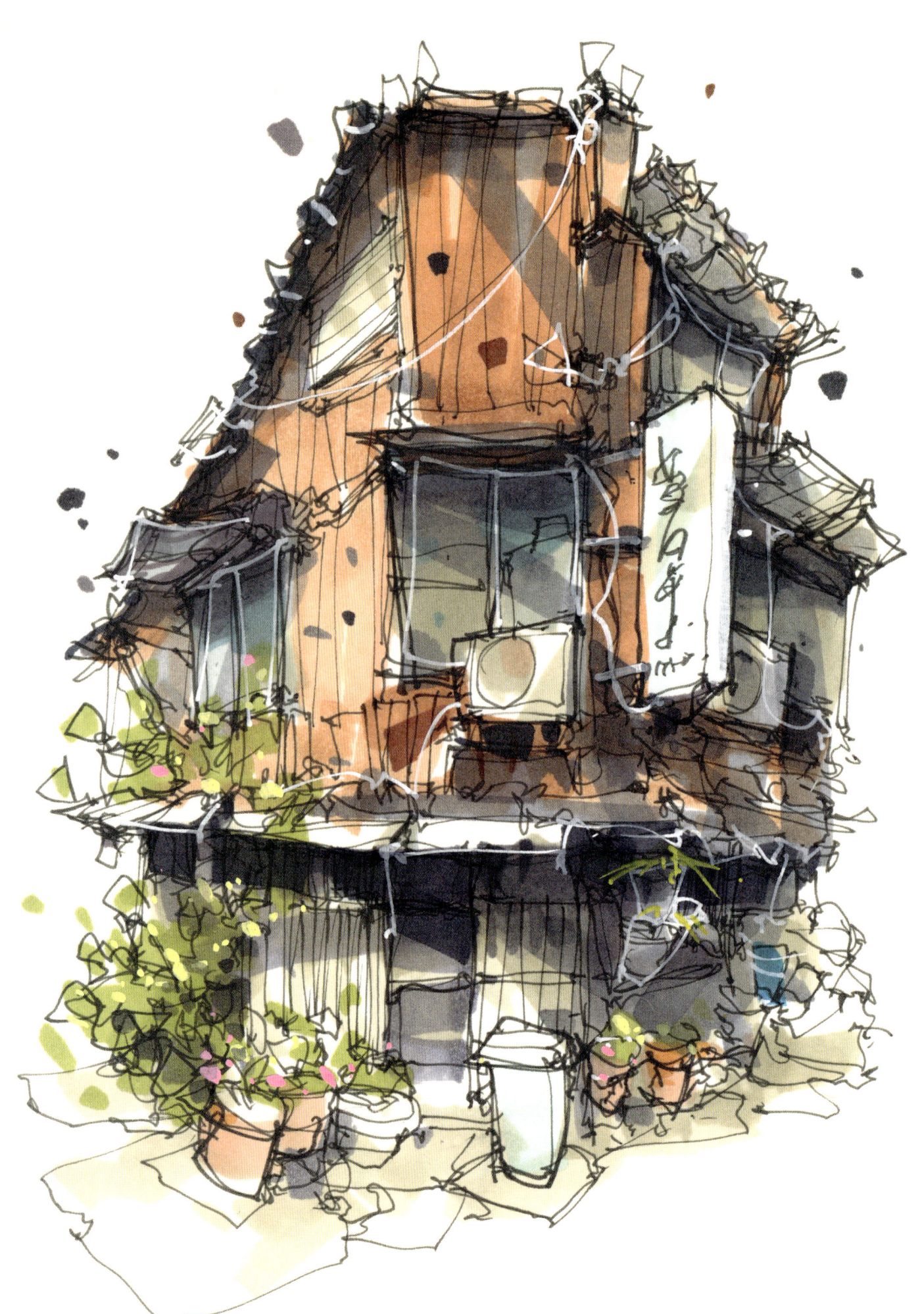

INTRODUCTION

Wow! You, holding this book in your hands, is something that was beyond my wildest dreams, when in 2016 I started picking up some random materials to try to get back into sketching again. Just something to rekindle my traditional drawing skills. No plans for markers and certainly not for sketching houses. And now look where we are!

With this book I would like to share things that I discovered and learned about sketching over the past seven years. By no means do I intend this to be a textbook on how to sketch. It describes the path I took to sketching, and how I figured things out that work for me and what things don't.

It will discuss the techniques of working with the combination of fineliners, markers, and white acrylic pens that I have slowly developed. What I want to stress is that this certainly is not the only way. It just turned out that this haphazardly chosen bunch of tools and materials worked wonderfully for me! Alcohol-based markers are an amazingly fast medium to color your sketches with.

I encourage you to look and work through this book, experiment, improvise, and explore. Hopefully this book will be a wonderful and valuable jump-off point for your own sketching endeavors. Through sketching, you are going to discover a brand-new and rich world that will open up to you. A world that has always been there. But, until now, you have never quite experienced this way.

Enjoy your journey!

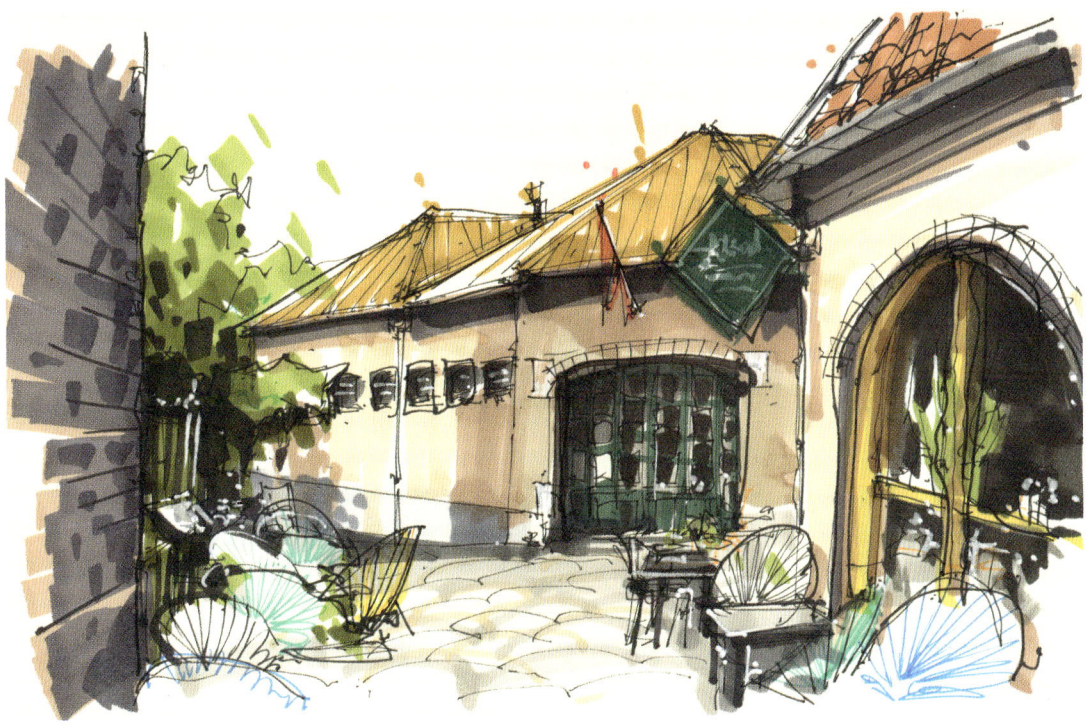

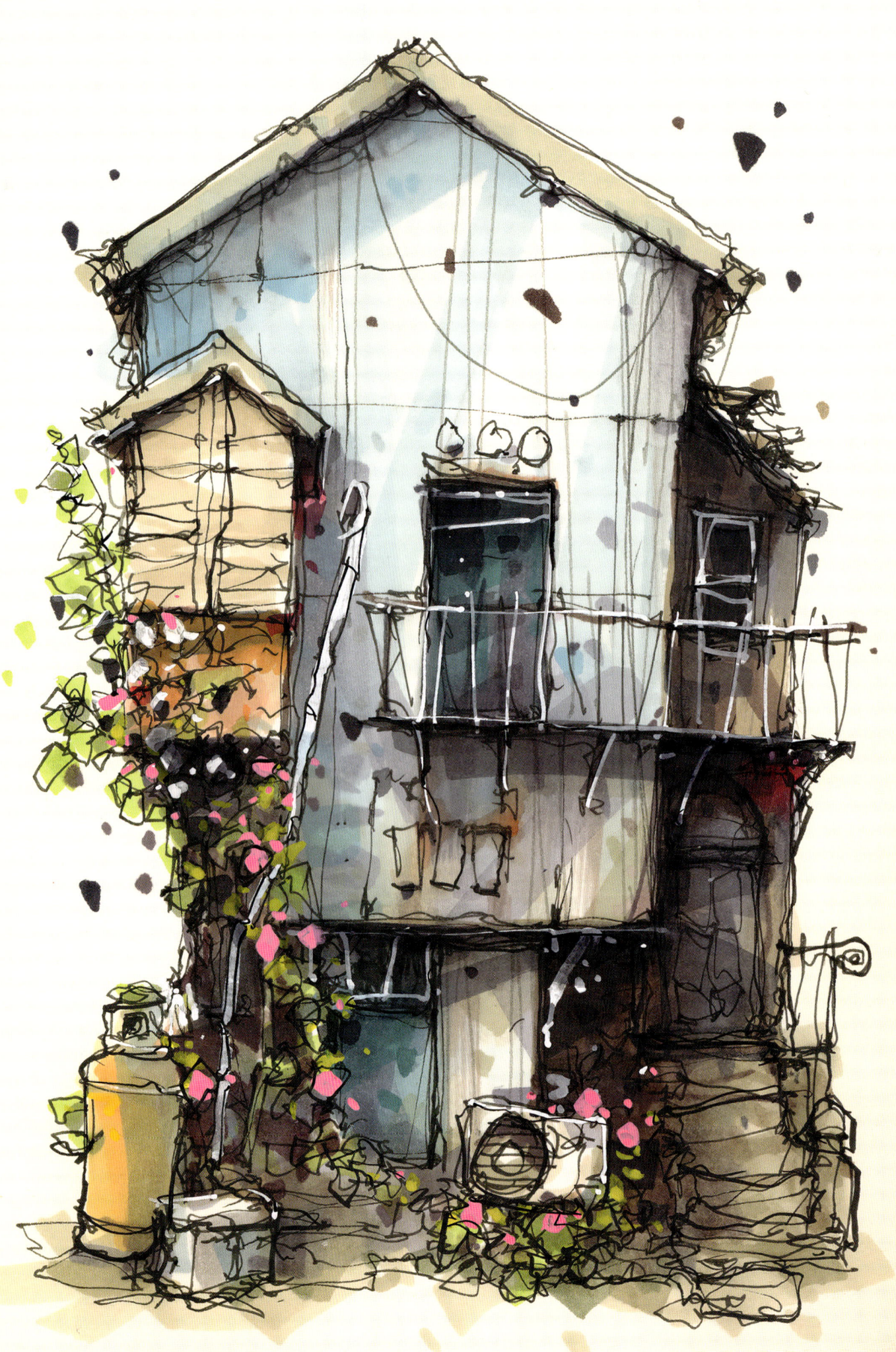

1

MY APPROACH

In this chapter, I will show you the way that I have
learned to approach creating sketches, from showing some of
my favorite materials (that I randomly bought but got to know
quite intimately) to gathering source material for inspiration and
explaining my way of thinking about how I look at sketching.

MY FAVORITE MATERIALS

There are so many types of paper, sketchbooks, markers, and other art supplies available that it can be overwhelming to know what to use. In this section, I will tell you why I use the supplies I do, but I encourage you to try others to see what works best for you.

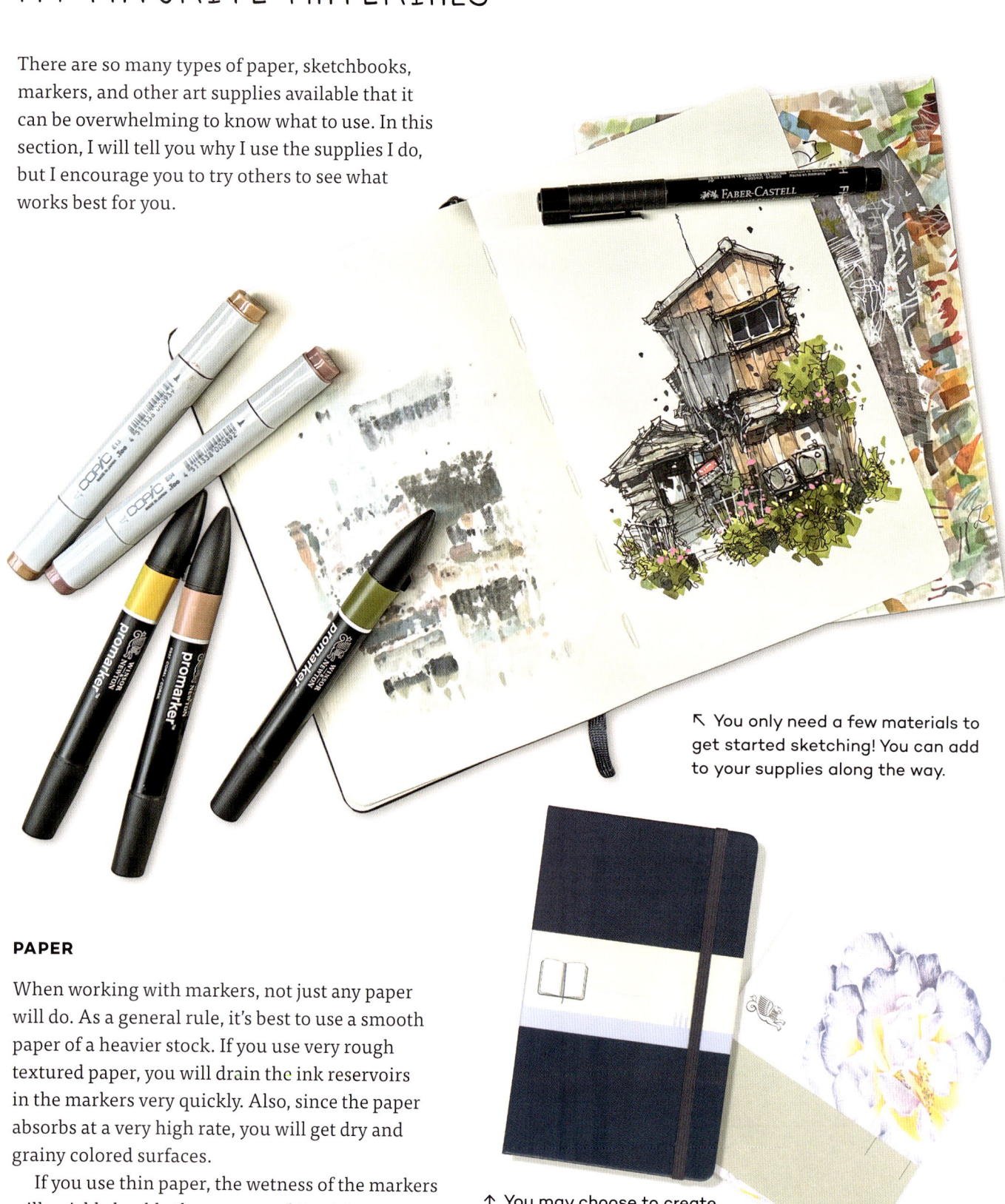

↖ You only need a few materials to get started sketching! You can add to your supplies along the way.

↑ You may choose to create your sketches in a sketchbook, on flat paper, or both, depending on the situation.

PAPER

When working with markers, not just any paper will do. As a general rule, it's best to use a smooth paper of a heavier stock. If you use very rough textured paper, you will drain the ink reservoirs in the markers very quickly. Also, since the paper absorbs at a very high rate, you will get dry and grainy colored surfaces.

If you use thin paper, the wetness of the markers will quickly buckle the paper, and it might even start to disintegrate. Luckily, the alcohol in the markers (I always use alcohol-based markers) will evaporate almost instantly and prevent the paper from falling apart, unlike with water-based markers that don't dry as quickly.

Sketchbooks

Ever since I started sketching, I've been using Moleskine sketchbooks. My favorite is the Moleskine Art Collection large sketchbook. It has a very nice and portable size and a pleasant 111 lb. paper that can take a lot of punishment from markers and fineliners. However, beware that the paint pens I use, which are water based, will quickly destroy the paper! Moleskine is not specially developed for markers. There is a special bleed-proof paper, but I don't like it because it's very thin and very white. I have come to like the warmth from the slightly off-white paper in the Moleskine Art Collection sketchbooks. There are several sizes to choose from: Pocket: 3.5 x 5.5 inches (9 x 14 cm), Large: 5 x 8.25 inches (12.7 x 21 cm), A4: 8.25 x 11.75 inches (21 x 30 cm), and A3: 11.75 x 16.5 inches (30 x 42 cm).

The larger sizes (actually, large is still comfortably small), starting from size A4, can be a little unpractical for marker use. This is due to the nib width of the markers. That width starts to look very tiny on a larger sized paper, and it diminishes the expressive, powerful stroke character that you see in my sketches.

Loose Paper

Whenever I need a flat sheet of paper, usually for commissioned works, I use Winsor & Newton smooth-grain cartridge pads. They come closest to the feel of Moleskine paper. These pads come in different sizes, from A5 all the way up to a gigantic (sort of) A2. Keep in mind that sketching on large sheets has its challenges. Even the broad strokes of chisel-point markers will feel small and feeble. And filling larger areas becomes an impossible task. So I limit my sketches to a maximum size of A3.

TIP If you do want a dry, grainy effect, use an almost-dried-out marker.

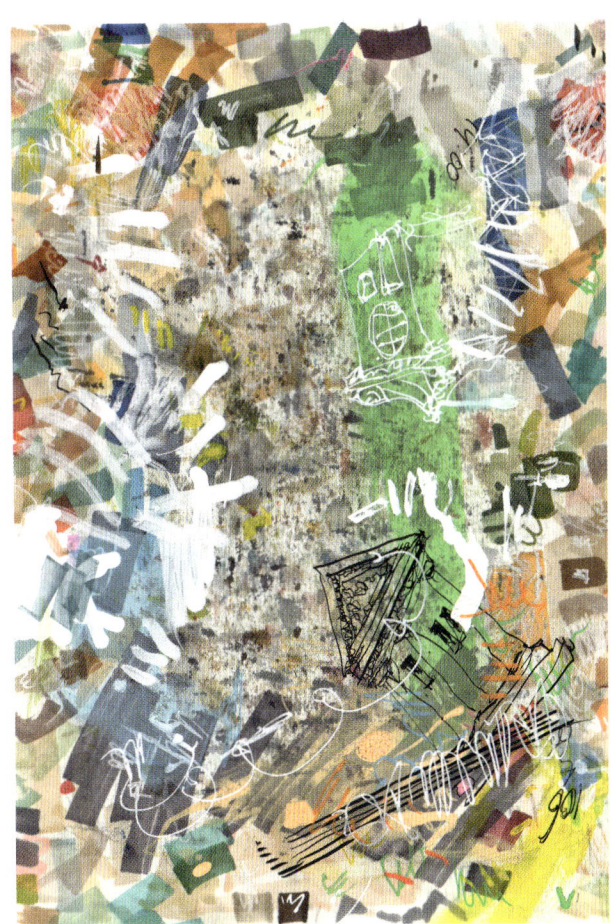

THE ALL-IMPORTANT BLEED SHEET

Then there is one very important piece of paper that does not need to be of any fantastic quality apart from being able to take a lot of punishment. And that is the "bleed sheet." If you're going to work in sketchbooks, this piece of paper will save you from ruining many valuable sketching pages. Alcohol-based markers bleed through the Moleskine and Winsor & Newton paper without mercy. You will easily punch through to the next page without protection. And with lots of heavy blending, you can even burn through two underlying sheets! So use that faithful bleed sheet. You will immediately notice when you forget to put it behind your current sketch page!

You may know markers from your times as a child. All those brightly colored pens of various shapes and sizes to color your castles and spaceships with.

What you might not realize is that they're very well suited for coloring your sketches in a wonderfully evocative way. Let's take a look!

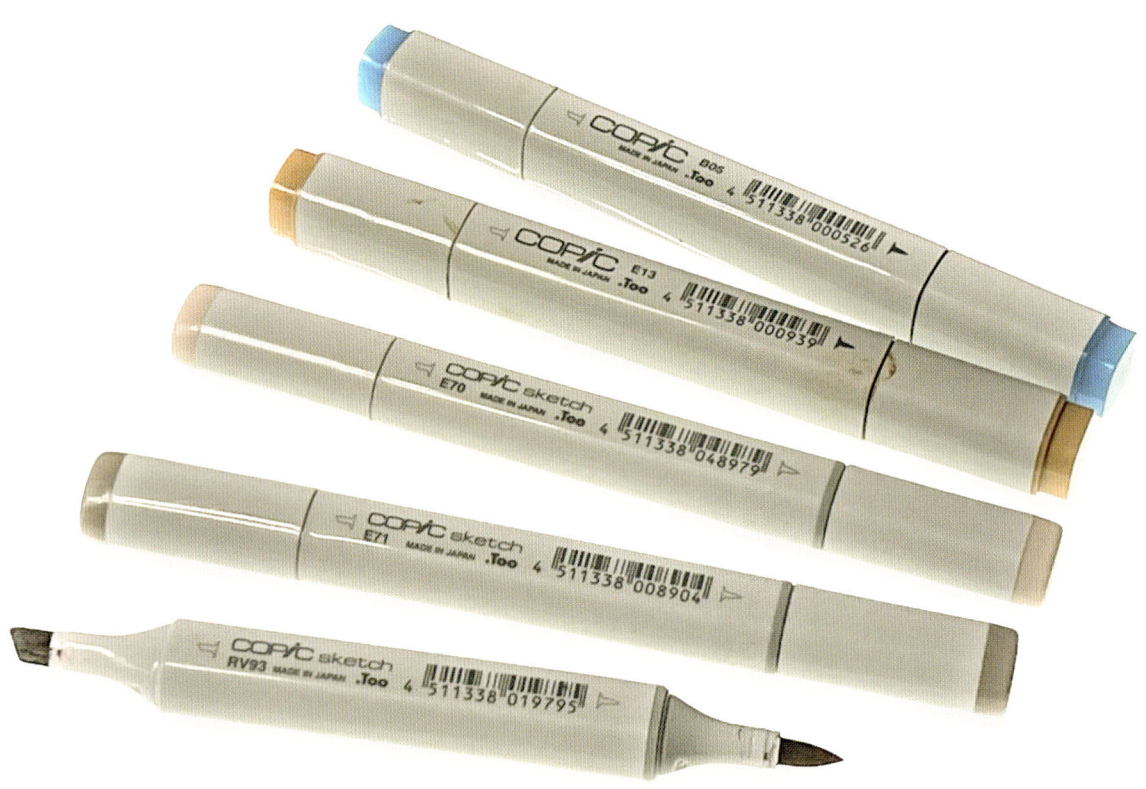

Copic markers.

Alcohol-Based vs. Water-Based

There are many different kinds of markers. But the main distinction is alcohol-based markers versus water-based markers. The type that I use is alcohol based. That has a distinct advantage: the colored sections dry almost instantly. So it allows for very rapid sketching and coloring. The disadvantage is that there is a very high bleed-through. If you don't put a "bleed sheet" between your sketching page and the next, you will see ugly stains appearing on that next page, ruining not only the backside of your current page but the following pages as well.

Another disadvantage is a result of that quick drying process. It is harder to create nice gradients and blends without really soaking the paper surface with ink. It is possible, but it will also result in heavier bleed-through, so always be sure to put a thick piece of bleed paper behind your sketch.

Water-based markers are great for blends and gradients but can quickly destroy a paper structure, especially if you don't use the right paper. Another big drawback is that they take a long time to dry. That's a dealbreaker for me.

Scan to watch a comparison of markers

Nibs

Most markers currently on the market have two nibs: the points with which you color your work. Depending on the brand and name, this is usually one broad chisel-shaped nib and either a sturdy pointed tip or a soft brush tip. It depends on the type of work you want to do if you need the brush nib or the sturdy pointed tip. In my sketches, I usually go for the chiseled nib.

Brands

There are a lot of brands of markers, and I will list some of them in the Resources section of the book. The two brands I use are Winsor & Newton and Copic.

Winsor & Newton (W&N) has an excellent range of colors, and some of their colors still rank among my favorites that I use all the time. They have two types: the Promarker and the Promarker Brush. They both have a nice broad chiseled nib, and the latter has a brush tip on the other side. The Promarker Brush is a little more expensive. Unfortunately, both W&N ranges are non-refillable and lacking in the darker ranges of values, so you cannot go quite as punchy as with the Copic markers.

Copic has three series of markers. The cheapest and least range of colors is the Ciao range. The Copic Classic is the range I like to use most. But actually, the Copic Sketch series has the broadest range of colors.

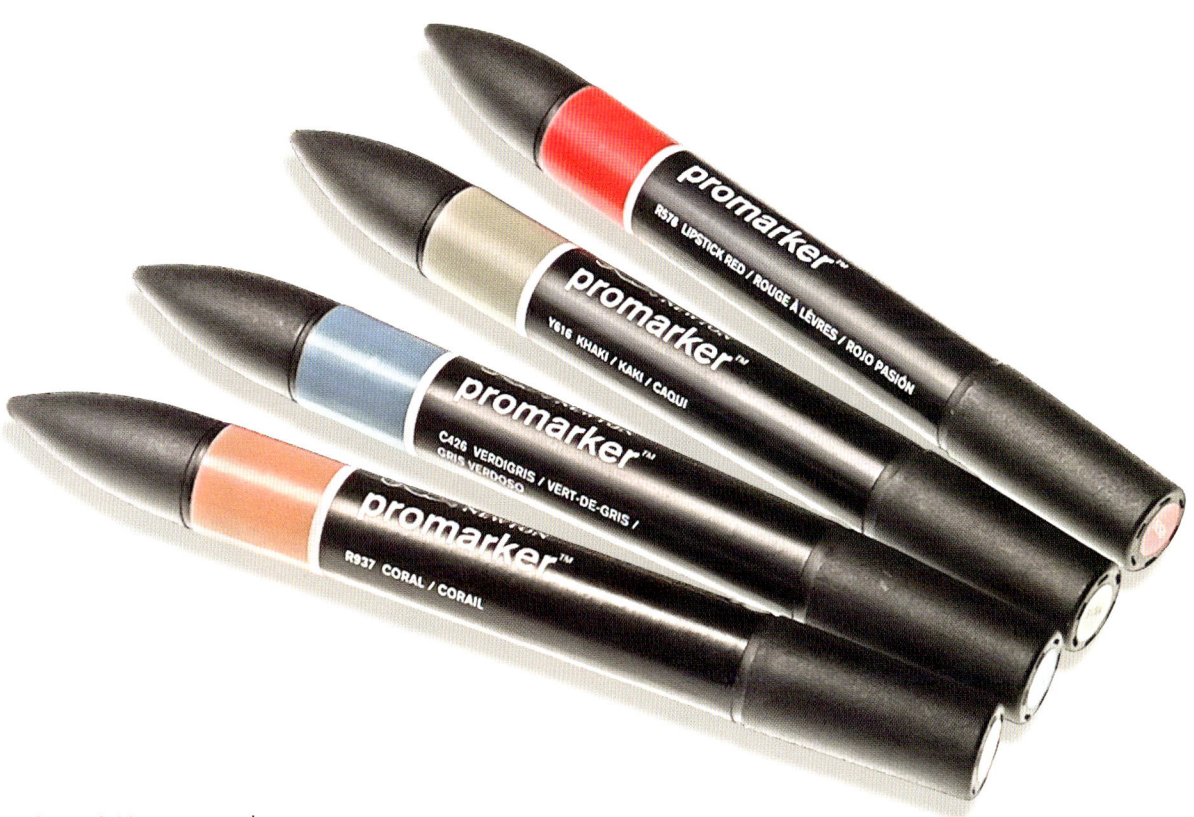

Winsor & Newton markers.

Fineliners

You need something to draw lines with. It's basically that simple. There's no fixed requirement for the type of tool that is. I grabbed a couple of fineliners when I first started—a thicker and thinner one. Using one or the other would allow me to vary the line width in my sketches. Let's take a closer look at the ones I have at the moment.

I use Faber-Castell fineliners in different thicknesses. I typically start my sketches with a 0.1 (XS) weight, and make accent lines with a 0.3 (S) weight. Currently, I'm also experimenting with a Fude nib from this brand. But that is a bit of a false name for that nib because it's actually more of a very sturdy brush tip. It's very stiff, but allows for a varying line width in a single pen. The ink in these pens is waterproof and lightproof, which is great. But don't let the waterproof fool you. Since the markers that I work with are alcohol-based, there will be some smearing. And the heavier the lines, and also the smoothness of the paper, will result in the ink giving way to the marker strokes. Having worked with the combination of these Faber-Castells and markers for seven years now, I don't find that little smearing a big deal. And it will add to the character of the sketch as well. But it's always a good thing to be aware of it.

There are many brands and options to choose from, and I will list some in the appendix of this book for you.

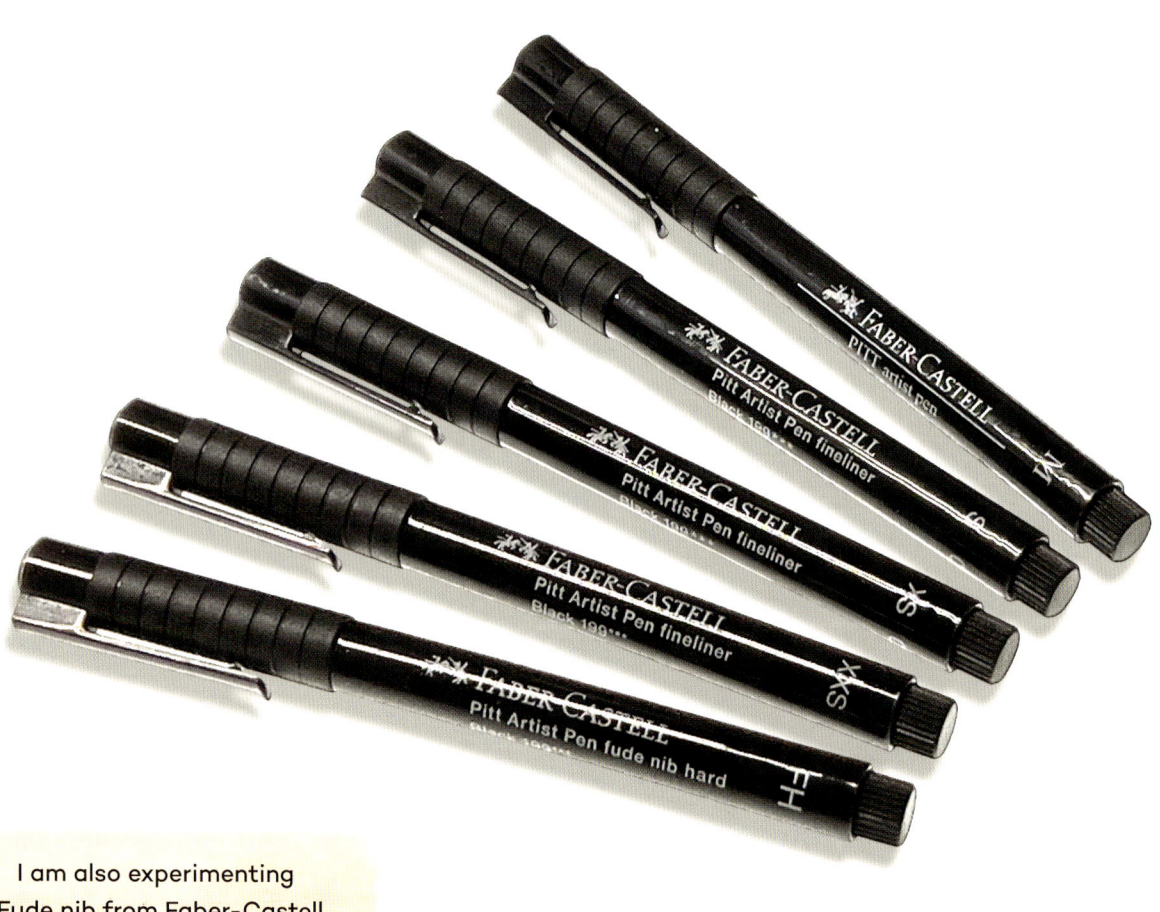

TIP I am also experimenting with a Fude nib from Faber-Castell. It's actually more of a very sturdy brush tip that allows for a varying line width in a single pen. It's very nice to work with.

Faber-Castell fineliners.

Paint Pens

I use paint pens to apply light lines over dark areas. Remember that when working with markers, you work from light to dark. When you finish most of your coloring, you will have some areas that would benefit from bringing back lighter lines. That could be window framing or flowers that are located in a dark shaded area. You could try to leave these areas untouched while sketching, but that would take both the speed and spontaneity out of a sketch, since you would try to avoid touching these places. One of the really important and characteristic traits of markers is their expressively flowing strokes. They radiate energy. When disrupting this flow and trying to avoid certain spots, you will get a very blobby forced look.

Paint pens all have the same annoyances to them. They clog up, and sometimes they give very washed-out milky lines that can hardly function as accent lines at all. But always keep in mind that things don't have to behave perfectly. It's all part of the process and, in the end, will add character to your sketch. A very important thing to keep in mind is that you don't get carried away by the white lines effect. This will turn your sketch into a white confetti fest. So after having applied the white lines or dots and blobs, I go over them with a medium-dark color or gray marker to blend them back into the sketch. This results in a really pleasing and convincing depth effect.

Just as with the fineliners, there are many brands and thicknesses of paint pens, and I will list some of them in the Resources. Here you will see the brand that I typically use—Uni Posca acrylic pens. They come in different thicknesses and sizes, depending on what type of effect you are after.

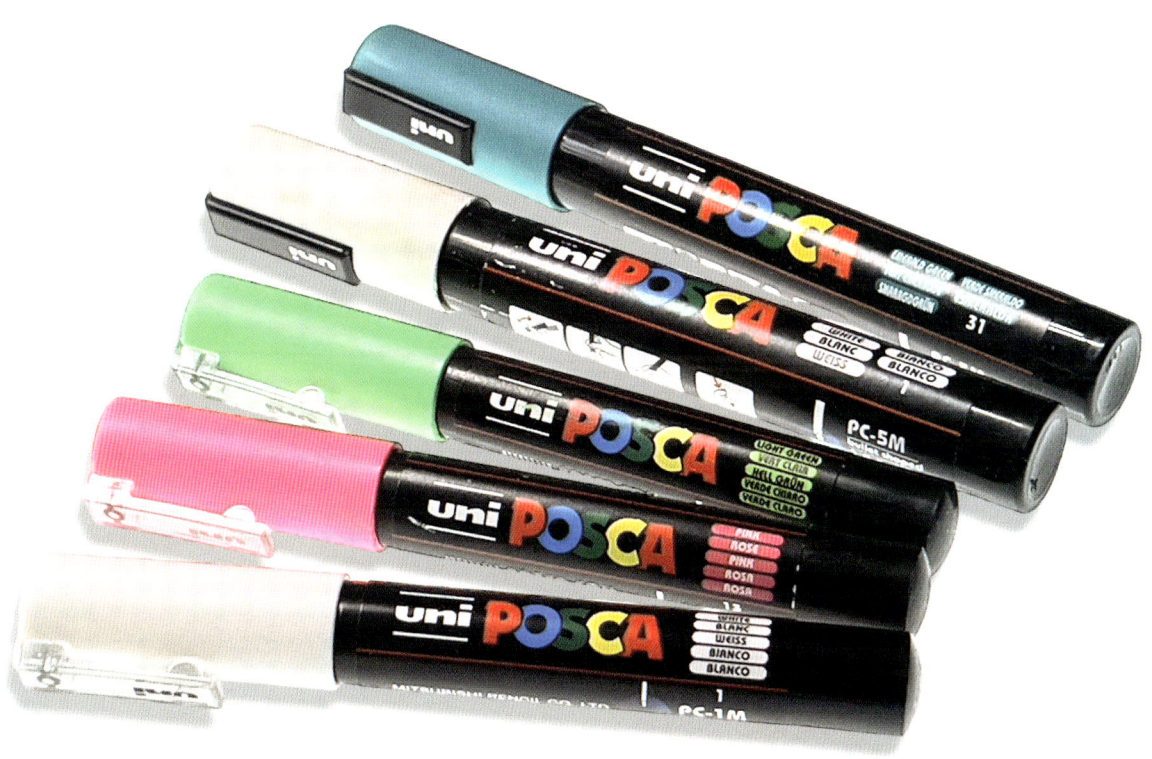

Posca paint pens.

CREATING A COLOR CHART

A color chart can be an invaluable tool in making color choices. Once you start accumulating lots of colors, maybe even from many different brands, it is essential that you know exactly what a certain color looks like on paper. Usually the colors you see printed on the label, or the plastic cap, can be quite far removed from the actual color. For that purpose, I create a color chart on the exact paper that I use the markers on.

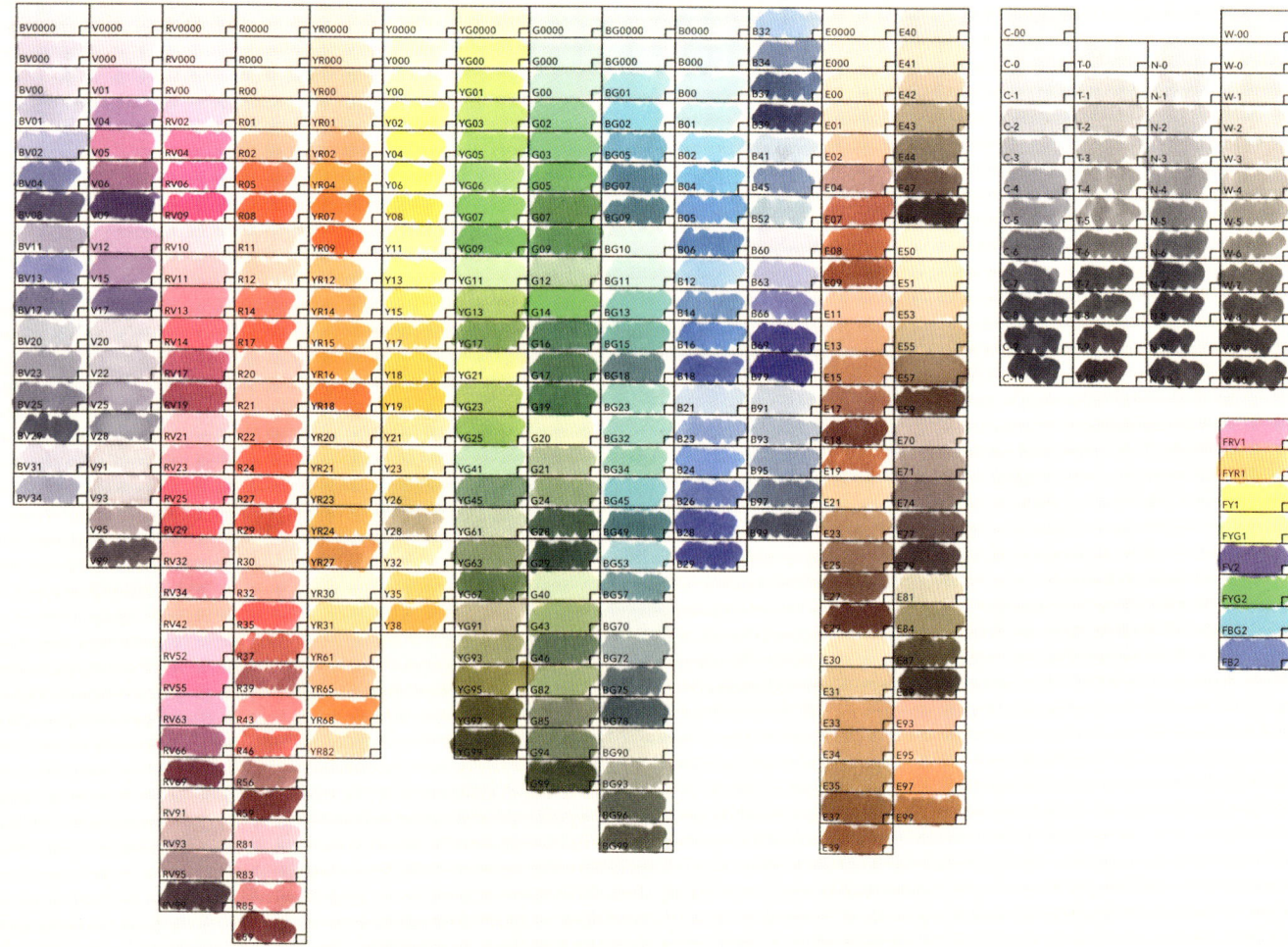

↑ I keep a record of my Copic marker colors on Moleskine paper, the same I use for my sketches so I can see exactly how they will look.

→ I also keep a record of my Winsor & Newton marker colors.

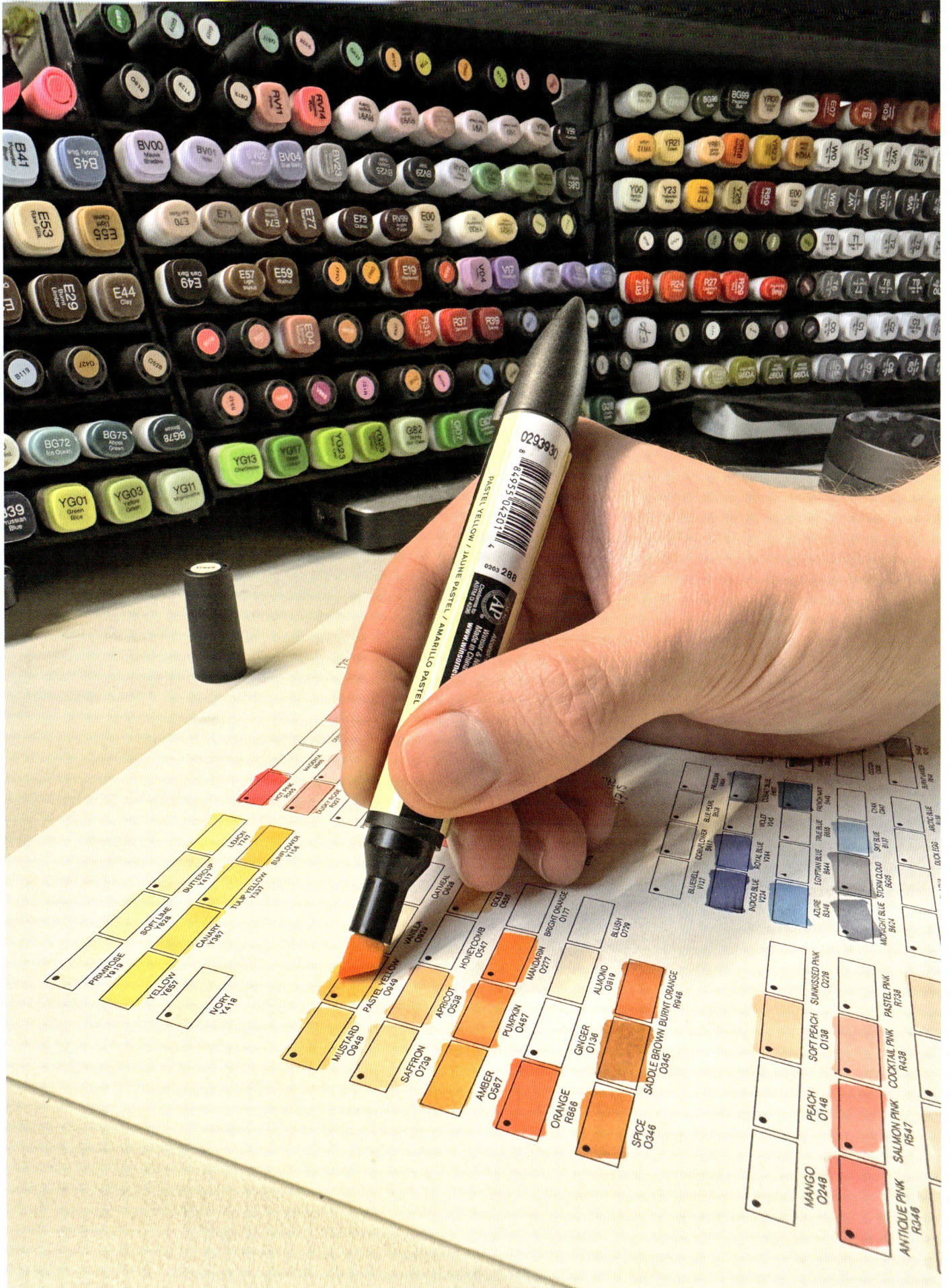

GATHERING SOURCE MATERIAL

The way I approach any new project involves a couple of simple steps. The first one is to pick a subject. I cannot understate the importance of that! I discovered when I started out that I lost a lot of time hunting for something to sketch. So a good strategy to minimize the search time and fully optimize the sketching time is to have subject matter at the ready all the time. This can be achieved in many ways, of course. Here are some of the ones I consider.

- On site
- Taking photos
- Look for online resources

ON SITE

On site, or *en plein air*, is a very tactile way to be involved in your subject matter. You can study your subject intensely, check it from various angles, and get a lot of extra information on the environment your subject is located in. And of course, you are right there sharing that same environment!

TAKING PHOTOS

Taking photos is another very nice way of collecting subject matter. It can be done very quickly and it allows you to store these visual memories for later use. Depending on your personality and available time, you are in control of when you want to make use of them. For me, I have a busy day schedule with my work as a CG artist. That means I cannot control the moment when I have time available to sketch. That might be at the end of the day, or even at night. Photos can also be advantageous in times when the weather is not playing nice. I am not a person who wants to sit in the cold while sketching or wants to get soaking wet. The main drive for me is to sketch as frequently as possible, so on site and working from photographic reference are the best for me. One disadvantage of photos is of course that they are flat. You cannot judge depth all that well, except for perspective cues, and sometimes it can be hard to interpret what you see in a photo.

ONLINE RESOURCES

And talking about photos . . . in this age of Google, Pinterest, Instagram, and other image-based services, it is a treasure-trove resource of finding great material to sketch! There are so many great references out there to choose from. So many, in fact, that it can become a time-drain. Before you know it, you find yourself browsing through all these wonderful photos, hour upon hour, without putting a single sketch line on paper! For that reason I would encourage you to create a folder, or use a software program, that can act as a visual reservoir for subjects to sketch.

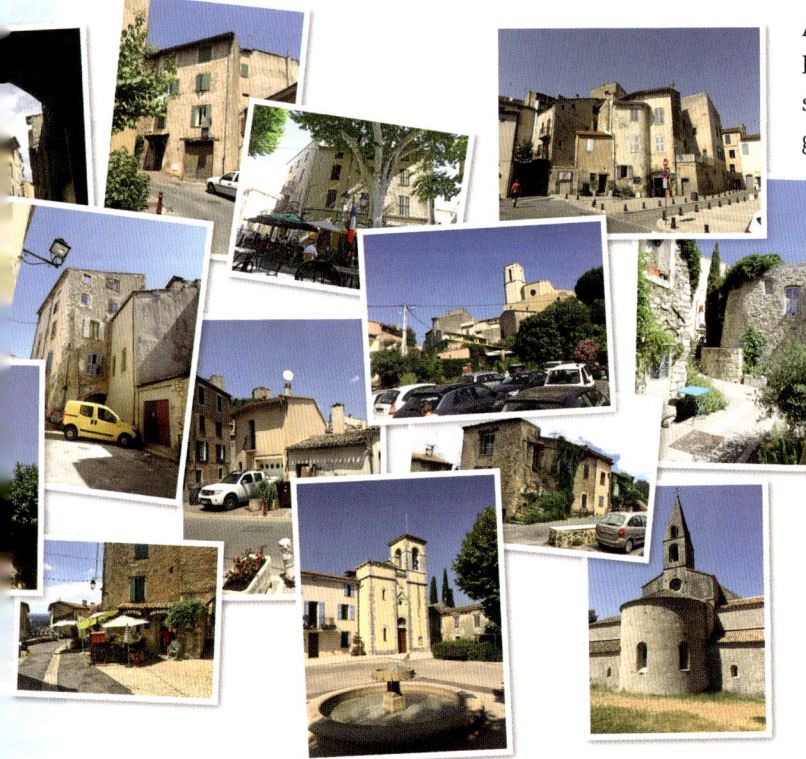

← Use your smartphone or digital camera to snap shots of interesting scenes.

→ Sketching on location is a great way to soak up the energy of a place.

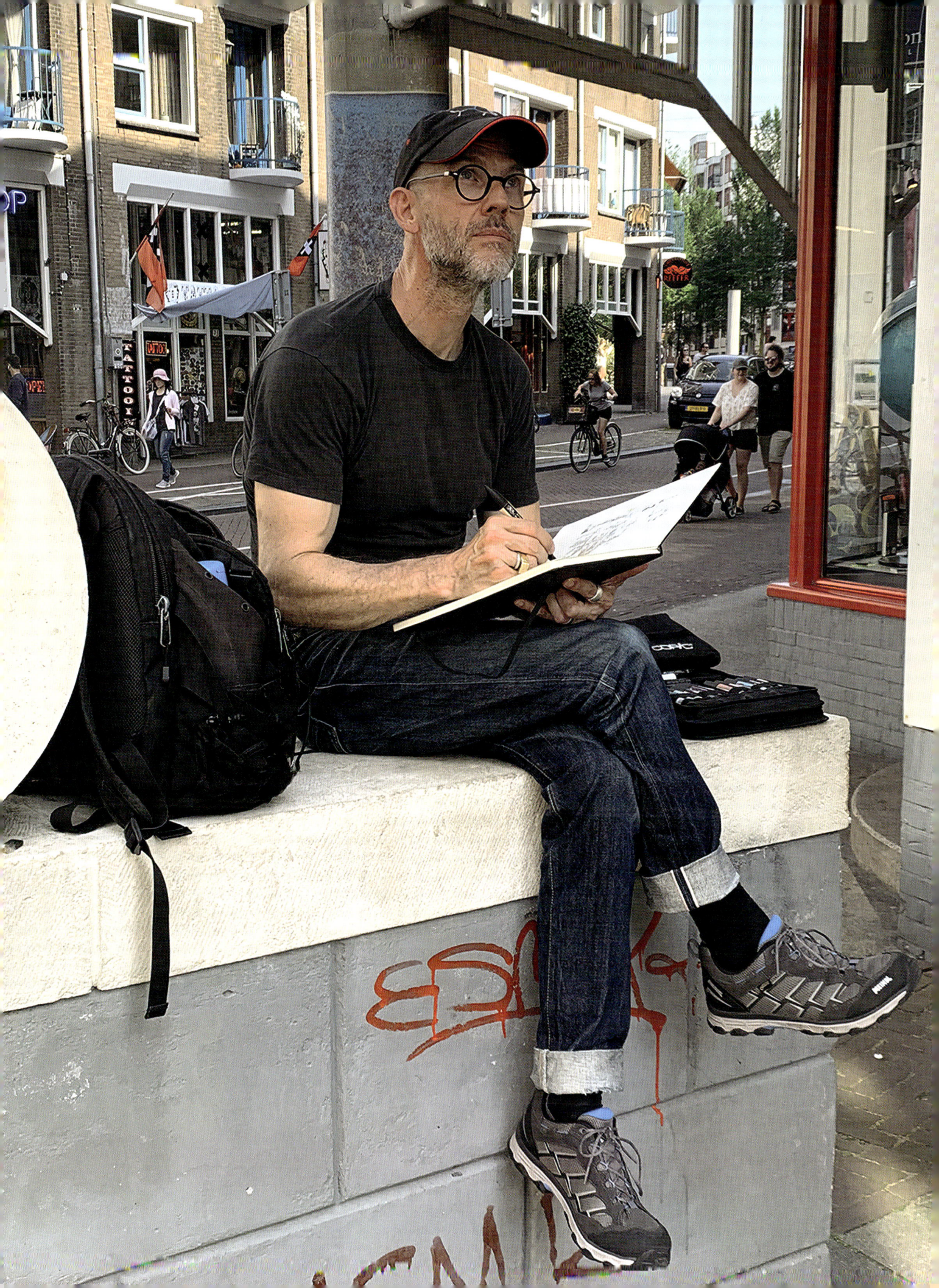

SKETCHING ON THE GO

I'd like to start out this section with a quote, attributed to the famous French street photographer Henri Cartier-Bresson. He was asked about what the best camera was for shooting photos. His answer was simple and very much to the point: "The one you have with you."

When you're planning to sketch on location or expect to be traveling about and intend to quickly capture a scene, it's vital to travel light. You're not going to lug along a huge set of materials and a big sketchbook everywhere you go. It's impractical. I happen to have a very nice digital camera with some great lenses that are interchangeable. But in practice, I shoot almost everything with my phone. It's always with me and I can grab it when I see something interesting. So, when I'm traveling or visiting a place, I usually just carry my trusted A5 Moleskine sketchbook, a fineliner, and a very limited set of colors that allow me to quickly jot down a scene. The colors always translate to a range of values (light to dark). The light and dark distribution, more than anything else, will give your sketch depth and "body."

Almost all marker manufacturers sell carrying cases. And of course, there are third-party vendors giving you great alternatives too. I have a couple of carrying cases from Winsor & Newton that I use while traveling. I organize the colors according to saturation and value and mostly in such a way that it mimics my setup in the studio. That makes it easy to grab the right colors all the time. Colors that almost always work are the less saturated ones. I combine those with some good contrasty ones for dark accents. These are usually from the very desaturated darker gray series.

One thing to keep in mind before going out with your markers is to check that they haven't dried out. I have encountered situations where I forgot to do that, only to get a coarse stripey mark. You can ruin a nice sketch with a single stroke. So, check your markers before you go out. In case of refillables, you might take some refueling cartridges with you, or for the regular mainstay color, have a spare at the ready.

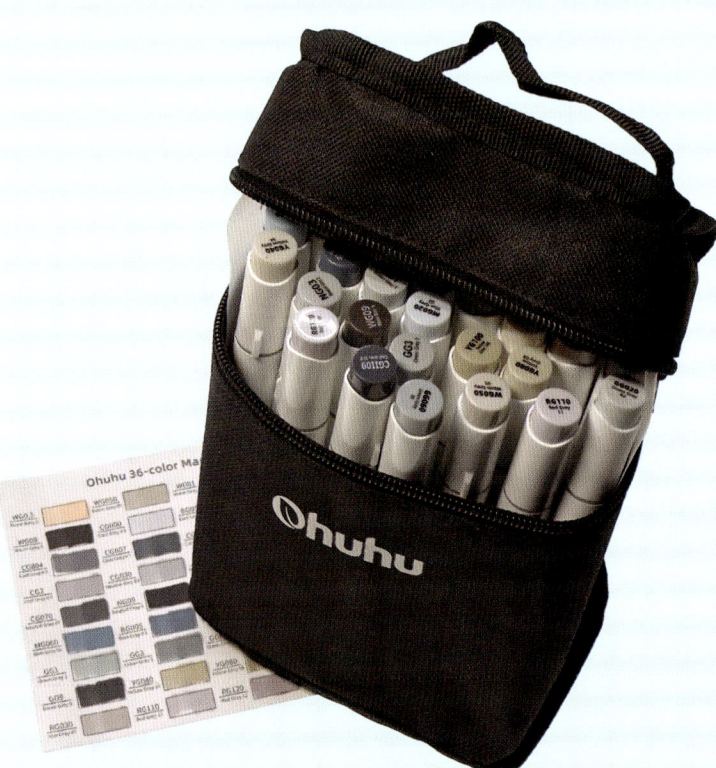

↑ OHUHU make a very affordable set of markers that is perfect for travel.

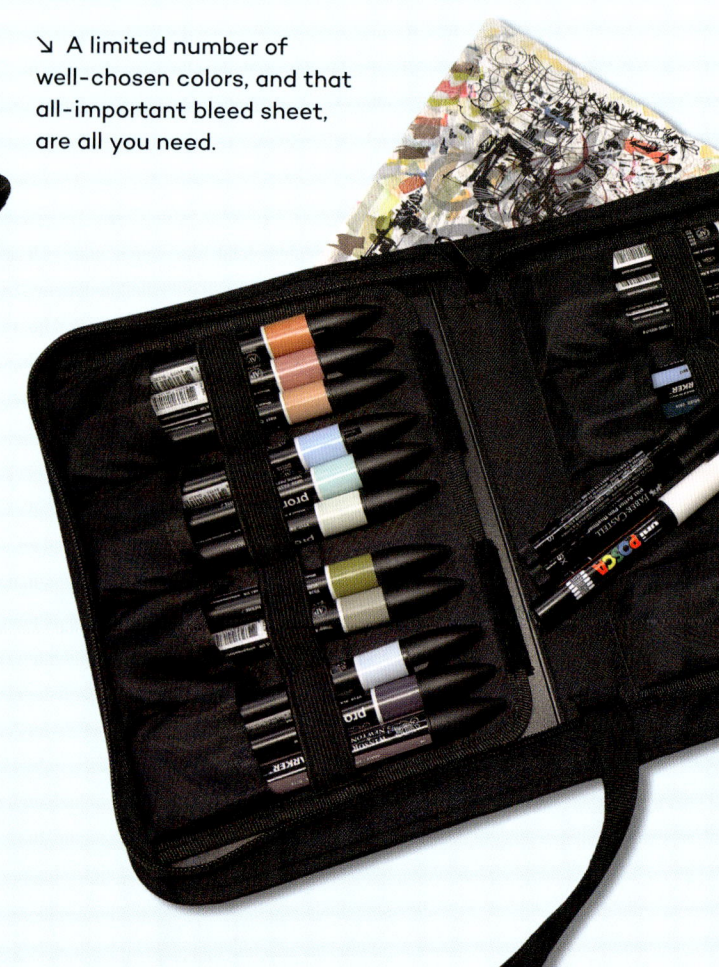

↘ A limited number of well-chosen colors, and that all-important bleed sheet, are all you need.

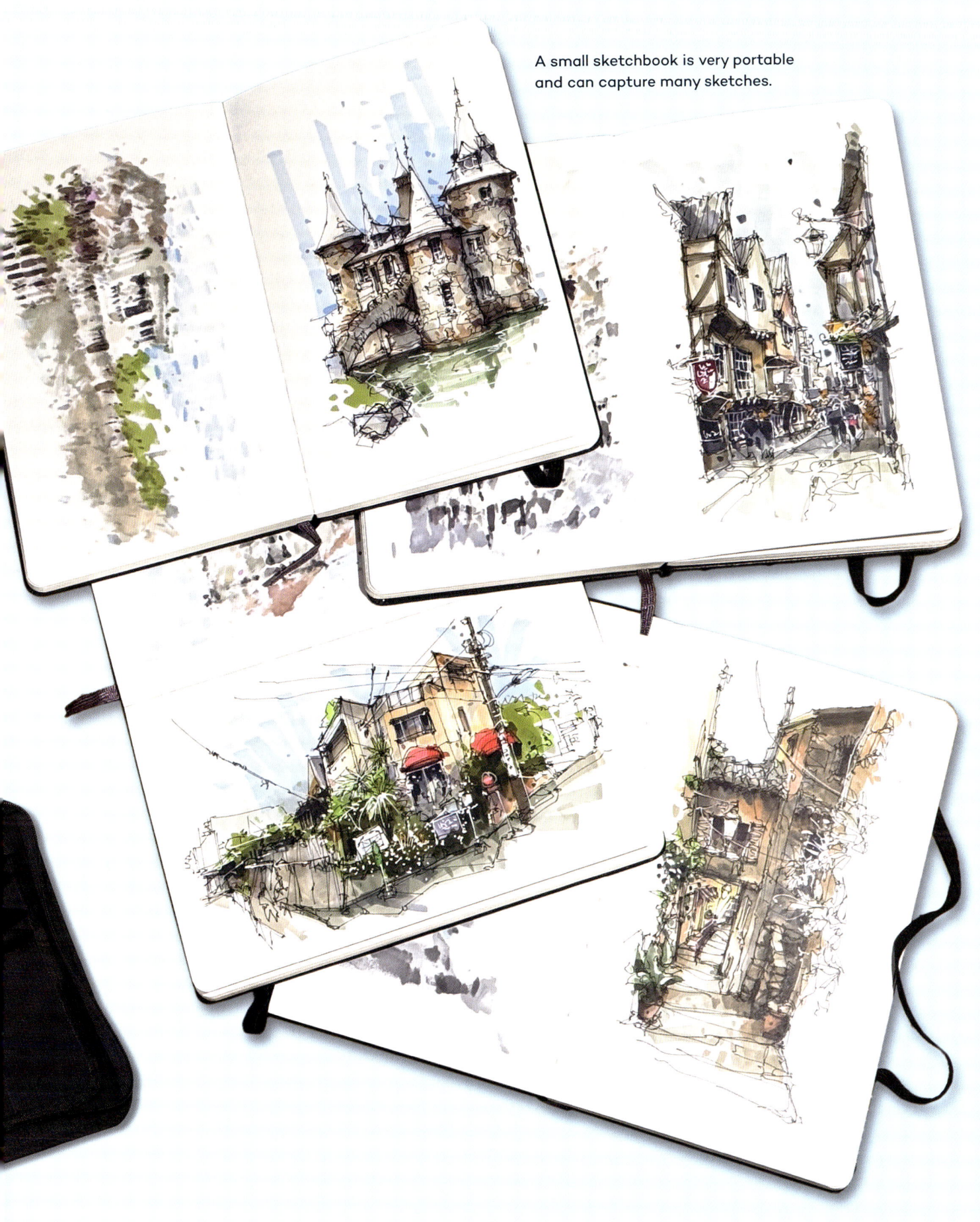

A small sketchbook is very portable and can capture many sketches.

FREEDOM FROM PRECISION

One of the most important aspects of my sketching intentions is to leave out mechanical representation. I'm not looking for a cold representation of a subject. I want my sketches to be alive and breathing. The foundation for that is laid down in the actual sketching process itself. I have already described it as flowing lines and writing the shapes that are the building blocks for my sketch. How I achieve that is to keep an almost continuous movement of my sketching hand. It comes very close to the way that sketchers apply a continuous line sketch. I am not really looking for a rigid way of applying a fixed technique, so I don't actually sketch with a single never-ending line. But the flowing movement certainly resembles that technique.

The advantage of this gliding over the page is that lines contain a pleasant flowing movement and feeling of continuity. Whenever I need to make very long lines (e.g., for a roof or vertical facade line), I add, now fully automatically, little jumps or "hiccups." This keeps such long lines energetic. I feel no need to make a fantastic perfect horizontal, diagonal,

or vertical line, so you see lots of jitters distributed over my linework. When I was in high school, I had a math teacher who could draw (almost) perfectly round circles on the blackboard. But perfection like that makes no sense to me because that might just as easily be drawn with a compass. I love to see lines that show the "hand" of an artist.

The easiest way to practice this kind of line drawing is to start describing simple forms this way. Start with lines, circles, triangles, and then move on to basic volumetric shapes like cubes and spheres and cones. Spheres are basically the same as circles. Practice pages full of them. The best way to get into the flow of things (pun intended) is to do some "loosening up" exercises. Of course, not for every sketch you make, but maybe just pause here and grab a loose sheet and warm up while reading this to actually *feel* what I try to describe. There is no need to make this a neat exercise (far from it, actually). Before you know it, this type of line treatment becomes second nature. And don't worry, your personal style will evolve from that over time!

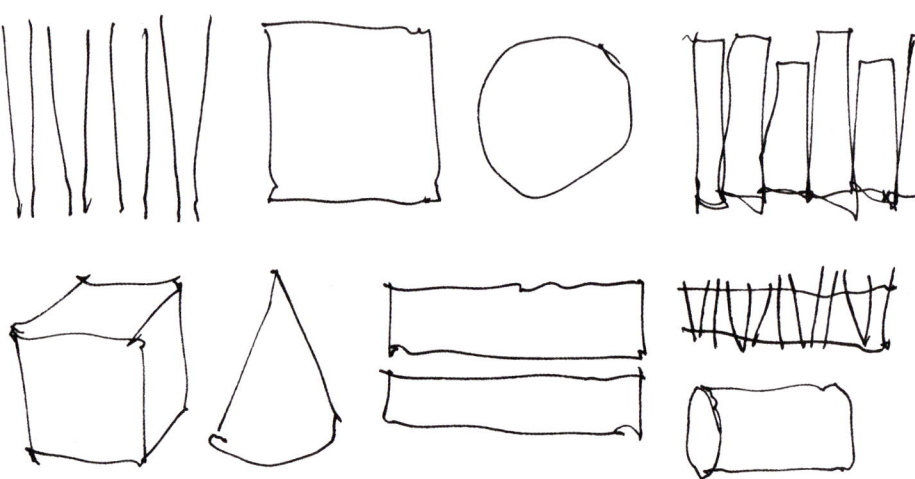

There's no need for straight lines or perfect curves.

Scan to watch a tutorial.

TIP Keeping almost-continuous movement of your sketching hand will result in sketches that feel alive.

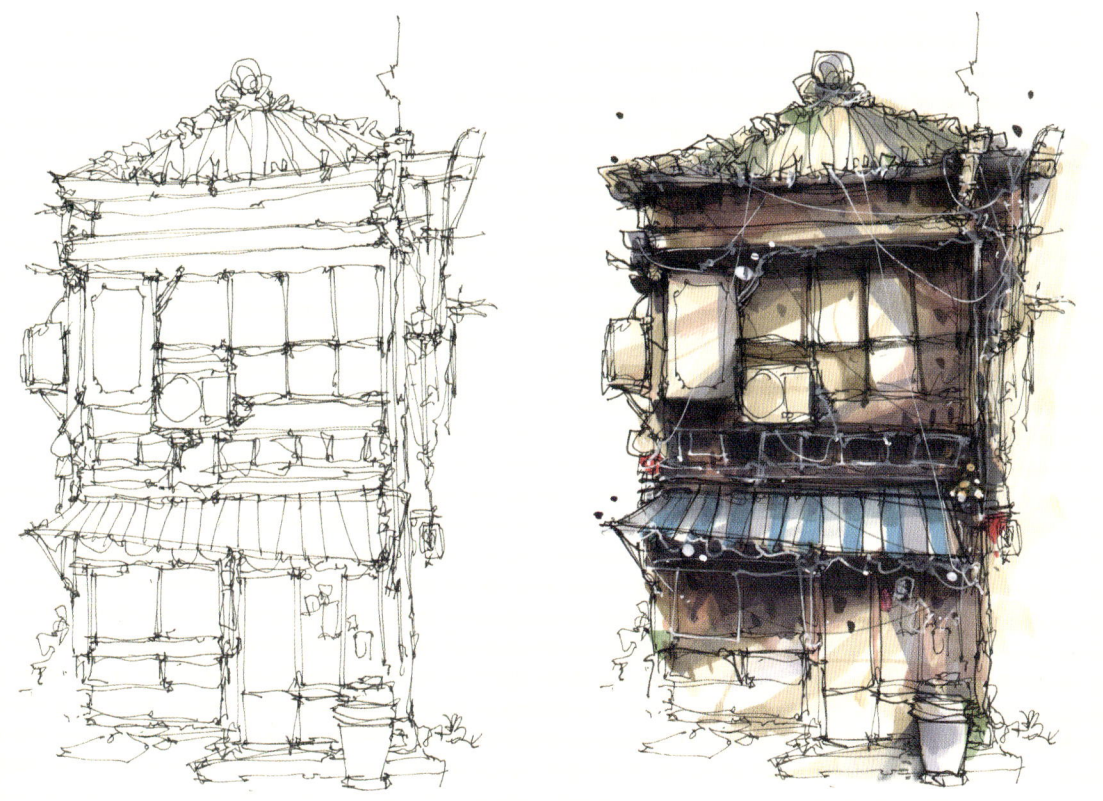

A "messy" line base is the perfect foundation . . .

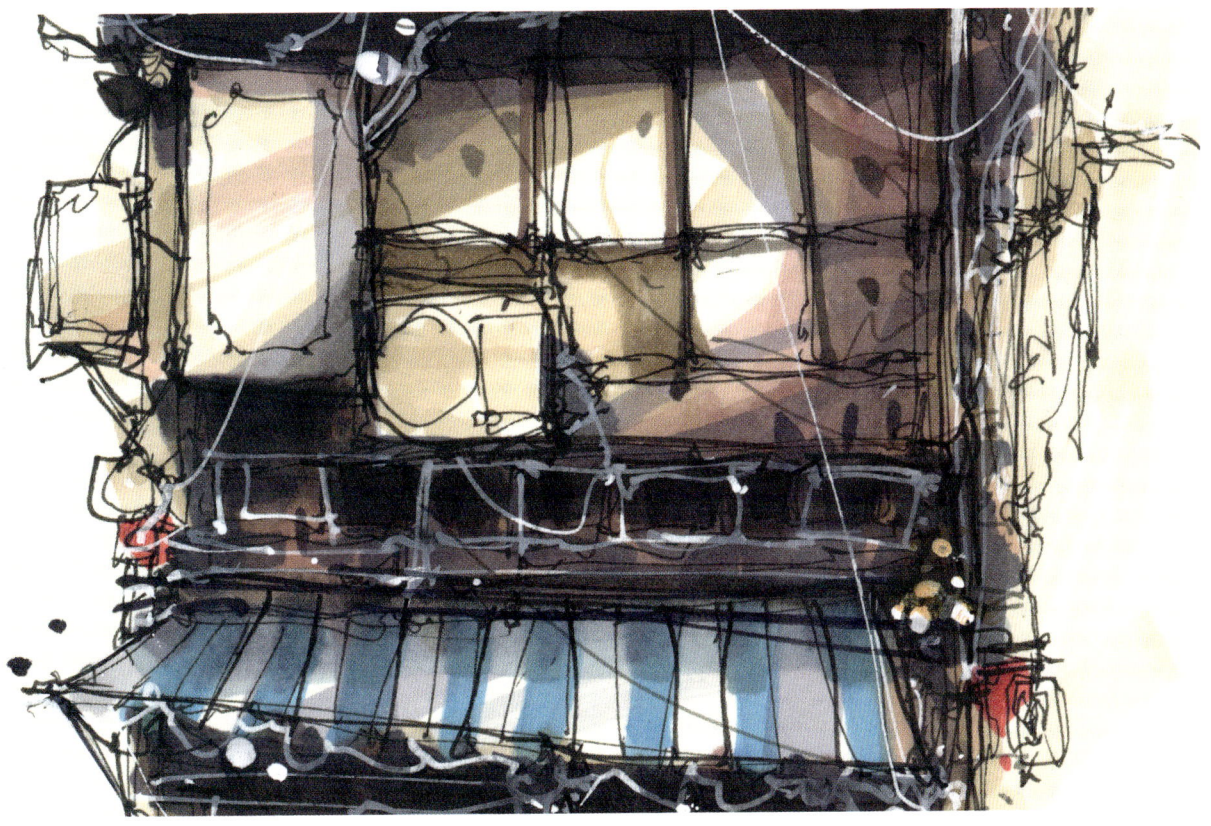

. . . for a sketch with great depth and expressiveness.

REPRODUCTION OR INTERPRETATION

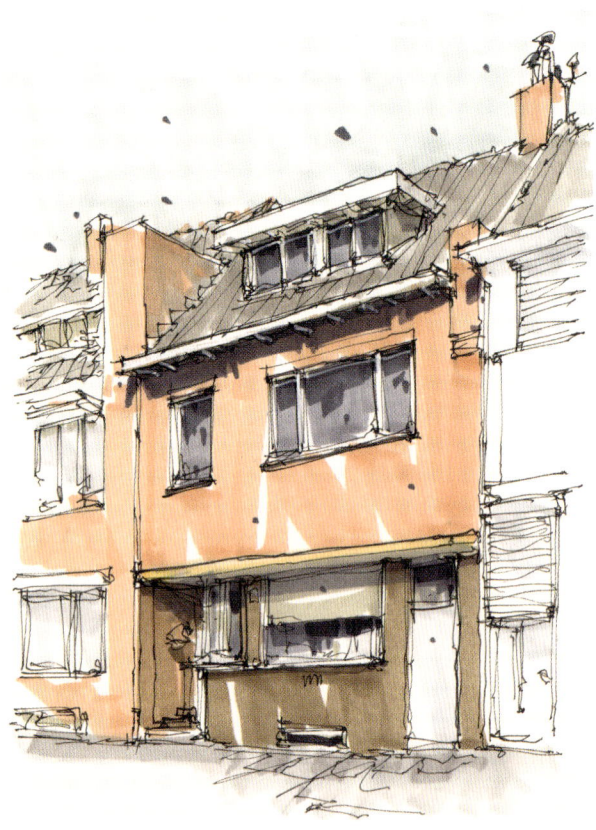

Adding dynamic strokes with visible "sharding" (leaving shards of the white paper) breathes life into this sketch.

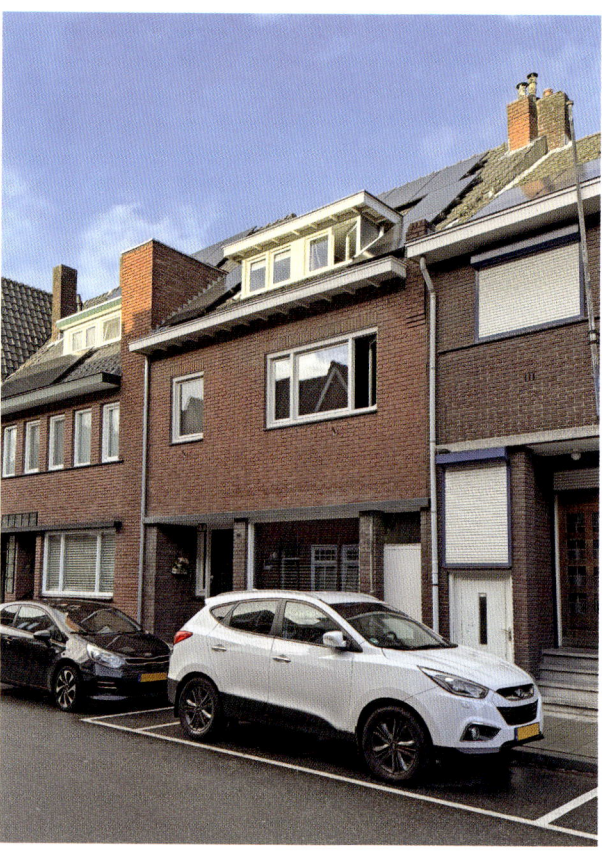

When sketching commissions, a more representative rendering is often more appropriate.

Starting a sketch always involves having a subject to sketch. That sounds obvious, but I clearly remember my first sessions where I wanted to sketch "something" but did not have a clue "what" I wanted to sketch. I ended up wasting paper while trying to scribble undetermined things. It all really started to click when that subject became clear. So . . . about that subject. When I prepare a subject for a sketch, I always decide beforehand how I'm going to approach it. Will it be a faithful reproduction of the subject, or will I take liberties with that and make my own version of it?

A more or less faithful reproduction will stay close to the original and have all of its characteristics, while an interpretation will take the essence of a subject and enhance or amplify that.

Looking through most of the sketches I have made, I see at least some interpretation. But in the case of interpretation, I take the exaggeration a bit further and also add "stuff" that I feel will be great additions to the character of the sketch. Those might be elements that are not present in the "real" subject. Usually when I'm in my studio, I have more flexibility since I'm starting from a photo. There I can typically go through different approaches: faithful, interpretation, or even fully improvised, based on a subject. The reason is that I prepare my subject in Photoshop. And there, things can develop in many exciting ways. Over the years, that is a process that I have really come to love.

When I am on location, I will usually gravitate more toward faithful representation, possibly with exaggeration to express what I think a subject needs.

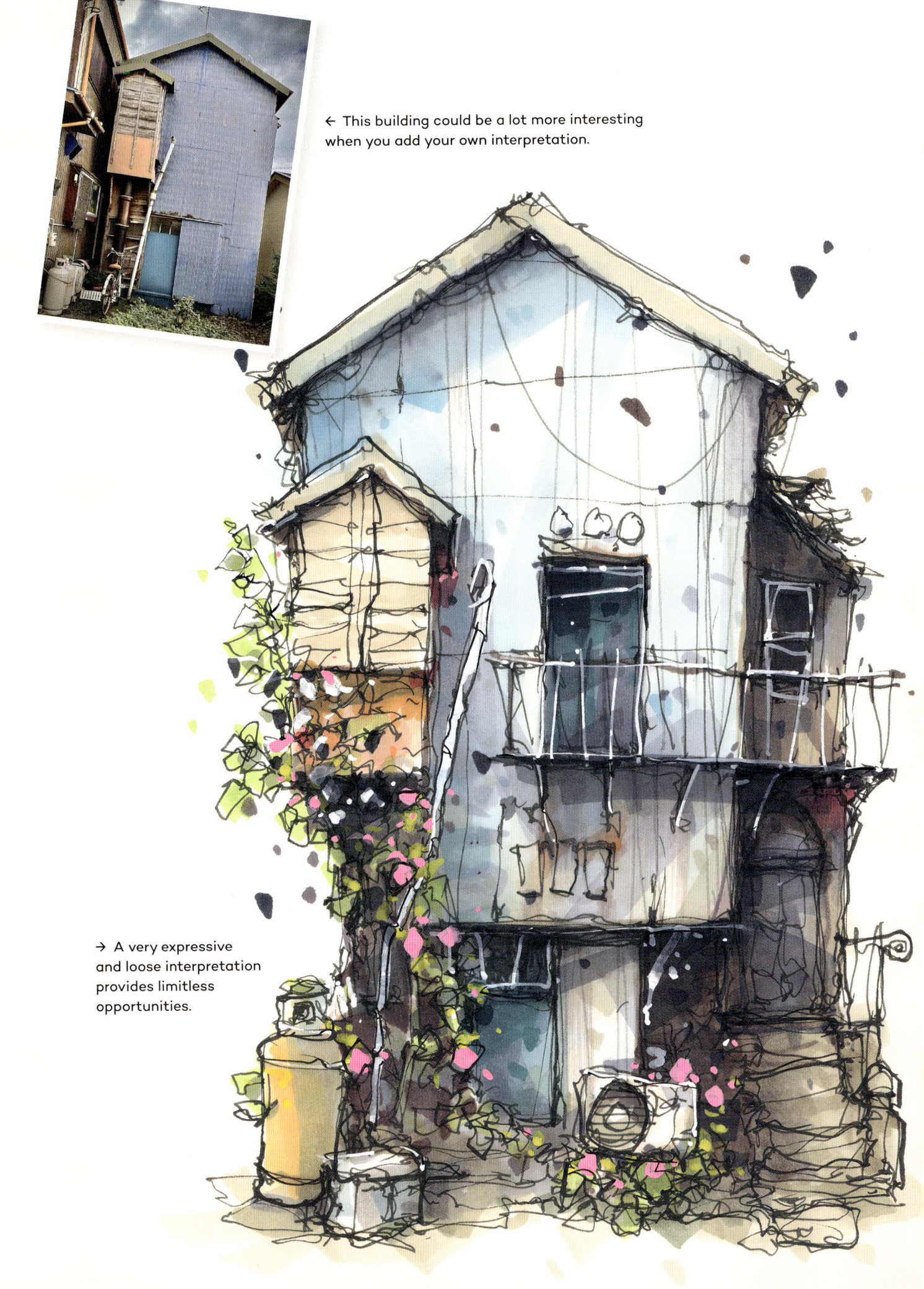

← This building could be a lot more interesting when you add your own interpretation.

→ A very expressive and loose interpretation provides limitless opportunities.

SIMPLIFYING AND SYMBOLIZING

Making a sketch is always about symbolizing the world around you or the world in your mind's eye. Of course it's possible to painstakingly try to draw everything you see exactly the way you see it. But the reality is that our mind actually filters everything we see in such a way that we discard what's not important and focus on the elements that may be important to us. Take for instance a lush bed of flowers, or a tree that is in full leaf, or a field of grass. If you try to put that all in a sketch, you will end up highly frustrated because, even if you succeed, everything would be in focus. And that would in most cases result in a confusing picture that makes you keep wondering why it doesn't look "right."

So symbolizing is key here. Now what do I mean by symbolizing? You doubtless have many examples you can think of. Take, for instance, the symbolic representation of a leaf or a rock. You can simplify these shapes while still conveying their meaning as a leaf or a rock. You will see that in many of my sketches the leaves and flowers and other details suggest what they are supposed to describe (e.g., triangular scribbles describing leaves) but are actually just a suggestion of them. A great advantage of this symbolization is that it also leaves room for

interpretation by the viewer of your sketches. That is so important. While hyper-realistic paintings are without a doubt exceptionally masterful, for me, they leave no room to dwell in these worlds apart from just marveling at the technical prowess such work conveys.

I have tried to come up with a word addition for that symbolization (I always try to make up words to explain something in a way that sticks): I add the term "-iness" to the objects. If you put that into practice, you'd get "leafiness," "grassiness," "rockiness," and "floweriness." So, make it look like leaves, grass, and flower, etc. That's more than enough to describe something. And it adds to the freshness and spontaneity of a sketch while also saving tons of time that would otherwise be wasted on too much detail. And the great thing about thinking of symbolization this way is that you can really take this concept very far. Just imagine "roofiness" and "crowdiness" in scenes where you need to suggest a busy city backdrop of a shopping street! In most cases you will discover that the suggestion of these elements is much more powerful to enhance the mood in a sketch or painting than meticulously trying to draw in all that detail.

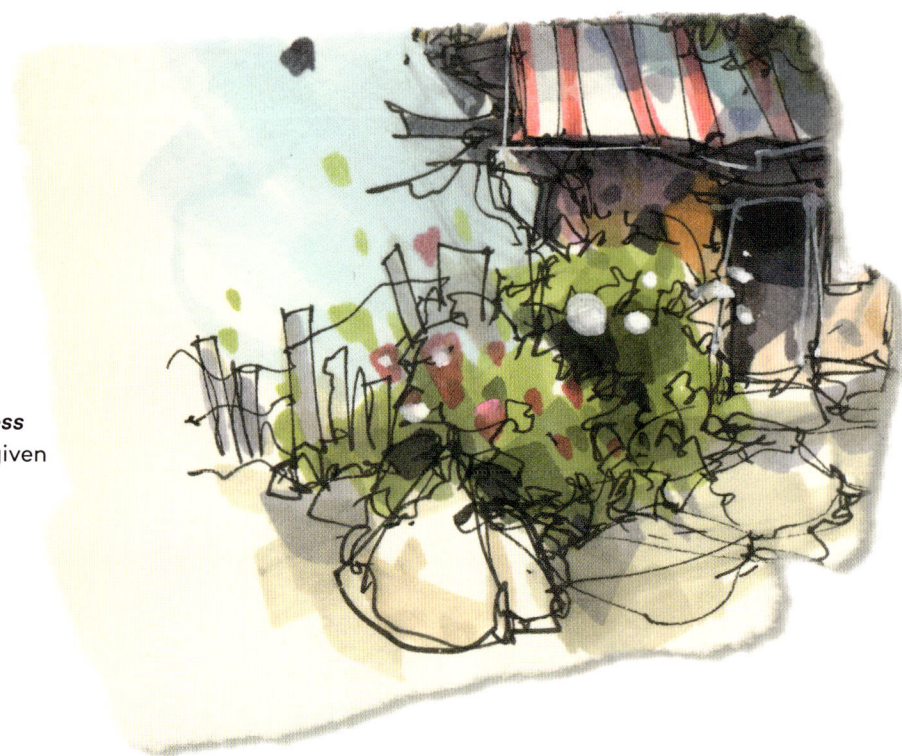

→ *Bushiness* and *fenceiness* in action. Loose lines are given context by coloring.

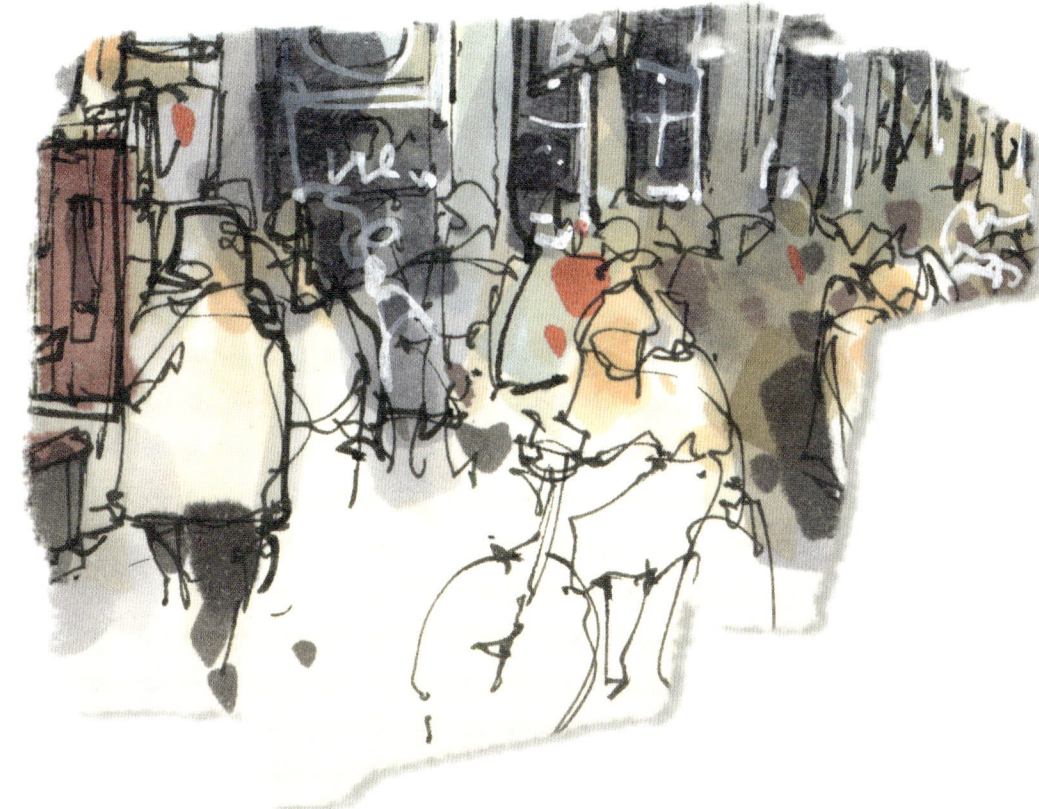

→ **Peopleiness** filling this street. All you see are basic head shapes and lines sticking out of basic trunks.

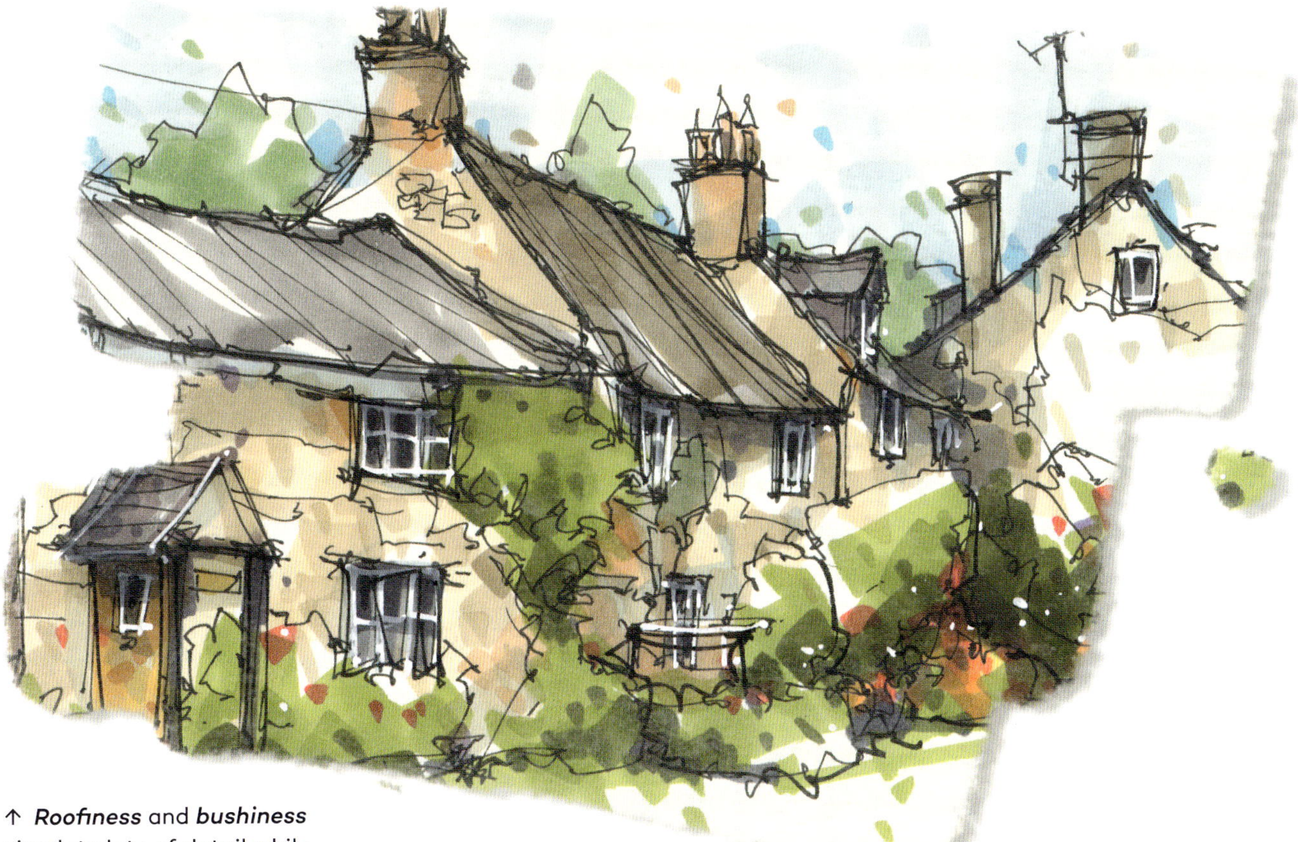

↑ **Roofiness** and **bushiness** simulate lots of detail while still maintaining a loose approach.

EXAGGERATION

It's very possible that the subject that you have picked might be interesting in general but still a little bland. In such cases, a little exaggeration can give that extra punch to make your sketch really stand out. Look for details in your building that lend themselves to exaggeration. You could treat your building as a caricature for a moment and see what "traits" really define your building. Does it have a crooked roof, some missing roof tiles, some interesting window details, maybe a door that is not completely straight, is it a little slanted? Maybe it's a very slender, tall building? Or a particularly

stubby small one? Those are all great cues for some attention-grabbing exaggeration. It's usually those interesting aspects that can define a house in the first place, and bringing these details out will help you "capture" the spirit, the essence of your chosen subject. It's up to you to determine how far you want to take this. But it's in the way you treat your subject that your personality, or at least your interpretation of a subject, will start to shine through. And that, in the end, can start to become your "personal hand" in the way your sketches turn out. Let's see how you can really make a sketch your own.

→ This restaurant has some very nice elements for a sketch.

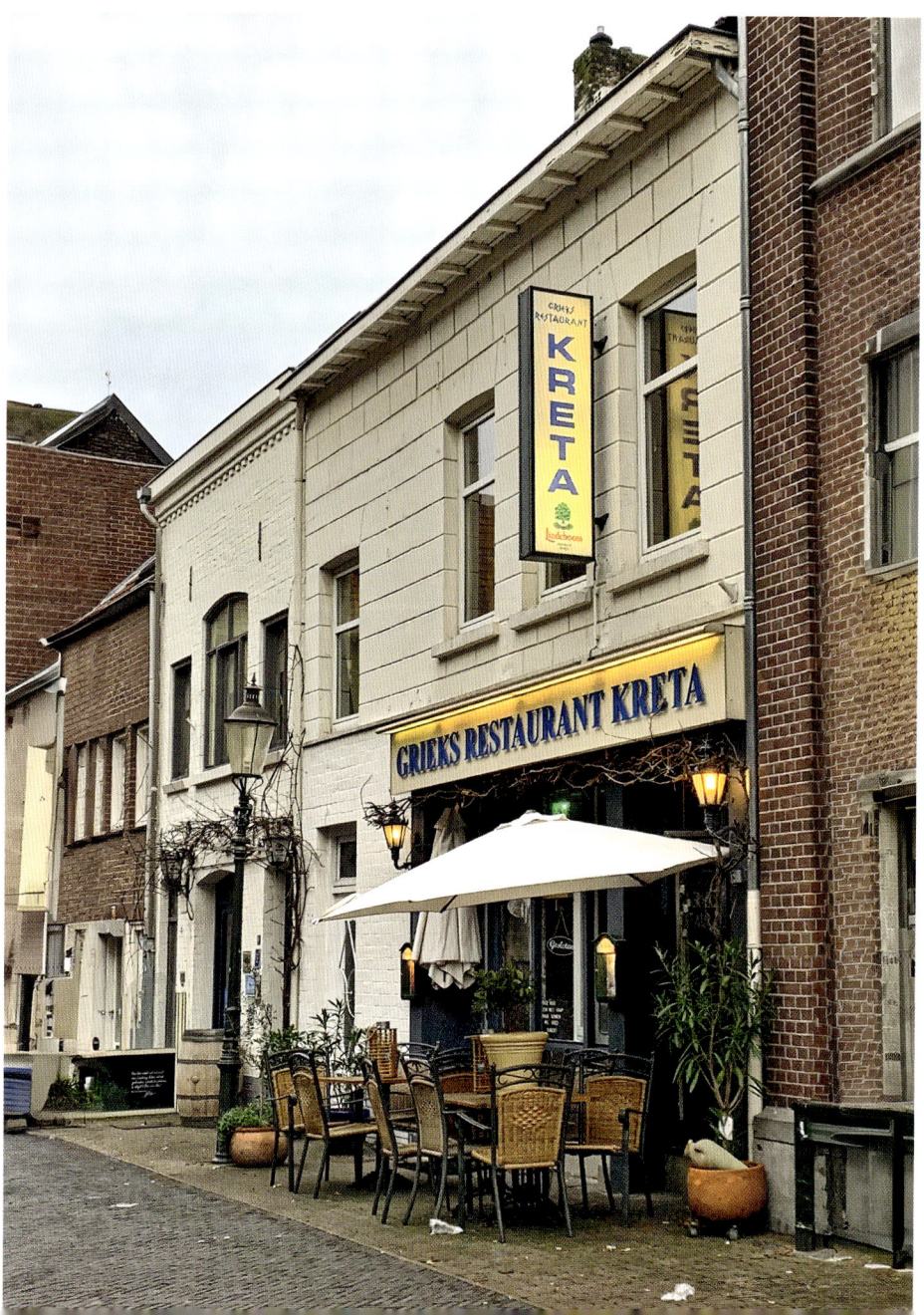

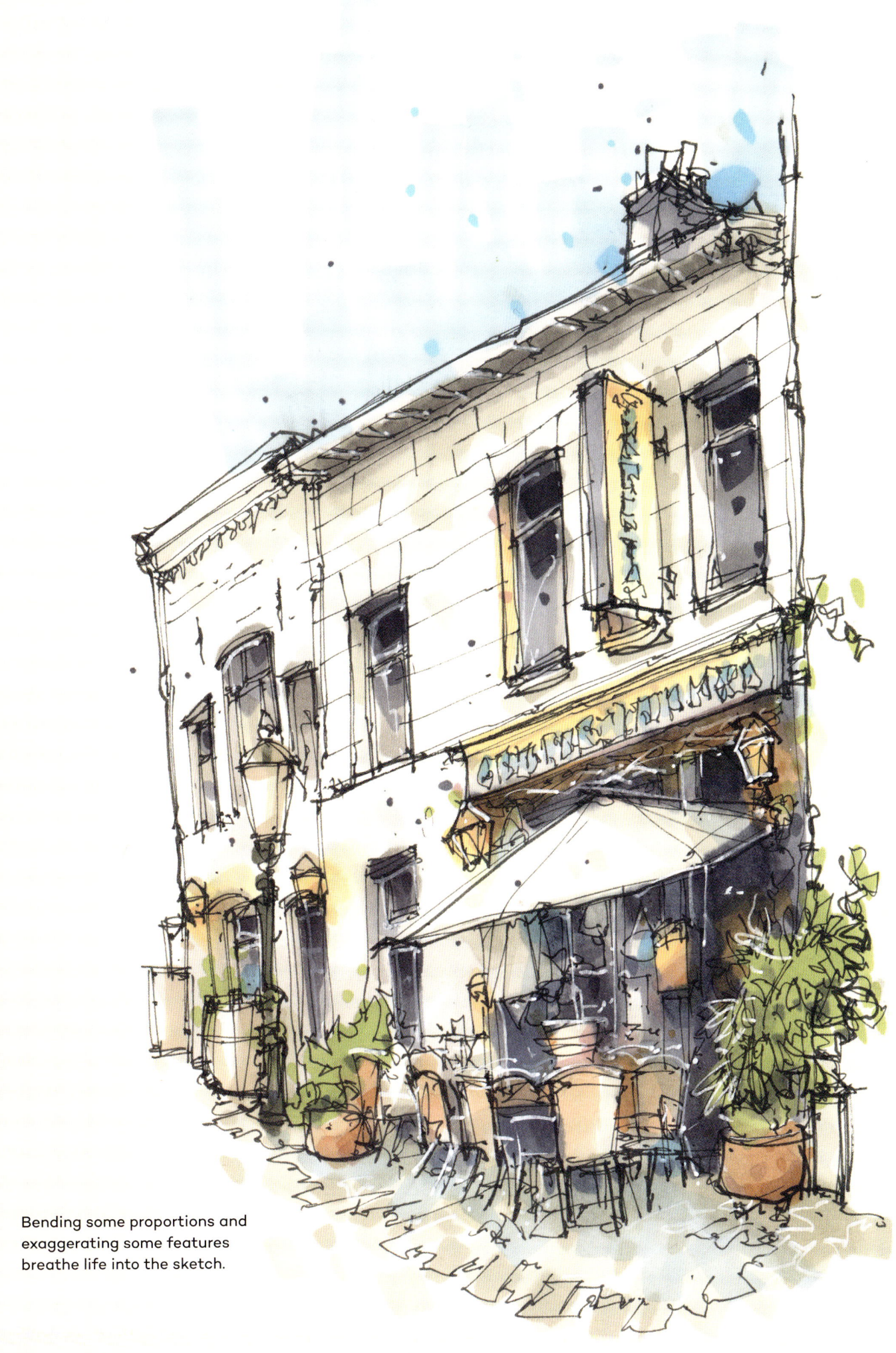

Bending some proportions and
exaggerating some features
breathe life into the sketch.

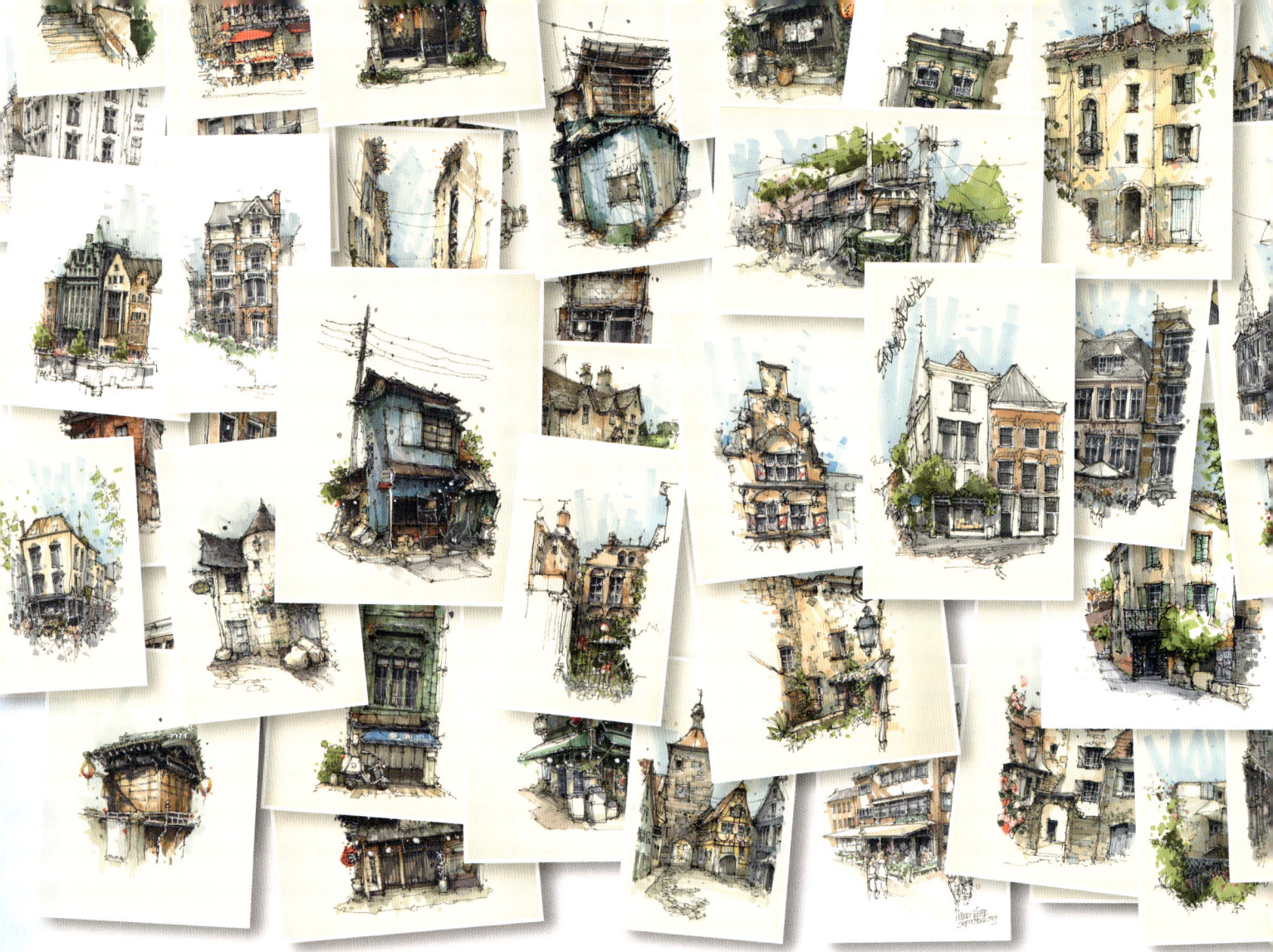

MAKING IT YOUR OWN

All the ideas I've just gone through will make a sketch your personal interpretation. And that, above anything else, will make for a sketch that is really your personal work. Don't expect this to happen right away on your first sketch. This whole process takes time. Don't get discouraged and keep an open mind to how you see things develop on paper. I know that you see all those great end results from others, and you can't wait to see your sketches turn out in such a unique way. But always keep in mind that the works of other artists, too, have taken time to develop. Nobody just throws a "masterpiece" on the paper from day one! Style develops over time after lots and lots of sketches. You will need to get some mileage under your belt, and there is no way to skip that.

Rather, try to enjoy this process! Be forgiving toward yourself and just keep turning to a new sketchbook page (or a new single sheet) every time you finish a sketch. Made a really great one? Great . . . turn the page. Made a sketch that really, really sucked? Too bad . . . turn the page! There's always that next one, and with every new sketch, you will see new things that give you a better understanding of the whole process. There's no such thing as mistakes. Of course we mess up things but think about it this way: Mistakes are actually very valuable moments of insight. You see that something is not the way you wanted it to be and that will help you see how you can fix, or avoid, such a situation the next time. Without this learning process, you will never get more experienced.

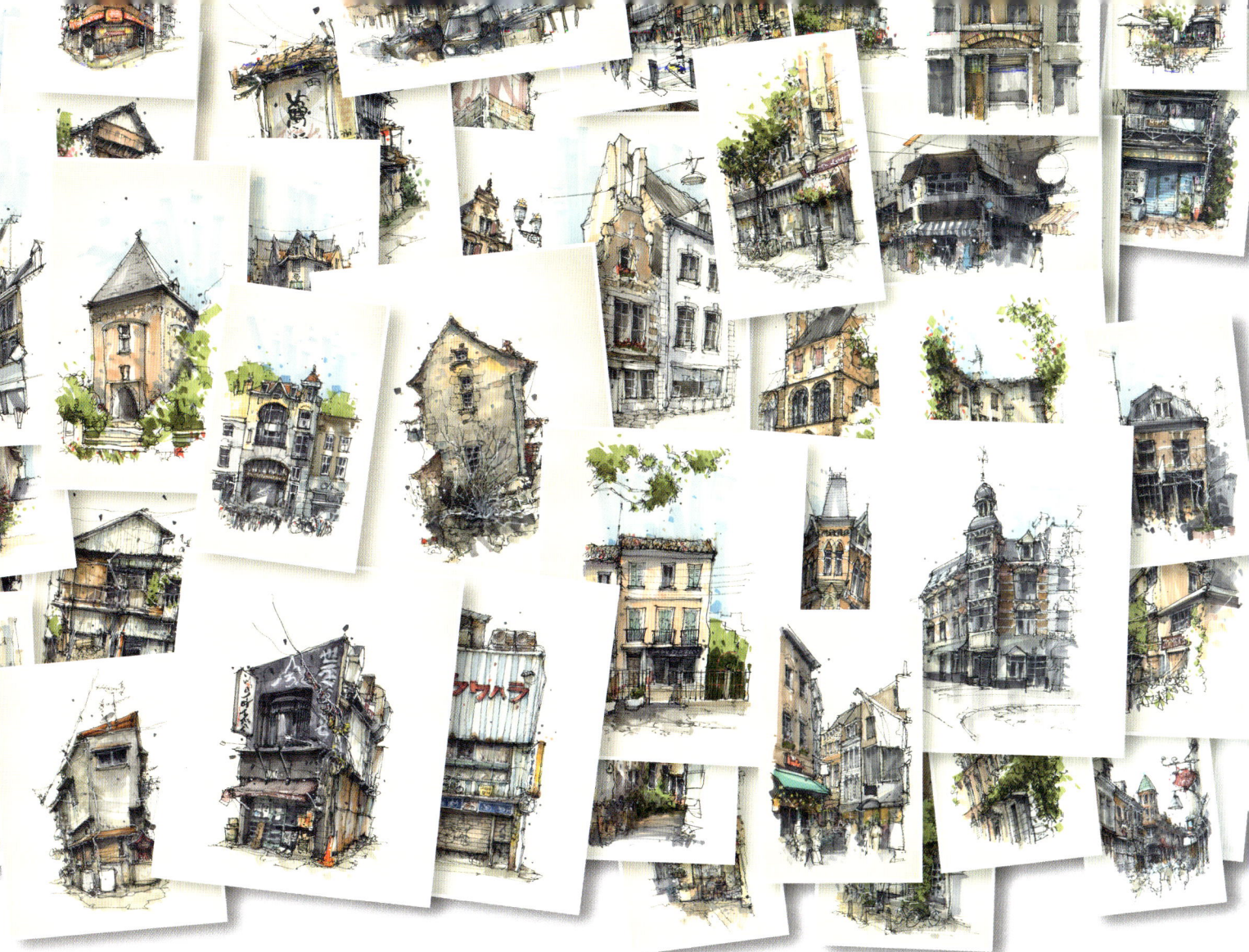

So grab a sketchbook or a stack of pages and go at it! The more, the better. Don't strive for that single perfect masterpiece; go for lots of learning. Before you know it, you will feel quite at home just sketching and expressing yourself without constantly getting in your own way. There's a saying that there are a thousand bad sketches before getting to the really good ones. Think about it this way: It will not take those symbolic thousand sketches before you see some nice result; it will gradually happen along that road that things start to go more and more to your liking.

↑ Developing a style is a journey, not a button. The more you sketch, the sooner your style will emerge.

TIP Nobody just throws a "masterpiece" on the paper from day one! Be forgiving toward yourself and just keep turning to a new sketchbook page every time you finish a sketch.

COLOR

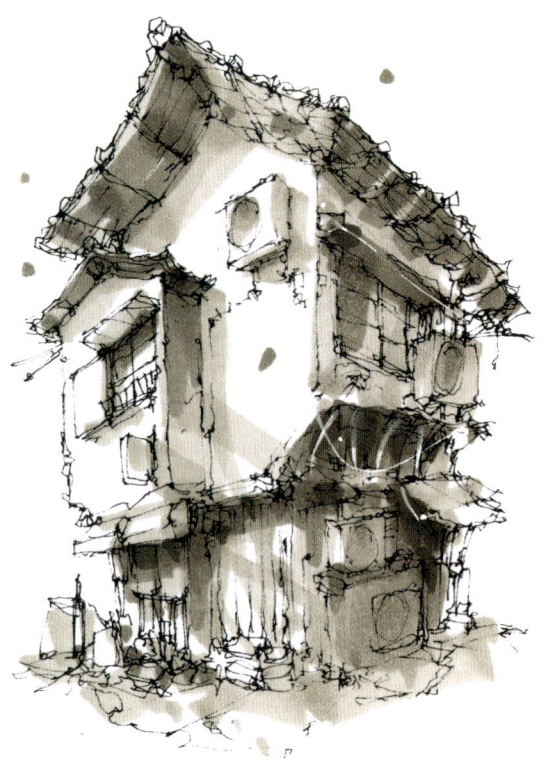

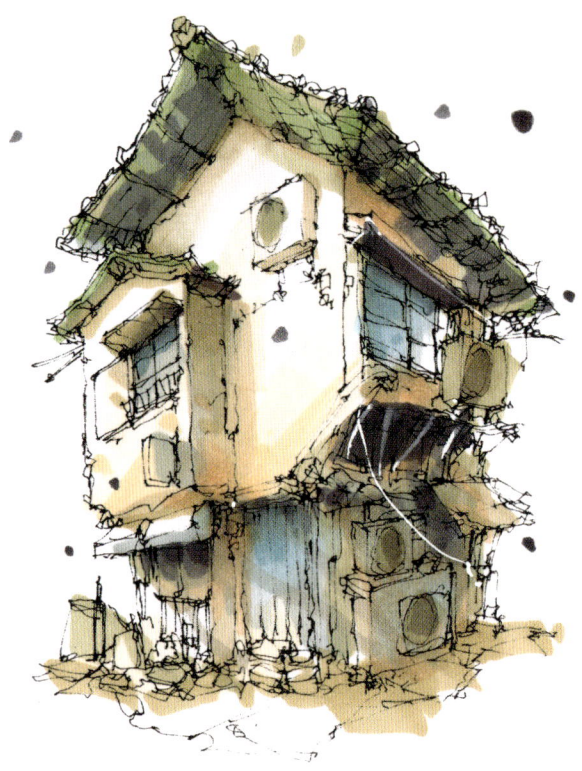

For me, color is a direct descendant of light. Without visible light, there is no color. Color, of course, is a great way to make your house sketch really interesting. But it's important to realize that you actually don't need color at all to still make your sketch very believable and interesting. Like I mentioned previously, it is the relation between light and dark that does most of the heavy lifting. And that is precisely what can be achieved with a set of differing light or dark values. These can be values of a certain color, but they can also be plain monochrome values of gray. In the following sketches of the same house I show you what I mean.

In the first version, you see the house built up with basic set of just three gray values.

The second version shows the same house, but now I have used colors while paying attention to the lightness or darkness aspect that a color has. You will discover that when your sketch has a flat look, most often is the relationship between the light values of colors that is "off." A good way to check if this could be the case is to make a black-and-white photo of your sketch with your smartphone. That photo will quickly show you how the values in your sketch define your building. If this value distribution is unbalanced, your sketch will look unbalanced. Another, even more low-tech way of checking your values is to squint. By almost closing your eyes while looking at your sketch you will see this relationship clearly.

Understanding this interaction between color and value is a very important factor in improving the way your sketches will look.

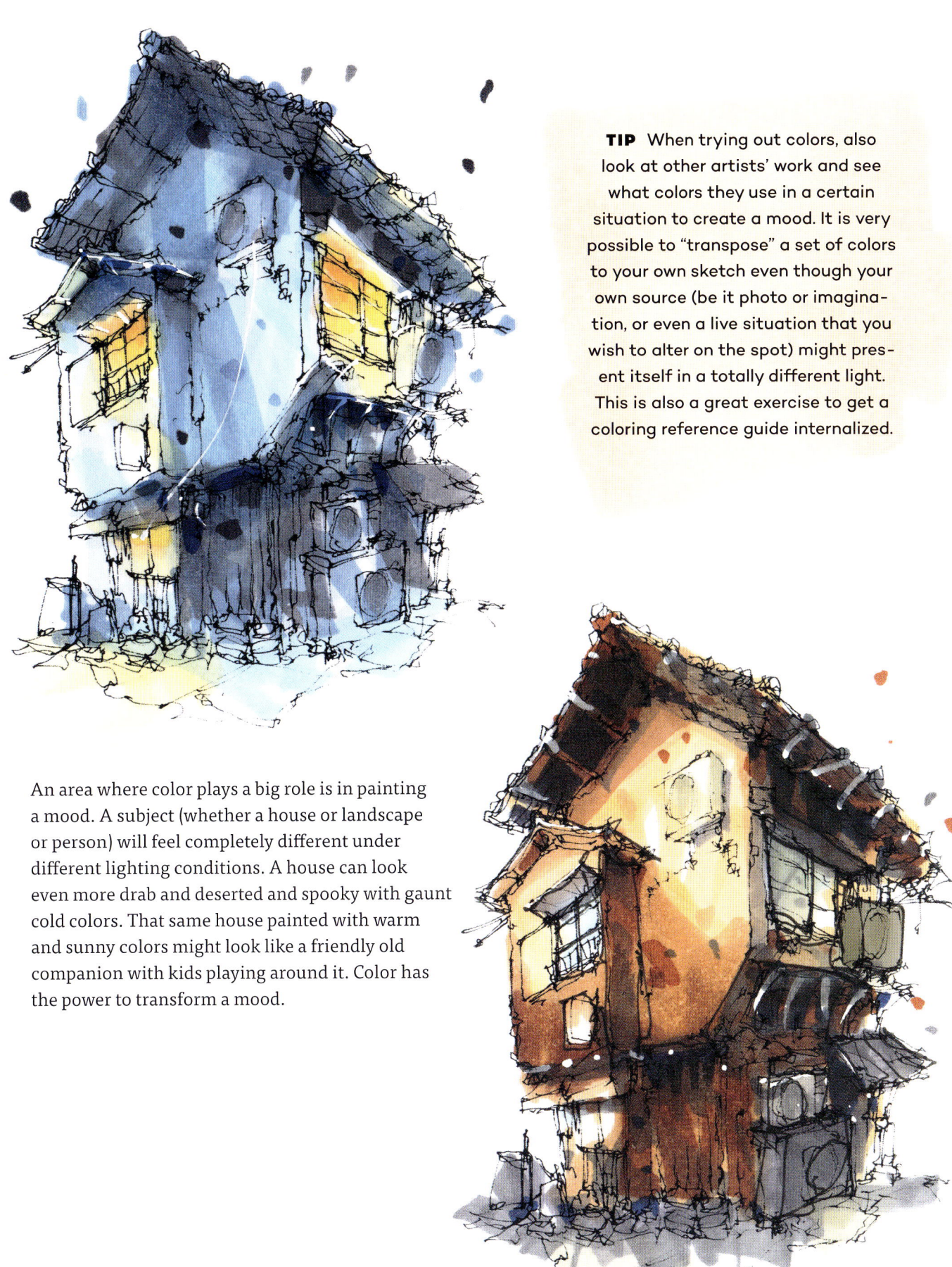

TIP When trying out colors, also look at other artists' work and see what colors they use in a certain situation to create a mood. It is very possible to "transpose" a set of colors to your own sketch even though your own source (be it photo or imagination, or even a live situation that you wish to alter on the spot) might present itself in a totally different light. This is also a great exercise to get a coloring reference guide internalized.

An area where color plays a big role is in painting a mood. A subject (whether a house or landscape or person) will feel completely different under different lighting conditions. A house can look even more drab and deserted and spooky with gaunt cold colors. That same house painted with warm and sunny colors might look like a friendly old companion with kids playing around it. Color has the power to transform a mood.

LIGHT AND DARK

Arguably one of the most important things to create a pleasing and interesting sketch is understanding the way light defines an object. Even more so than color, actually. Whether that object is just a simple box, an apple, or a highly complex temple. That might sound very daunting, but it doesn't have to be. Breaking complex objects down into simpler forms will help you a great deal in understanding, and consequently even predicting how light will behave on a given surface. Of course, there are other factors influencing how light behaves on a surface. For instance, if a surface is made of a shiny reflective metal it will look different than if a surface is a sheet of glass or a rough patch of grass. But let's take a look at the most basic behavior of light on a matte type of surface and use that in making sense of a building. You will see how much clearer things become once you "see the light," so to speak.

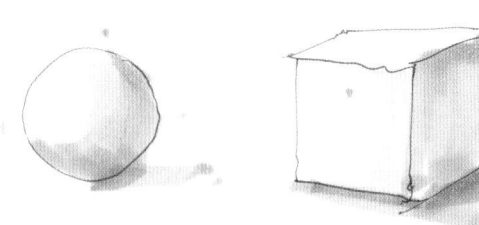 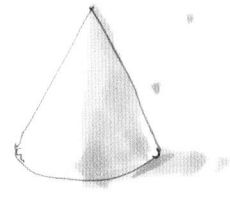 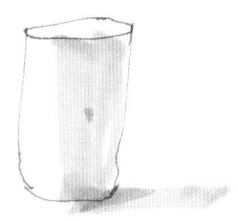

Simple volumetric shapes shaded with light coming from top left.

PAINTING LIGHT BY SKETCHING THE SHADOWS

In the example, you see the line sketch of a building. I have included some well-defined elements to help you see how you can quickly give this building depth by looking at the way light plays on the forms, and how shadows would fall in areas where the light cannot touch it. A word of caution: I'm not going to construct things! Just like perspective, shadows cast from a light source can be constructed to a great degree of precision, but for me, as with perspective, constructing these phenomena would make a sketch rigid and boring. So keep in mind to use it as a guiding principle.

USING THE WHITE OF THE PAGE

One way to make great use of "painting with shadows" is to use the page-white as the areas of your building that are hit by direct sunlight. Then use the colors (or light and dark values) to sketch in the shadow areas defining the shape and surrounding environment (for example, tree branches and leaves) onto that building. This is a very powerful way of modeling your building. It's also an effective tool to very quickly create your sketch. Keep in mind that it doesn't necessarily have to be the page-white that needs to be the base of your building (even though it's the fastest way). You can also quickly sketch in a base color, or blend and work with powerful shadows on top of that. Regardless of starting from page-white or base color, painting or sketching in the shadows is a very quick and highly effective way to capture your building on the page.

Scan to watch a tutorial.

Scan to watch a tutorial.

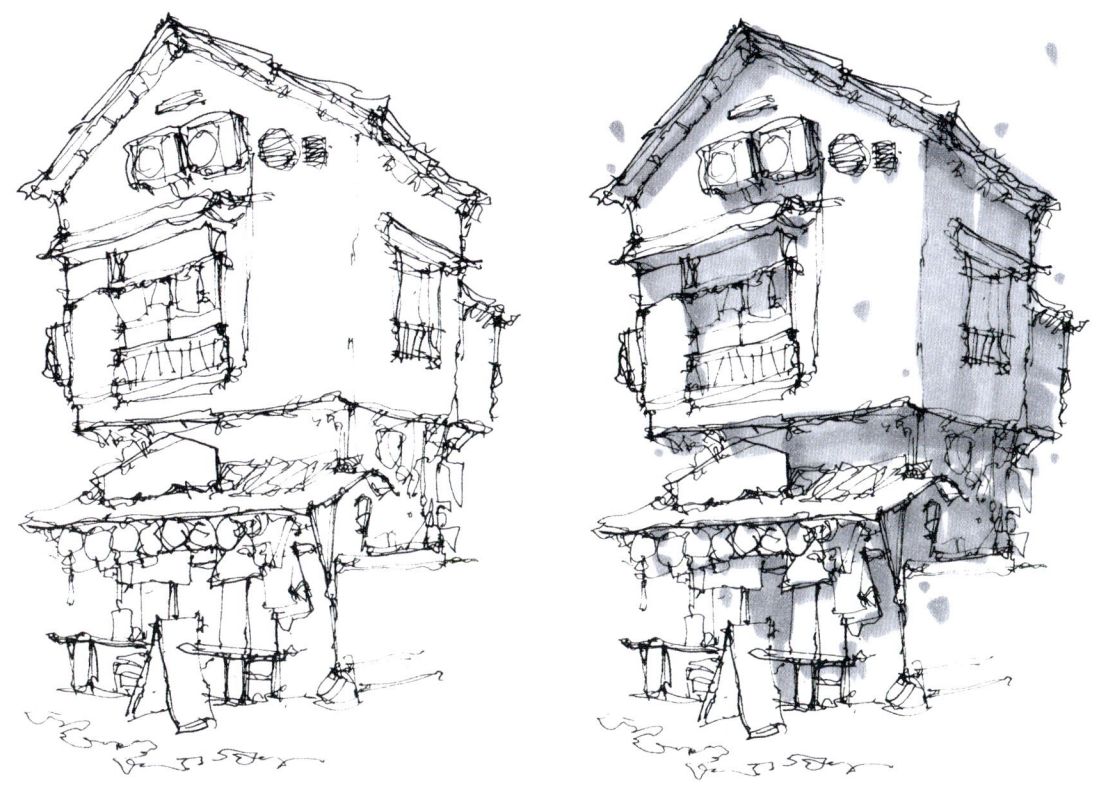

↑ Quickly create depth by painting the shadow areas only.
↓ The shadows on the wall are painted in the wall's colors. The page-white is used as the lightest area.

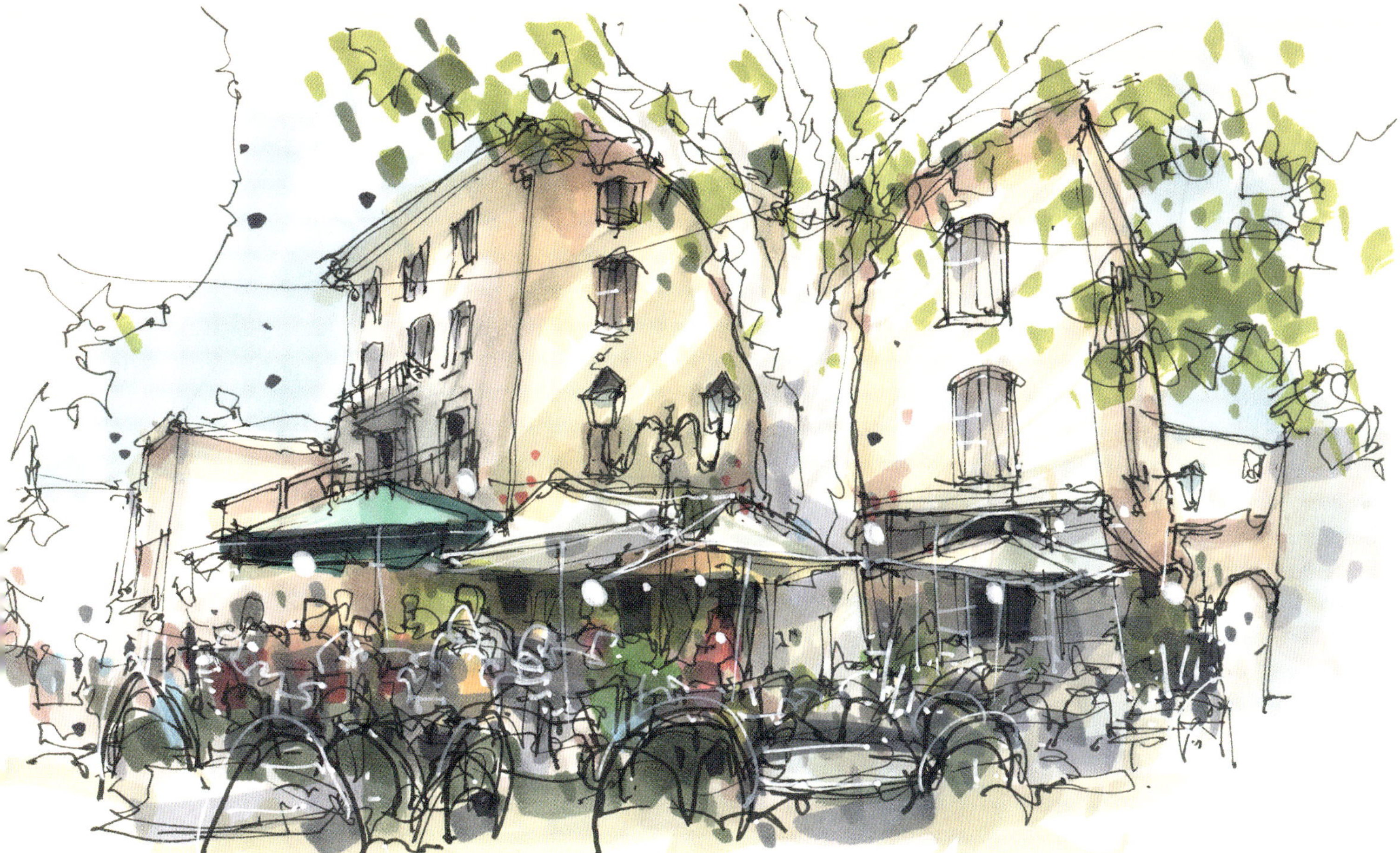

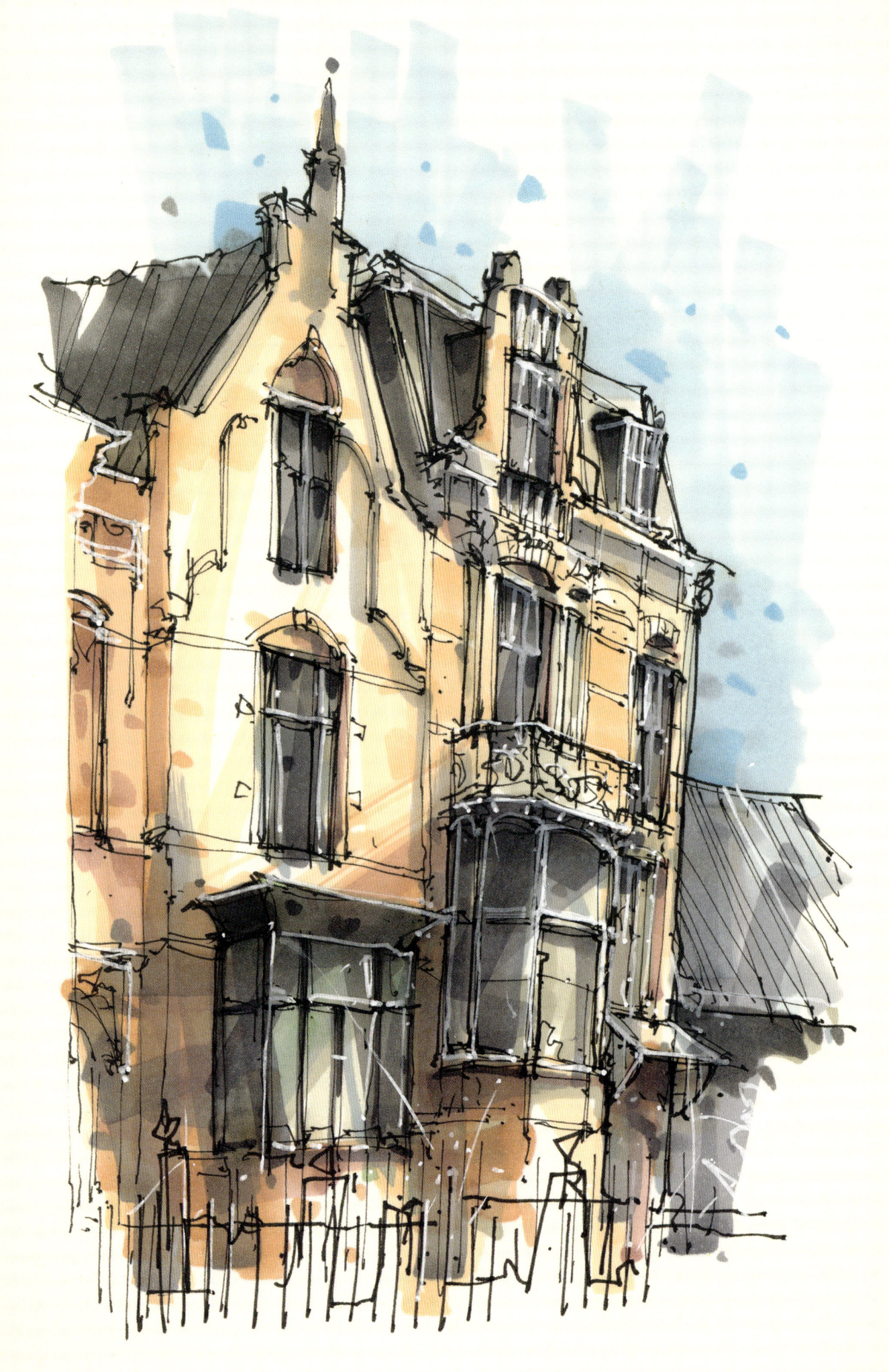

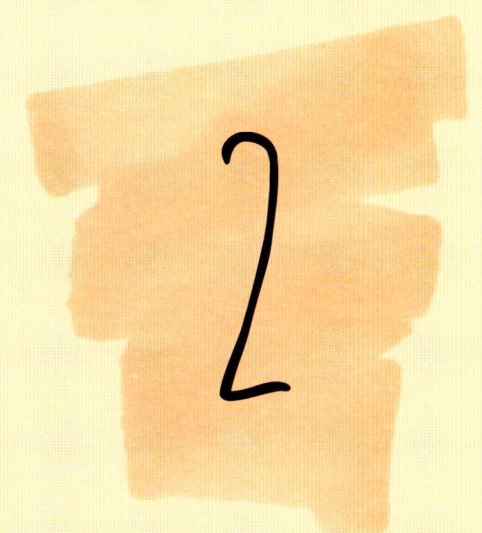

HOUSESKETCHING

— THE PROCESS —

Now that you know a little bit about my approach to sketching and have your materials ready, I'm going to walk you through my process in detail, from choosing a subject to adding the finishing details. You'll then be ready to sketch along with me in the next section of the book.

PICKING YOUR SUBJECT

It obviously all starts with picking something you want to sketch. Once you have that clear, you're on your way. So, how to pick a subject? Since this book is about sketching houses, there is already a clearcut subject matter ready and waiting for you. But what type of house or structure do you want to sketch? Is it a small, ruined shack somewhere out in the field, a shiny temple bathing in sunlight, or your local pub or art supply store? There are so many great types of buildings to choose from. In my case, I started sketching local buildings in my hometown of Venlo. I loved the buildings from the 1700s and 1800s, of which there are many nice examples to be found close to where I live. But maybe you like modern architecture, or churches, or dark alleys with a few interesting structures that catch your attention.

When you are starting out, it may be a good idea to start with a set of simple "readable" buildings, by which I mean that you can clearly see the way it is structured (see the Anatomy of a House on page 42). This will give you an easier way to simplify the building in your mind's eye. And that, in turn, will add to your understanding of what you're going to draw.

If, on the other hand, you start out with something like a Gothic cathedral, with lots of highly decorative spires and sculptures adorning its form, you run the risk of easily getting lost in all that detail. The trick is to start seeing the foundational shapes, even in those very complex looking structures.

Now, where do you start looking?

TIP When you are starting out, it may be a good idea to start with a set of simple "readable" buildings, in which you can clearly see the way it is structured, to see the "anatomy" of the house.

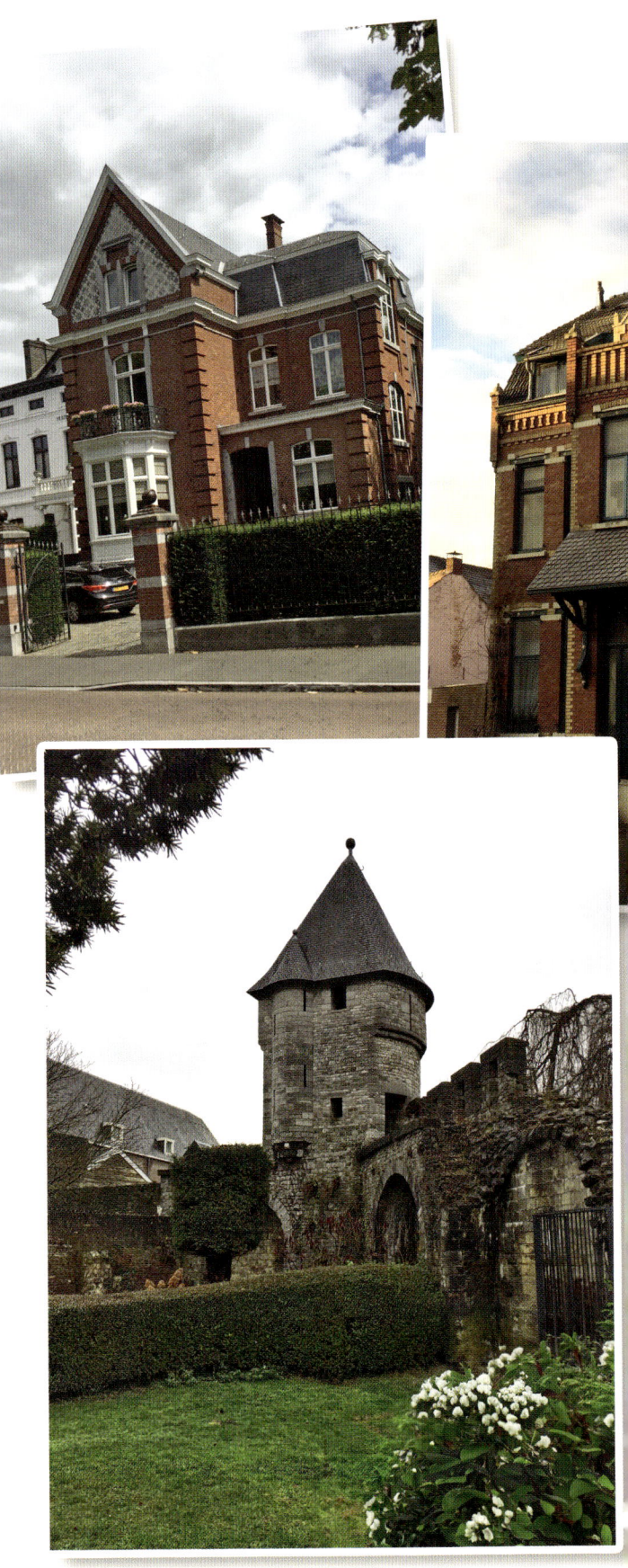

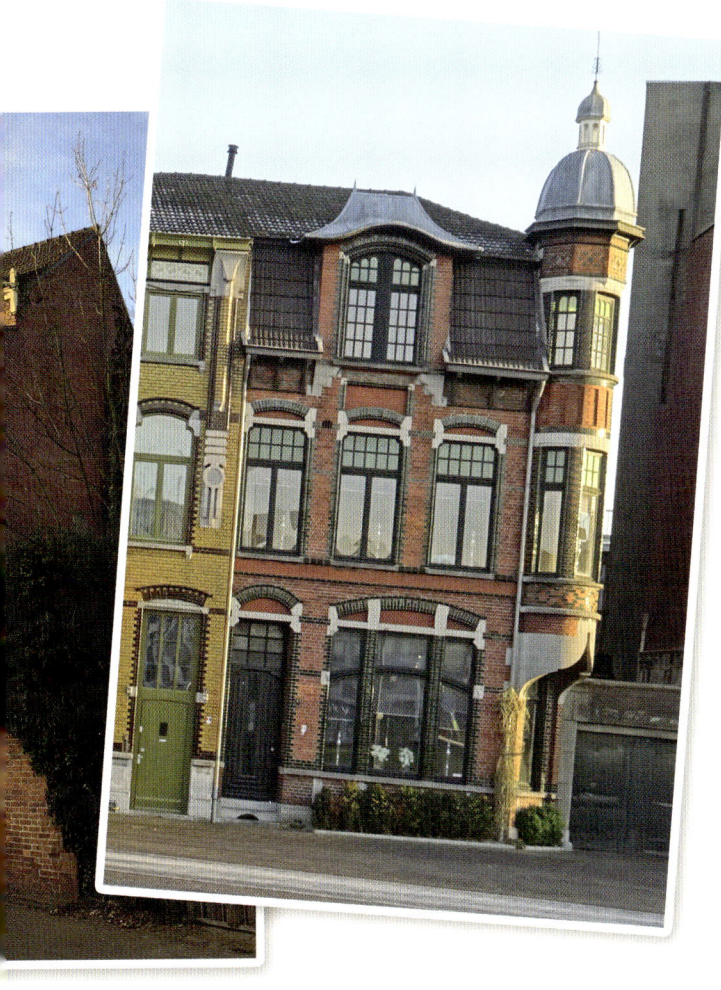

← ↑ In the Netherlands, where I'm from, I have lots of interesting buildings to choose from. These are buildings from the late 1700s and onward. All have very rich ornamental brickwork arrangements that I love to sketch.

PINTEREST

Pinterest is a real treasure trove of subject matter where you will find an enormous number of inspirational buildings in all shapes, sizes, and architectural styles. And the nice thing about Pinterest is that the algorithm presents you with loads of new pictures with every search and click. Unfortunately, since the advent of AI (artificial intelligence)-generated images, I have started to see loads of generated houses appear on the Pinterest pages, making it harder to find "real" buildings. Also, beware of the "magical forest" syndrome. You may spend countless hours in that forest without ever getting started on a single sketch, because of all that great content that you can look at.

INSTAGRAM

When I first started out, I really used Instagram only to post some family photos since I did not know how to use that platform. Things have changed a lot for me in seven years. Now I see such a wealth of artists there, and if it wasn't for Instagram, probably many of you would not have known me. But also, it was on Instagram that I found some wonderful street photography of not just Japanese houses but wonderful buildings in many countries around the world. And I have since connected with many people that have graciously allowed me to sketch based on their photos, as well as publish some selected photos of them in this book in the Projects section.

MAPCRUNCH

During the COVID-19 period when traveling was discouraged or even prohibited, I stumbled across a web service used by artists to paint "virtual outdoors scenes" from a random location round the globe. It is like Google Maps, but it opens up a completely random location every time you do a refresh. You can end up in the most incredible locations this way. And if you look for virtual plein air on Google, you will find some incredible art to be inspired by.

ANATOMY OF A HOUSE

A house can be daunting in all its visual complexity. But if you take a moment and analyze it, you'll discover that there is an underlying system at work, even in some of the most chaotic structures! Try to discover that structure and use that as the foundation for your sketch. So, into what foundational components can you break down a building?

→ This, and any house, can be broken down into easy-to-understand components.

↓ Looking at a silhouette of a building helps you decide if it will make an interesting sketch.

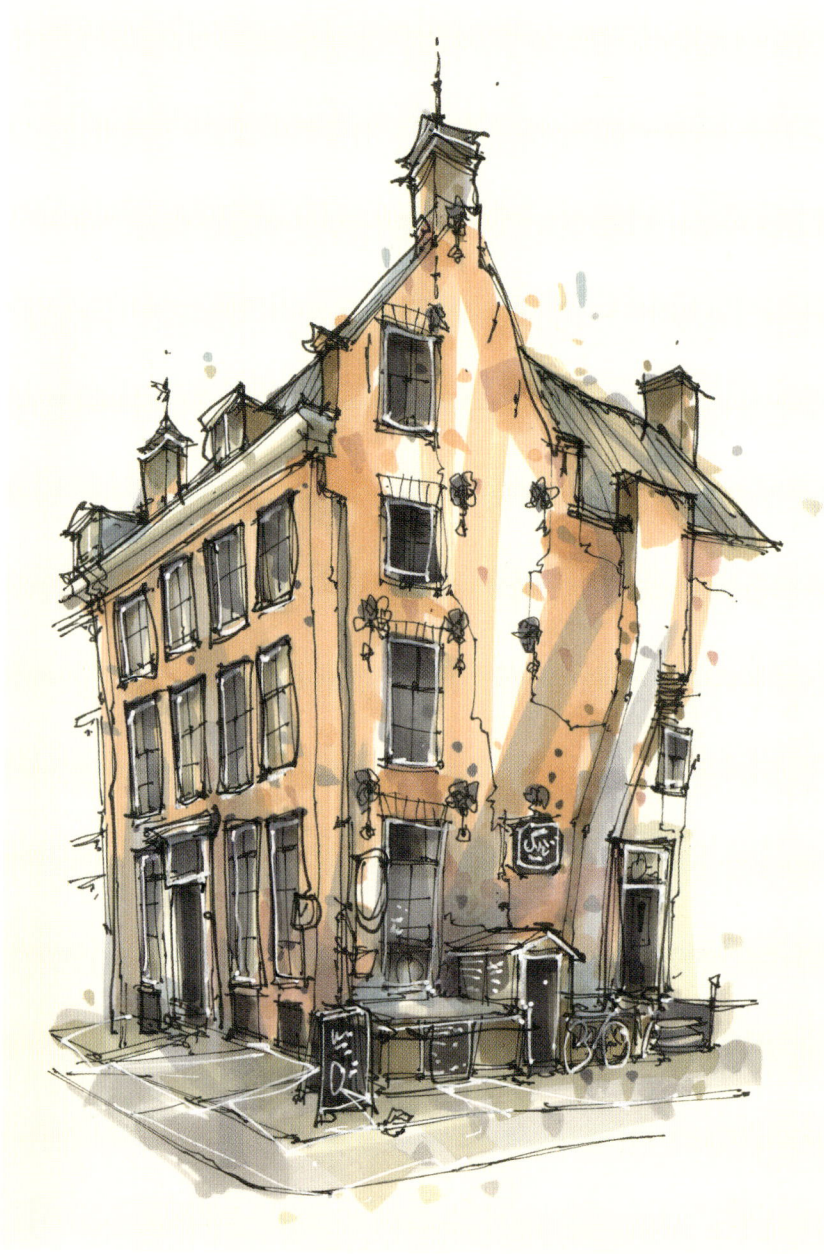

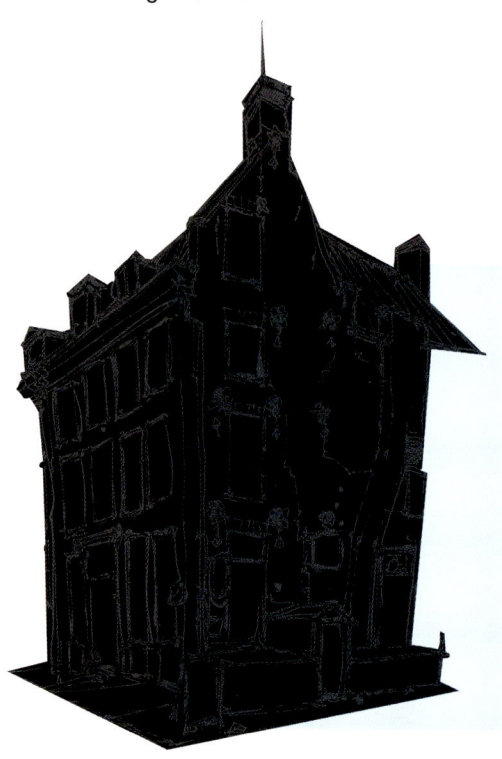

THE IMPORTANCE OF THE SILHOUETTE

You might think that this very basic unit is only a placeholder. And in many cases it is, especially when you're using it as the prime compositional element. But you need to pay close attention to it. The silhouette of this shape is actually very important. Without an interesting outline, you might end up with a really boring sketch, regardless of how much attention you pay to coloring and adding interesting details. If that silhouette is just a flat uninteresting rectangle, your whole sketch will still look quite boring!

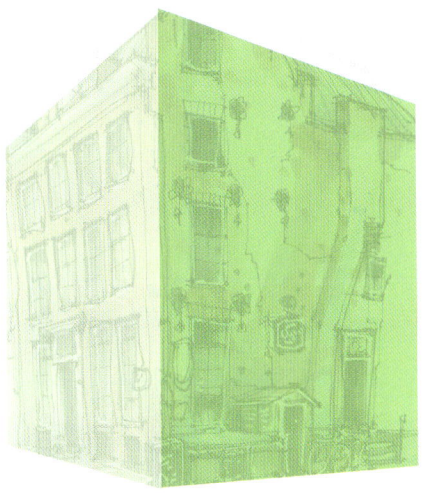

The overall shape of this house is a little bit taller than a square.

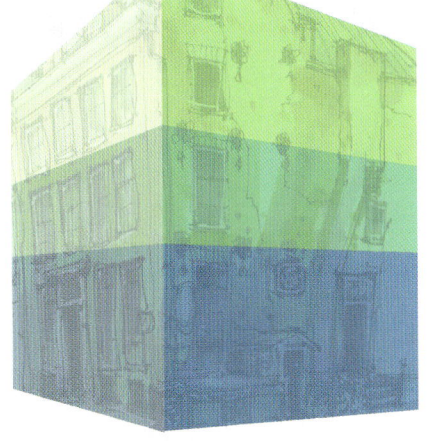

This building has three floors of slightly different heights.

THE BLOCK

The biggest unit of a house is the overall shape. And that overall form is the main volume that you can use as a compositional element on your page. Forget about all the distracting detail and chaos (though that is certainly a lot of fun to sketch, and we'll get to that too!). Analyze the shape of that block: Is it a vertically oriented shape or is it a nice square chunk? Maybe it's more horizontal? That primary volume is a great way to help you put that element down and base your sketch around it.

FLOORS

Now that you have established the big chunk, it's time to see how it's subdivided. With larger structures, you will discover there are one or more floors stacked on top of each other. This stacking can be very obvious or quite minimal. In medieval houses, for instance, you can see a big difference between the different floors. The ground floor mostly has a very small footprint and then the first floor starts to overhang that, and then upward it goes. In some more "organically grown" buildings, like a lot of the Japanese structures in my sketches, you see floors stacked on top of each other. They might have no planned intention to them at all but were just built as the need arose (I love that aspect!). It's easy to spot the segmentation in those types of buildings because they usually have lots of different building materials applied to them. These layers also provide you with a great "hook" for exaggeration in your sketch.

Every vertical division usually has its own function. For instance, a ground level will be a store or a living room area or a kitchen. It will have some sort of access way like a door, and some windows. The second floor might be a bedroom also with windows. You can think of doors and windows as holes in the walls, usually covered by a surface like a door or a window. But still, they are holes. These are in many cases just rectangular areas or rectangles, sometimes with an arched top section. Have a look around and observe how different and interesting these can be.

ROOFS

You can basically group roofs into two categories: slanted or flat for more box-type structures, and domes or conical roofs for cylindrical structures (like temples, castles, and church towers).

This makes it quite easy to analyze your subject.

TIP If you feel like your sketch is lifeless, have a look at supporting elements, such as bushes, air-conditioning units, chimneys, dormer windows, flowers, and balconies.

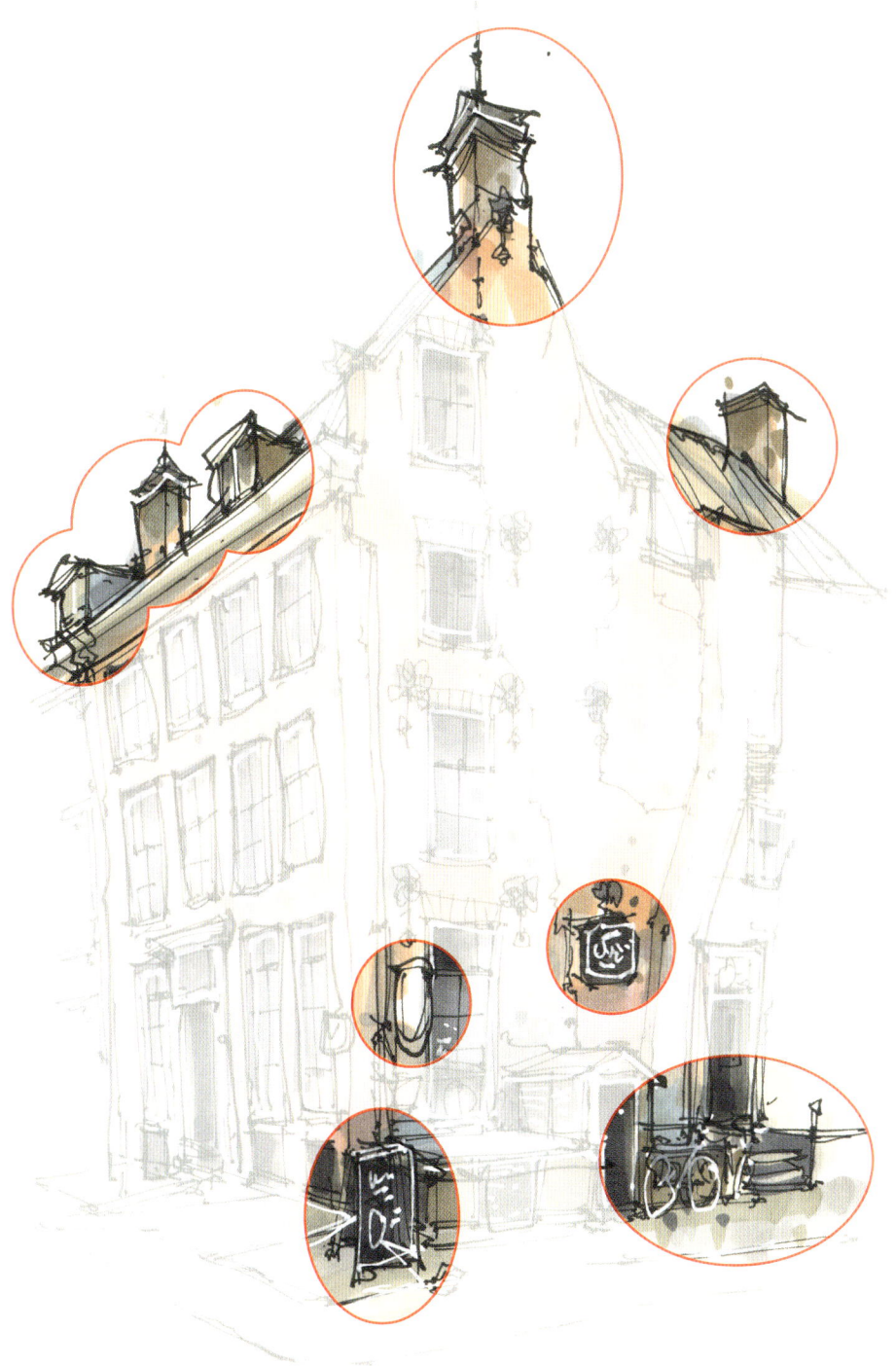

SUPPORTING ELEMENTS

Once you have a good idea about the base structure, you can group the rest of what you see into a category of entourage or supporting elements. Think about bushes, air-conditioning units, chimneys, dormer windows, flowers, balconies, etc.

If you feel like your sketch is lifeless, have a look at these important elements. Are they present in your sketch? Always remember when you are sketching, you make your own reality, and if you feel that a house would benefit from adding some things, even if they aren't there in the photo or on-site, by all means add them. It will make all the difference.

COMPOSITION

Almost always, before anything else, you are looking at a blank page, beckoning to you to do something with it. And that empty sheet is actually your stage. This is where everything will play out. So, first of all, how will you go about placing elements on that stage? That's what composition will take care of.

So how can you do that? Again, for this book on house sketching I will concentrate on how to place a house on that page. That's not going to be a complicated thing. But still, I'm going to give you some pointers on what is good to keep in mind.

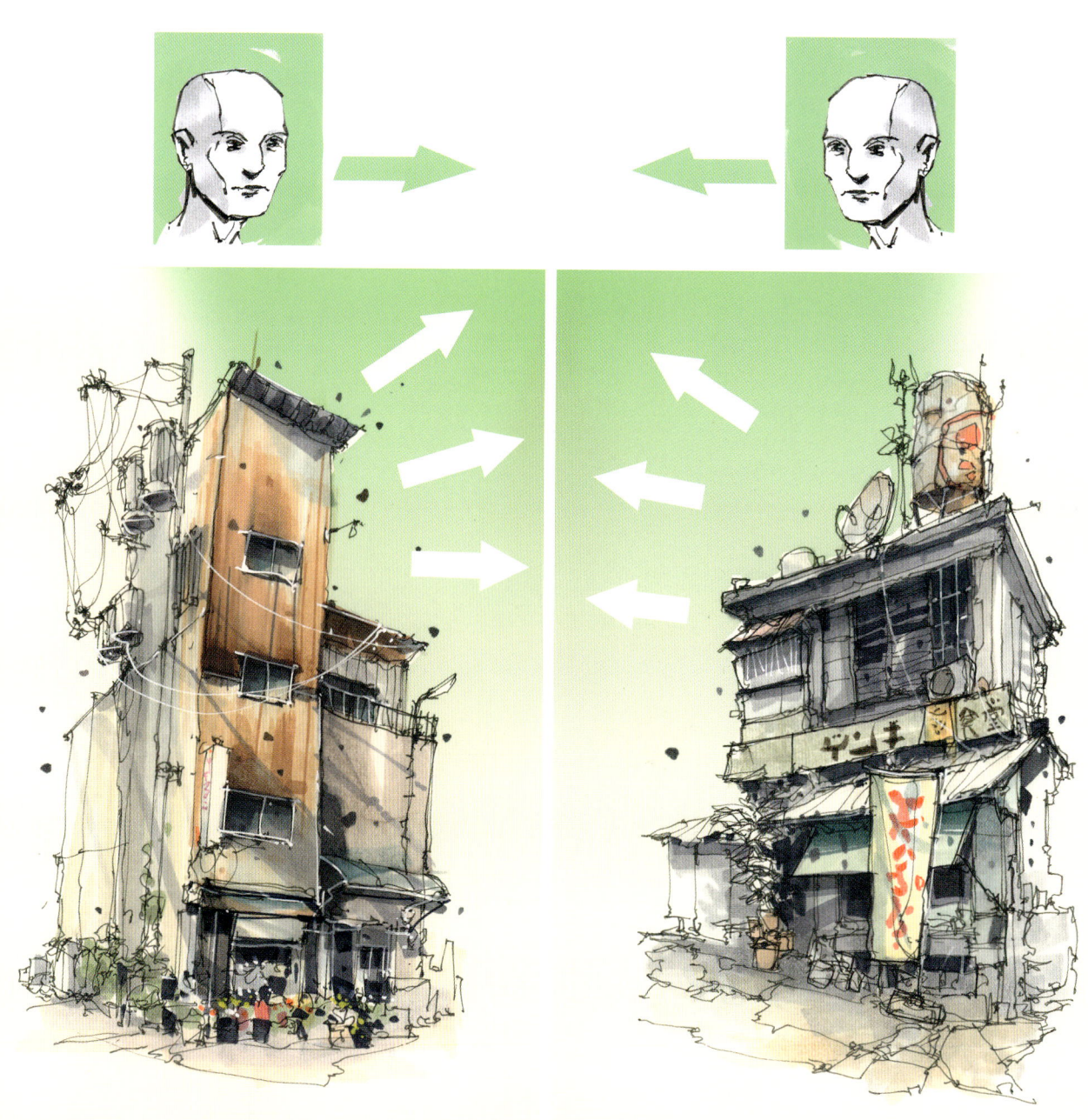

Looking at the facing direction of a building helps you place your subject.

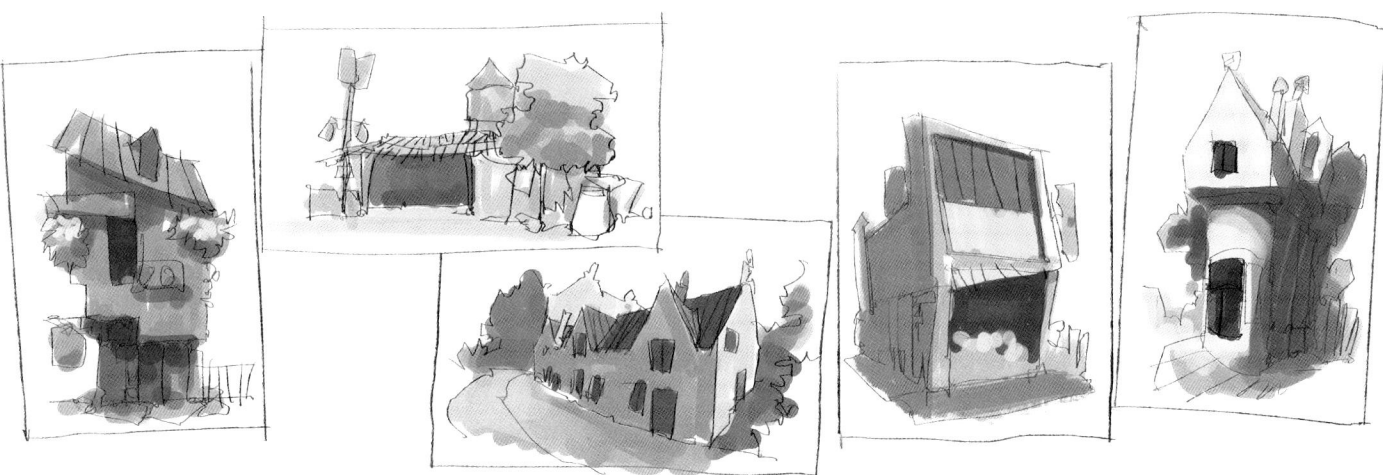

LET'S FACE IT

This might not at first be something you would think of, but it helps a lot if you would imagine your subject, yes, your house in this case, as having a face. Why? This will help you give a watching direction for your subject. The face, or the most storytelling side of your building, needs to have some space to look out from. If you quickly replace the house by an actual person's head, you'll immediately see why that makes sense. If you don't leave room for the head to look away from the page, things start to look cramped and "not right." As soon as you add some more room to the viewing side of the face, it gets more relaxed. And that works for the building as well. Your house will have that "main" side in your sketch. And from that side, add breathing room. You'll see this at work in the illustrations.

THUMBNAILING

Of course it would be cumbersome and a lot of work sketching houses to actually find that perfect spot on the page. That's why it can help to create some thumbnails, tiny sketches. Like I said, for houses as single units this will not be too complicated a process. You basically have two orientational options: portrait and landscape.

If you have a structure that is taller than it is wide, it will usually best fit in a portrait-oriented page layout. Buildings that are wider than tall best go in landscape orientation.

Of course you can play with this. Especially if you start exaggerating aspects of your house, it is easy to stretch a building that is actually very low and wide into a taller structure that fits a portrait orientation. And vice versa, you can squish a tall building and pound it into a landscape frame of reference. This will not work for sketches of structures that you intend to keep more or less truthful to their real proportions. But for more loosely interpreted work, this is really a great way to have fun.

DEPTH

Now that you have seen some of the main perspective construction methods, you might think that is all there is to it. But it's not! Perspective is a great tool for getting things structurally right in your sketch, but there's something else that is of vital importance to give your sketch that visual oomph: depth.

I don't mean depth by vanishing points and things getting smaller toward the horizon, but in a much more direct way. And the cool thing is that you don't even have to construct it! You just have to be aware of it. And once you realize that, it's going to be a very powerful ally!

OVERLAP

A really powerful way to create depth in your sketch is by using overlap. It's a technique that is very widely used by artists in paintings, photography, and in stage and film design. Overlap is also a great organizing and compositional tool. At its simplest form, you can arrange items into a foreground, mid-ground, and background "plane." Just like you would see it in a theatre. Most of the action plays out in the mid-ground, with the fore- and background giving context and depth to the scene.

→ Schematic and final composition making use of overlap.

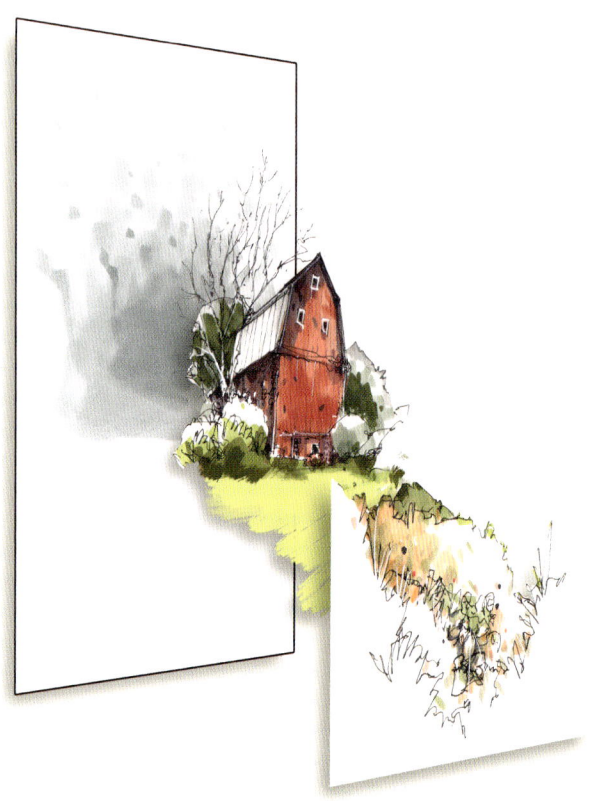

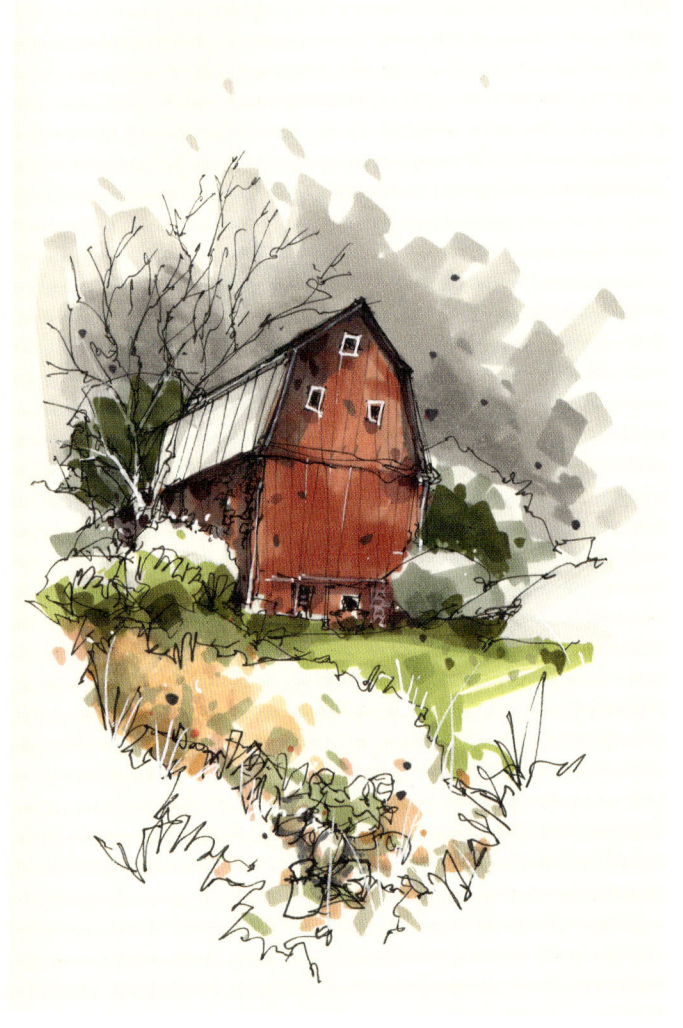

Scan to watch a tutorial.

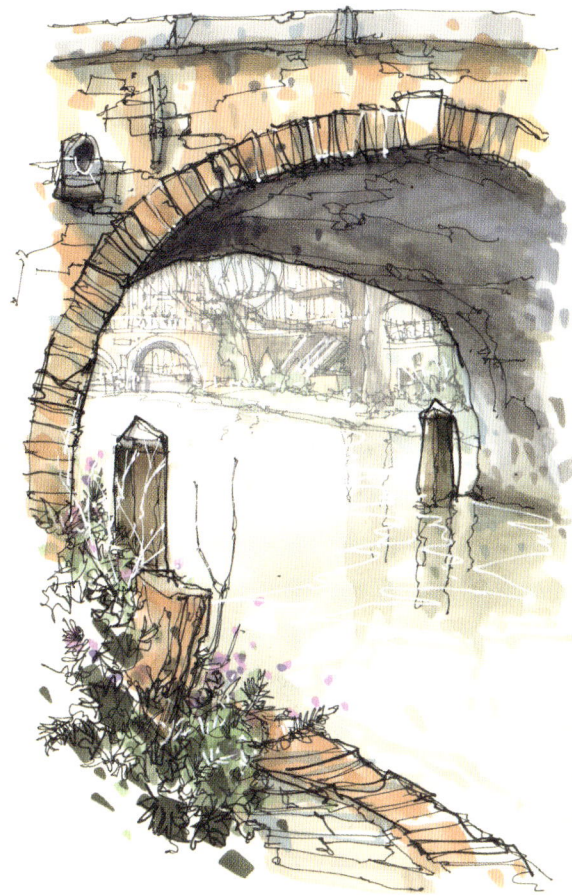

I did a little Photoshop magic to enhance the light haze in that arch.

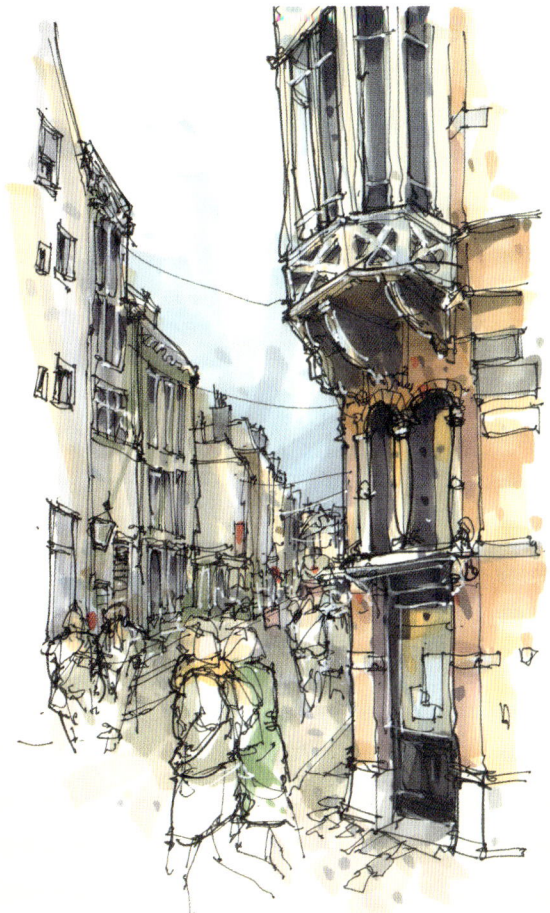

Strong bold lines on the foreground building create more depth.

VALUE

Remember that things get smaller when they are farther removed from you. Many of you will have probably made use of that phenomenon at one time or another by taking a photo where you are pinching a tower or tree between your fingers (because they are a distance away from you). Well, there's also another thing at play here. If you look at things in the distance, often times the colors start to fade too. Things get lighter and a bit hazy. That's probably where the phrase "fade into the distance" comes from. Well, that fading into the distance is a very nice indicator of depth. For sketching single buildings, you will probably not need this depth cue that much. But for larger scenes, such as cityscapes or buildings in a landscape, keep this one in mind.

THICK AND THIN

A seemingly odd one out for depth is line thickness. But I use it a lot and it is quite effective. In technical illustration, line thickness adds to the dimensionality of a shape. Usually outline edges are made with thicker lines, and interior edges that bend away from the viewer also get that thicker line weight.

Scan to watch a tutorial.

Scan to watch a tutorial.

PERSPECTIVE: THE LEAST YOU NEED TO KNOW

You experience the space around you in 3D because your left and right eye have slightly different views that your brain combines into a three-dimensional "image." You can see depth this way and judge distances and relationships between objects within that space. But there are more cues. Things that are closer to you appear larger than things farther away. Large objects like houses and trees appear as tiny things when they are farther away from you. Of course, you know the size of these things, so you immediately understand that it is the distance that makes you see these forms smaller than their actual size.

On a piece of paper, there is no actual distance between objects. You need to create that illusion of depth by drawing things that are farther away smaller than shapes that are closer by. But how can you do that in a consistent way? That's where perspective construction techniques come into the picture (so to speak).

Regardless of what type of perspective construction method you want to use, the primary question is: Where are you, the observer? The observer is vital because it determines how you're going to use the construction method. Since you're going to sketch your house or scene from your vantage point, it's you, the observer, that this perspective will be dependent on. And the nice thing is that once you're done, the viewer can easily swap places with you and see the world in your sketch, literally, from your point of view. So, where are you? There's one important line that plays a key role in establishing your viewpoint. And that's a simple, horizontal line. And, yes, it's the horizon! And to make that stick even more, you will see a lot of things lining up horizontally along that horizon line if you look straight ahead. To illustrate how that works, let's look at some examples.

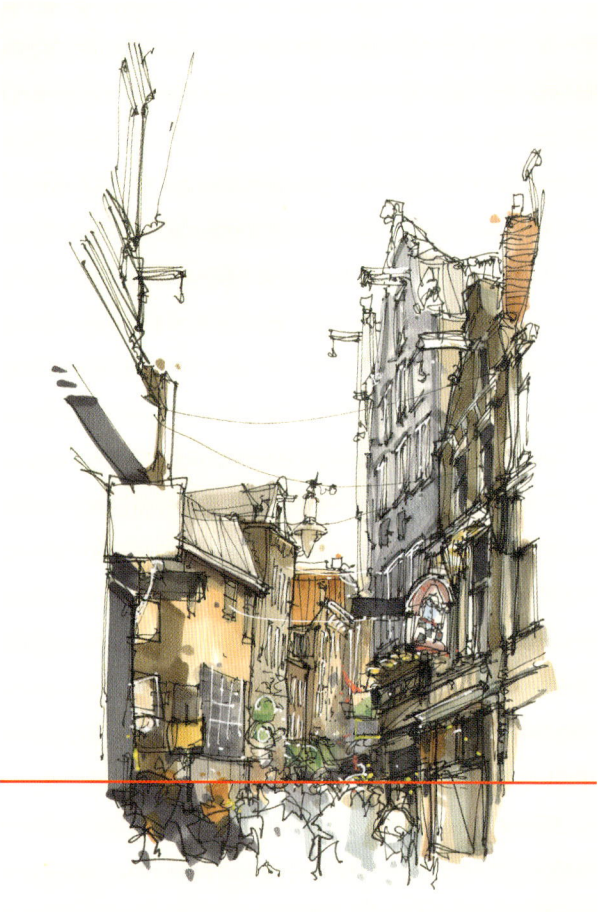

In this case, the horizon line is at your normal eye level, while standing straight. What this means is that everything that is on that line is all the same height as your eye-level height.

HUMAN'S-EYE VIEW

Let's have a look at the most obvious one first. You're just standing around in a street and looking straight ahead. People that pass by are more or less at eye level with you; you can look them in the eye, so to speak. And all other objects, buildings, cars, trucks, and trains look the way you're used to seeing them. This provides a very nice and comfortable frame of reference.

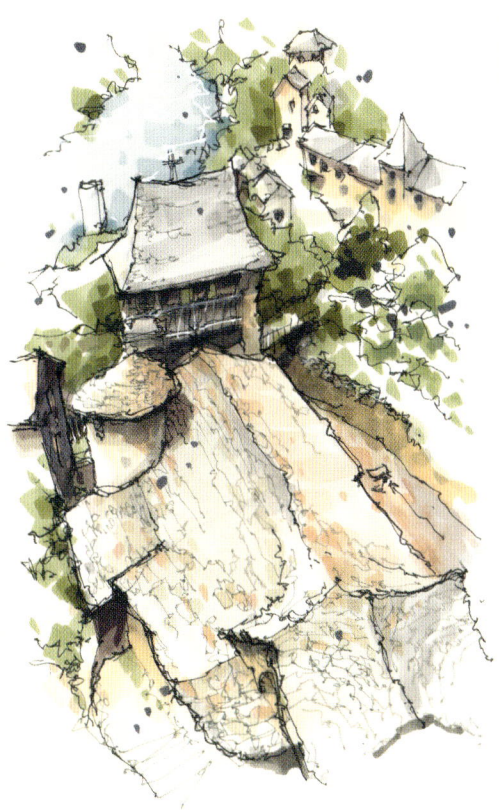

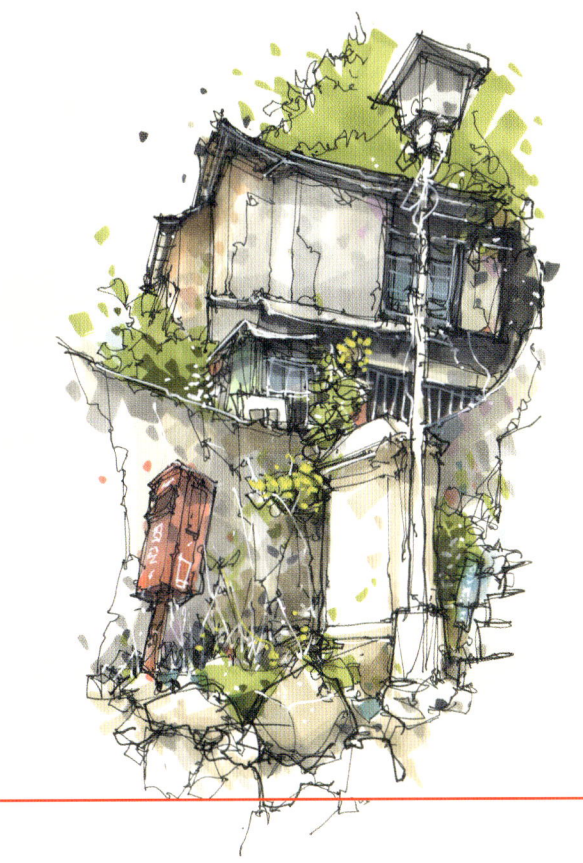

In the case of a bird's-eye view, the horizon line moves way up.

With a worm's-eye view, your horizon line moves all the way down and only tiny things will match its height, like pebbles or a matchbox. Everything else will tower way above that horizon line.

BIRD'S-EYE VIEW

Now imagine that you could take to the skies and fly high up in the air, or just take a balloon, to be more practical. Suddenly, you see the world as a bird would see it. It's quite unfamiliar for us to look at things this way. But it gives a dramatic impression. Buildings look tiny, and you see mostly roofs or facades of skyscrapers that tower even higher than you. Looking at the world like this can make things seem insignificant.

WORM'S-EYE VIEW

The total opposite of a bird's-eye view is the worm's-eye view (or other preferred creature that lives close to the ground). Like the bird's-eye view, this is a view that you don't usually experience in your day to day. It can provide some very nice dramatic effects for a sketch of a building or a scene. Ordinary items, even people, look majestically impressive, seen from this close to the ground.

TIP Since you're going to sketch your house or scene from your vantage point, it's you, the observer, that this perspective will be dependent on. That way the viewer can easily swap places with you and see the world in your sketch from your point of view.

TYPES OF PERSPECTIVE

So now that you know a bit about the relationship between the horizon line and some key viewpoints (human, bird, and worm), you can start to combine this with the construction methods that I am going to discuss next. There you're going to see the importance of that single horizontal line!

Let's take a look at the most common perspective types. Knowing these three will already get you quite far in understanding and deconstructing many of your typical spatial situations when it comes to sketching houses. Remember the vantage points from earlier in this chapter? They all depend on where you, the viewer, are in space and in what direction you're looking.

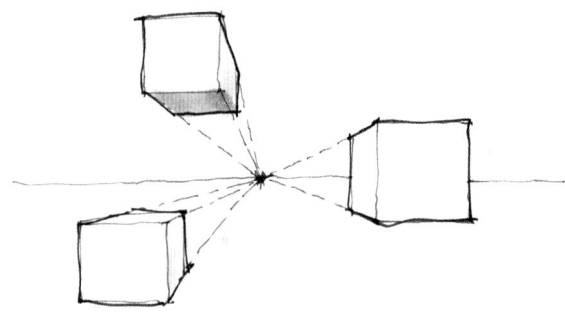

Central Perspective

Central perspective, or single point perspective, is one of the most basic of the constructed perspectives. The first thing to establish is that horizon line. Once you have that drawn on your sheet of paper, you simply add a point on the horizon. That's it! Now you can start to draw shapes and give them depth by drawing lines from the corner points of these objects right to that vanishing point on the horizon. That's all there is to it. Central point is already a great method to construct a house or even a street scene and give it some believable spatial quality.

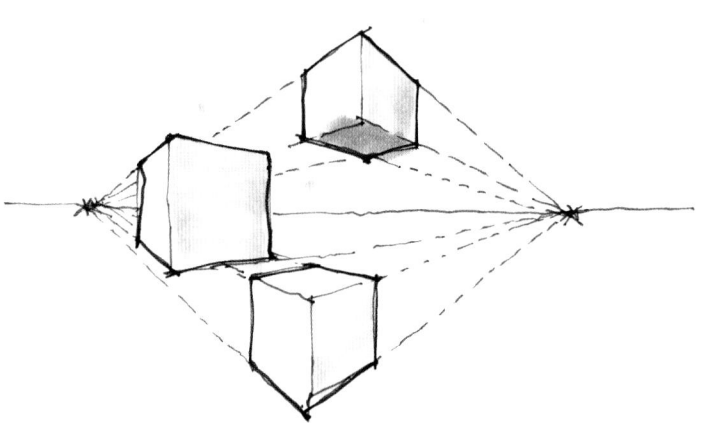

Two-Point Perspective

Although central point allows you to add depth to your scene, the way in which it does this can be a bit limiting. As you can see in the schematic, all objects (you can substitute them for houses, cars, boxes) somehow all "look" straight at you. That gives it a very forced, rigid feel. And that's certainly not what you're after. So, let's see what happens when we add another vanishing point on that horizon line. Now that's starting to look much more dynamic! By adding that second vanishing point, both sides of a box that you can see each go to one vanishing point, and you clearly get a more believable and less forced shape. Two-point perspective is great for showing houses when you see more than just the facade.

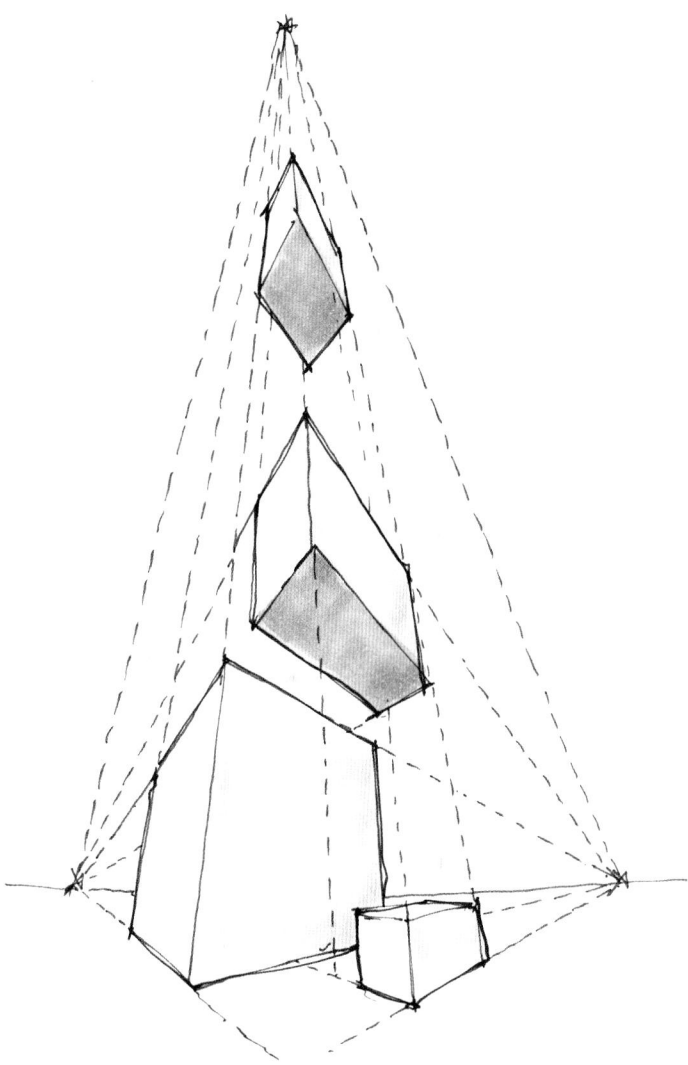

Three-Point Perspective

In three-point perspective, we take that dynamic up another notch—yes, by adding a third vanishing point. But unlike the two earlier vanishing points, this one does not lie on the horizon line. This one you can think of as lying in the direction that you're looking. So, if you look up, that third vanishing point lies above the horizon, and if you look down, it lies below the horizon. This third vanishing point gives your scene a sense of grand scale or of a really dramatic intensity for everyday objects. Normally you are not used to seeing regular objects in such a distorted way (even though your photos might suggest otherwise). But by exaggerating perspective with that third vanishing point, you can amplify the sense of depth.

Keep in mind that these construction methods are simplifications of what we see. Regardless of where you look. There will always be vanishing points both on the horizon and in the direction (up or down) that you are looking. But usually, these vanishing points will be much, much farther apart than what you can construct on paper. When you put the vanishing points on paper, things tend to look really huge. But then again, that might be precisely what you want!

A FINAL THOUGHT ON PERSPECTIVE

I am always hesitant to show perspective as a construction means to my students. The reason is that often, when you start constructing something, you run the risk of losing the spontaneity in a sketch. You start to mechanically trace what you have set up in your perspective schematic. This would result in a technically more or less correct sketch, but you may have killed all life and soul in it. So, try to be cautious about applying perspective too much as a set of rules. Use it more as an underlying principle and soft guideline to orient some key shapes in your house toward.

SKETCHING

I consider the way I sketch much as I would write a letter to someone. I want to let my pen skate across the page in a fluent way. I search for the landmarks in my subject and "flow" to the next point of interest. But of course, that is a very poetic way of describing it. Still, it helps to think about it this way. Let's take this analogy a little further and compare the writing you would do in your day to day against writing that you would do when you want to write beautifully. As soon as you want to make it beautiful and gracious, you will have to slow down and start to think about your movements. And as soon as you slow down, you might freeze in your linework and things will start to look rigid and forced. So, keep it flowing.

You can also carry this over to what you are sketching. In houses, rhythms will play an important role. That can be in the way the levels (floors) in a house, the railings surrounding a balcony, or the ways roof tiles are arranged. But also, how pavement is organized on ground level or how picket fences are sketched surrounding your main house. You can of course space out these elements which are arrangements of lines or shapes and make them more alive by actually breaking away from the normally regular patterns. In fences, you can break them up in lines that are not exactly parallel to each other. The same goes for tiles on the roof. Vary the lines in such a way that they are not perfectly and neatly ordered. Check my sketches and you see me use that aspect a lot.

You have to remember that I have a lot of experience in three-dimensional work from my day job as a visualization artist. That knowledge comes to me automatically. I have explained the basics of that knowledge in the previous section. But what I would like to stress is that you really should not get too involved in the construction of perspectives. Knowing the basics is more than enough to create your work. Placing too much attention on the technical side will soon let you fall into the trap of dead, mechanical drawings without much soul.

When you are sketching with the intention of subsequently coloring them with markers, you have to keep in mind that you don't fall into the trap of "coloring" in your sketch while still in your line-

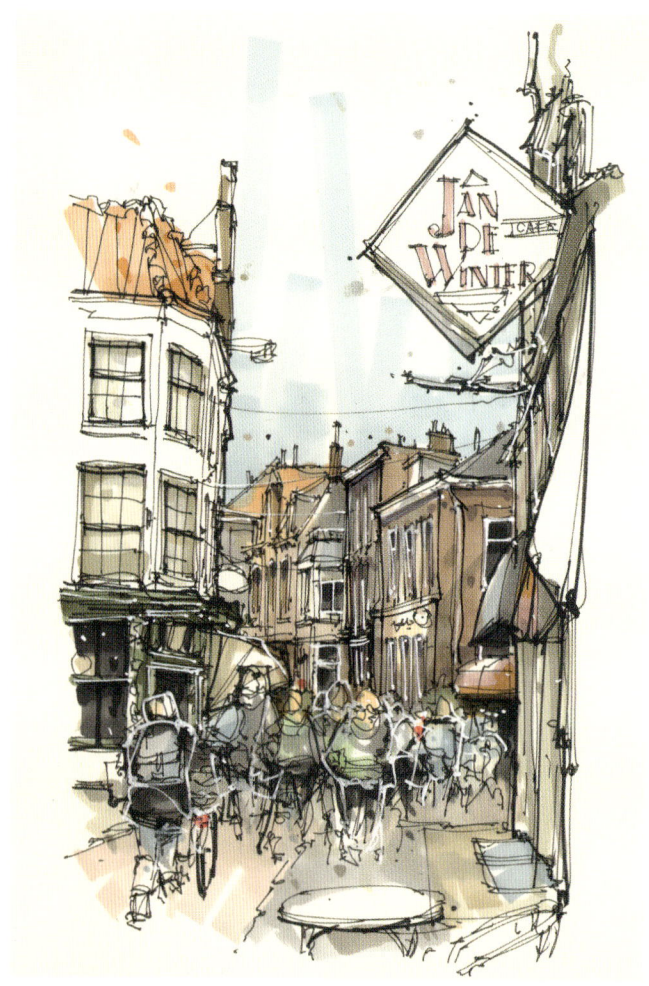

Play with depth using fore-, mid-, and background.

sketching phase. Doing shading work with your pen in this stage, like hatching and cross-hatching areas that are in shade, can start to look dirty and chaotic when you start coloring over these areas. Try to keep the linework as clean as possible. Even those very dark spots, like windows or deep shadows, are best left for the coloring stage. Black in a colored sketch will almost always look like very black holes. When you use a dark gray (even an almost black or deep dark blue or other hue) you'll keep these areas alive. The linework can still show through these areas and that looks much almost all the time. Of course, if you are going for a more graphic, comic look, feel free to punch in those blacks during your sketching phase.

Where this graphical look can also be very pleasing is when you are making a pure minimal value sketch where you use just two or three shades.

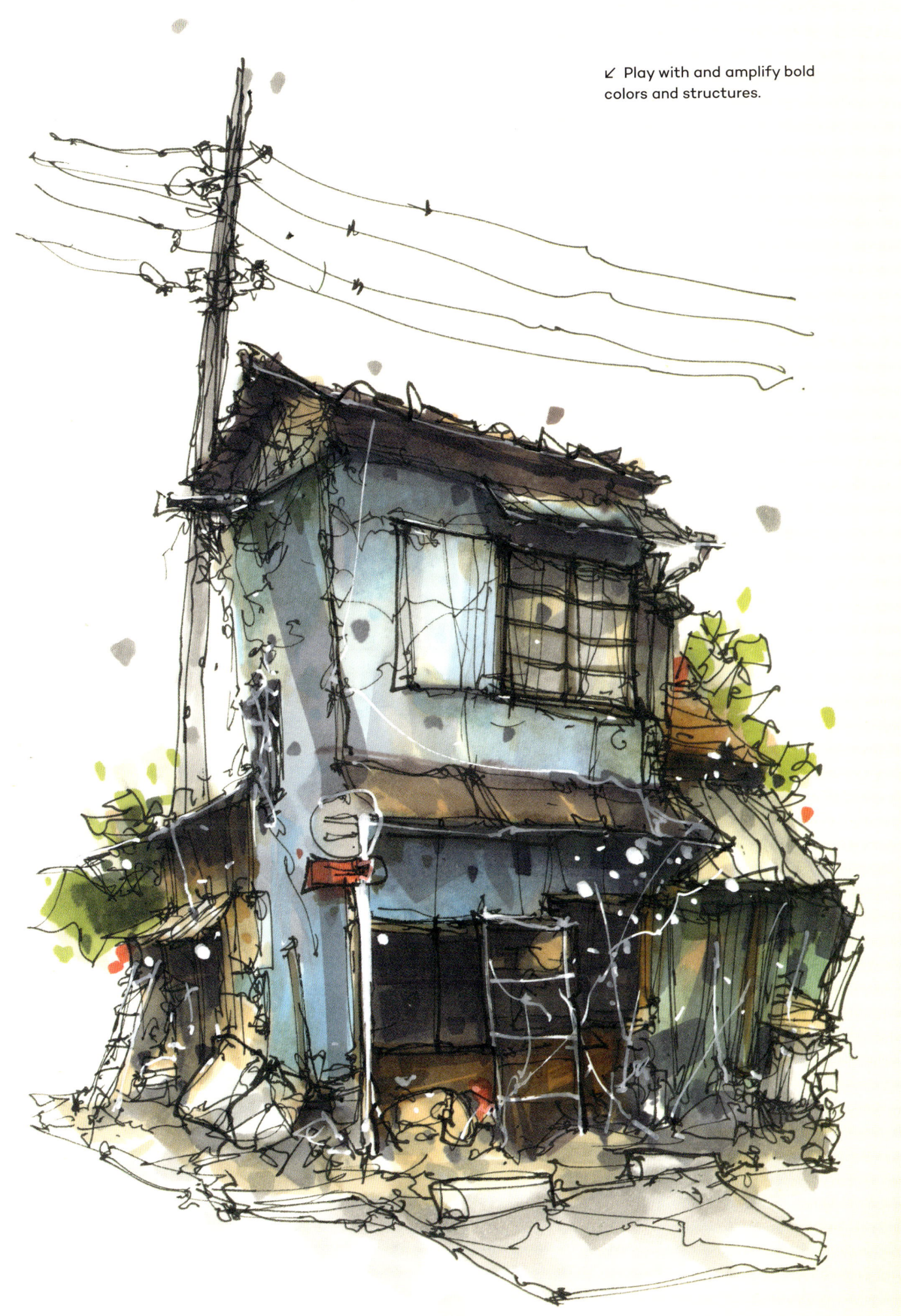

↙ Play with and amplify bold colors and structures.

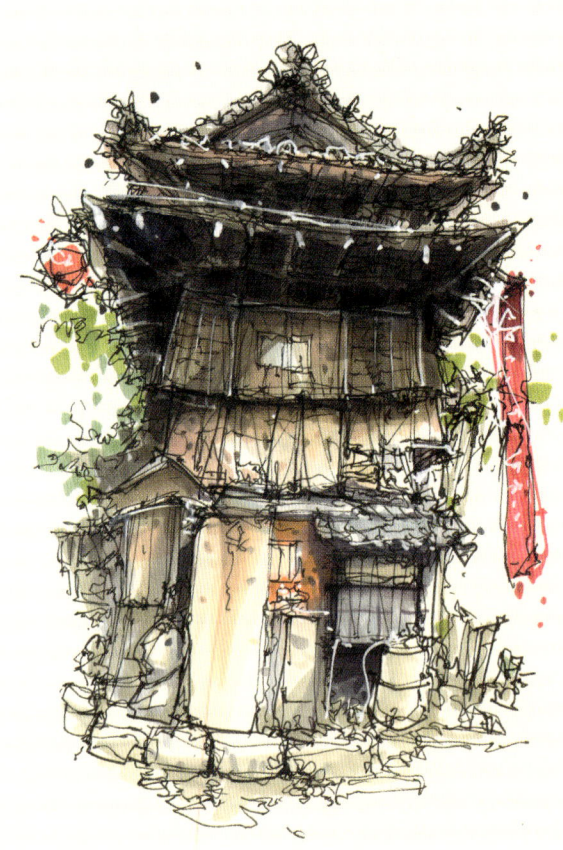

Use minimal, but harmonizing, colors and bold shadows.

Black can be very effective there in powerfully establishing volume and mood.

Sketching is a highly personal way of expressing yourself. And so the tools that you will be using to create your marks and lines will add a lot to the way your sketches will look. There are artists who use fountain pens with a variety of nibs that create variable line thicknesses. Others use calligraphic pens with a flat chisel nib for a highly variable thickness in line while drawing, from very thick and bold to thin and delicate. By turning and tilting the pen, you can achieve that in a single flowing stroke of the pen. You can use dip pens and even pointy thick branches dipped in ink to make highly personal marks for your sketches.

The small drawback to creating dynamic lines with these tools is that the ink that is used takes longer to dry before going over it with your color markers. That can be a problem when you are on location or if you have a limited amount of time. A (battery-powered) blow dryer can speed up that process of course, but that also takes extra space in your kit.

Like I said, when I picked my materials, I chose them at random, but they turned out to work really well together. So, the fineliners I use have the advantage of more or less drying instantly to receive color right on top. I use mostly two and occasionally three different line weights for expressive lines. When you sketch with fiber-tipped fineliner, you can "break" or bend the tip out of its structured shape and have something of an irregular broken tip. That allows much more random marks to play with in your sketching work.

The key to discovering what you like is to experiment. There is absolutely no need to stick to just one tool! Use fineliners, fountain pens, pointed sticks, butchered nibs glued to a pen, and maybe even heavier gear like really chunky black markers. Somewhere there lies the discovery of your personal means of expression, something that will immediately tell viewers it's *you*. In that sense, don't view what I describe here, or use personally, as the stuff to use for a successful sketch. I never chose the materials in a conscious way, but I learned to explore their possibilities to express myself. I am still experimenting and so should you!

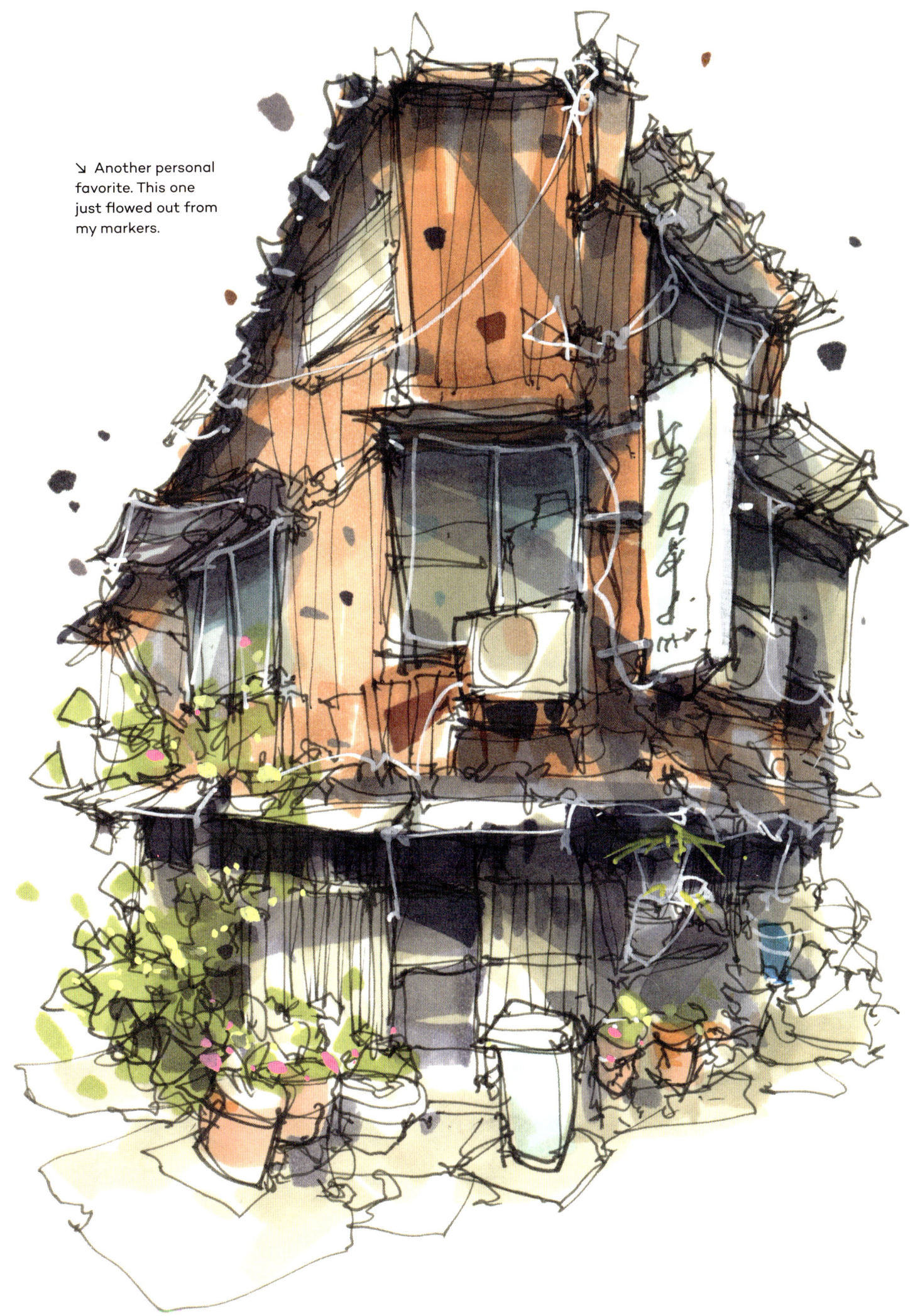

↘ Another personal favorite. This one just flowed out from my markers.

COLORING

While the line sketching is a very foundational step, the coloring phase will really bring your sketch to life. It's critical to realize that your lines are important, but in service of your coloring. What I mean is that you should prevent yourself from drawing too much texture and too many details in your line work. That is the domain of colors. So have a look at some techniques you can use to bring your work to life!

BASE COLORING

Let's start with some very simple but important and effective techniques. The simplest being a single flat color. This is the easiest way to start. When I first began sketching, I only had six or so colors to work with and I applied them simply to my sketch. But if you pick out a set of nice hues this can work really well!

→ For this sketch,
I used only four colors!

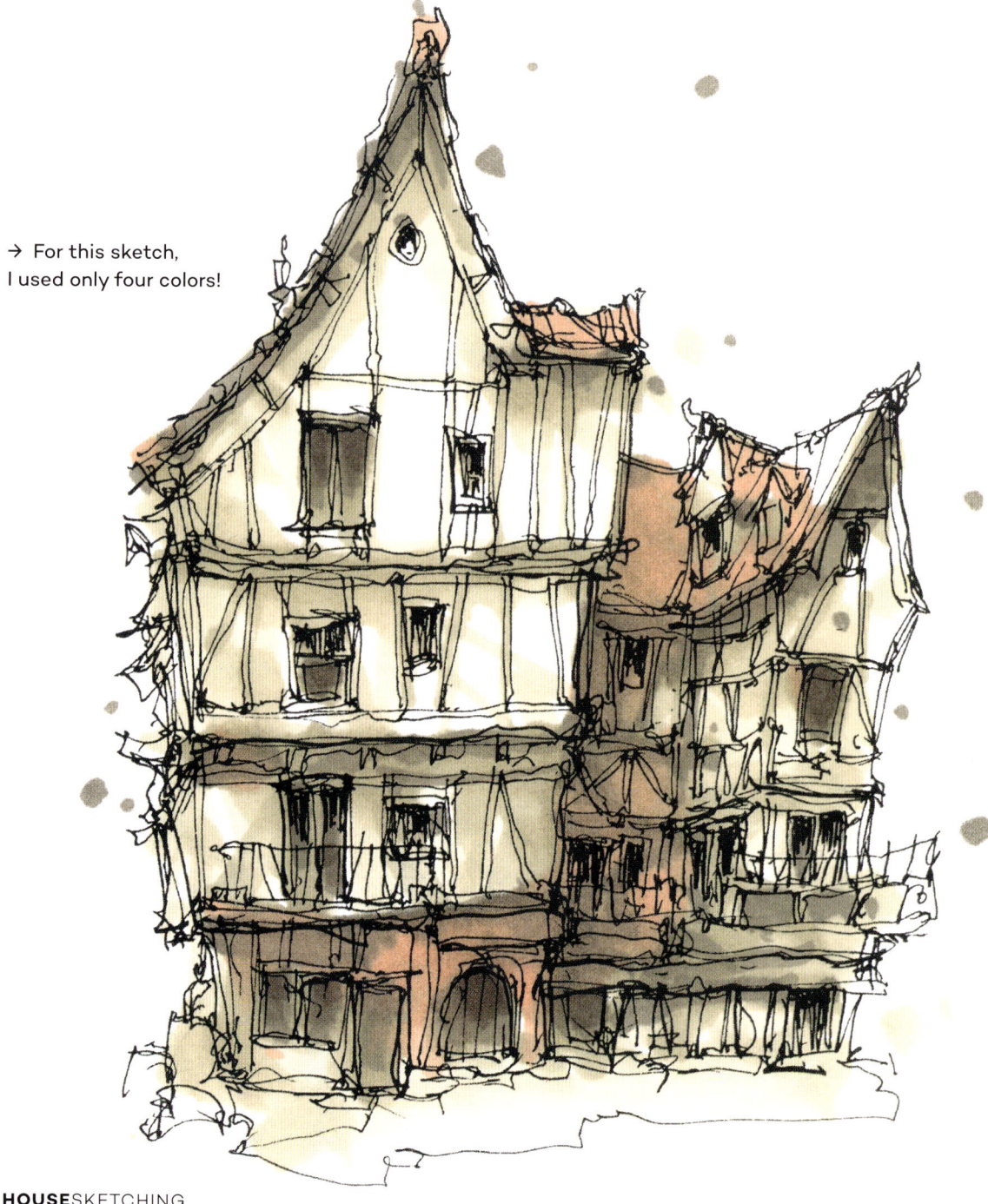

FROM LIGHT TO DARK

Since markers are transparent, you need to slowly build up your coloring and shading. If you start out too dark, there's no way to go lighter again, and your sketch will most probably be ruined. So start light and gradually build up with darker shades. Keep in mind that colors on your page will not necessarily stay dark when you apply multiple coats of a single shade. They may dry up in exactly that lighter shade of the first pass. It is the moisture that temporarily will darken things more. That said, there will be some difference in value. But a good light to dark is best with a series of actually darker values in markers. The simplest, of course, is a set of gray values. You can start with a 20% gray for instance, and then add a 40%, a 60%, and more (if you want to go really dark).

Scan to watch a tutorial.

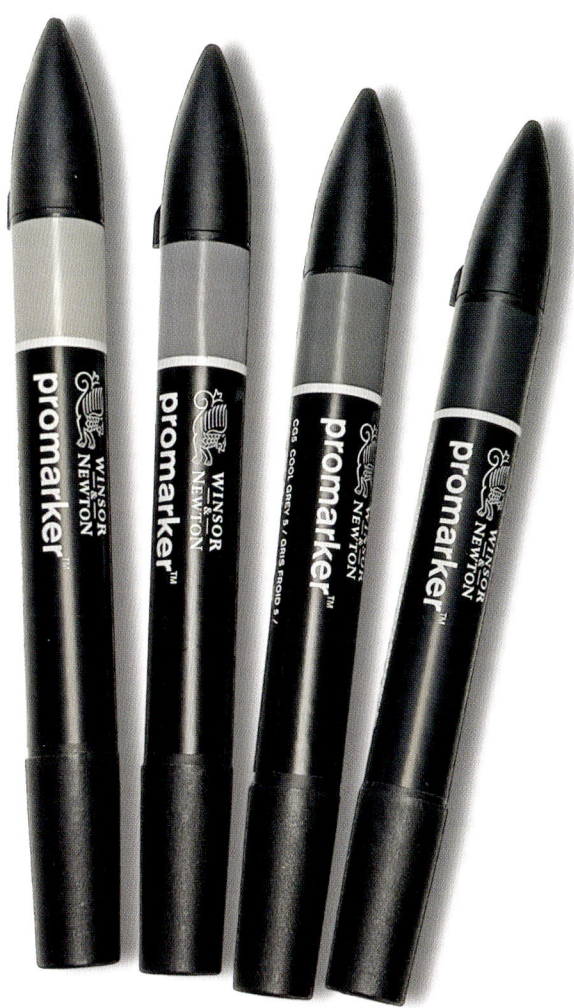

↑ Sketching with a range of grays is a great way to learn about values.

GRADIENTS AND BLENDS

There are two ways to make a color or value go from one to another: either in a step-by-step way with visible layers of changing colors, or as a smooth gradient where you almost don't see the changes. Both have their own use in coloring your sketch.

Layered gradient.

Scan to watch a comparison of layered and smooth gradients.

Smooth gradient.

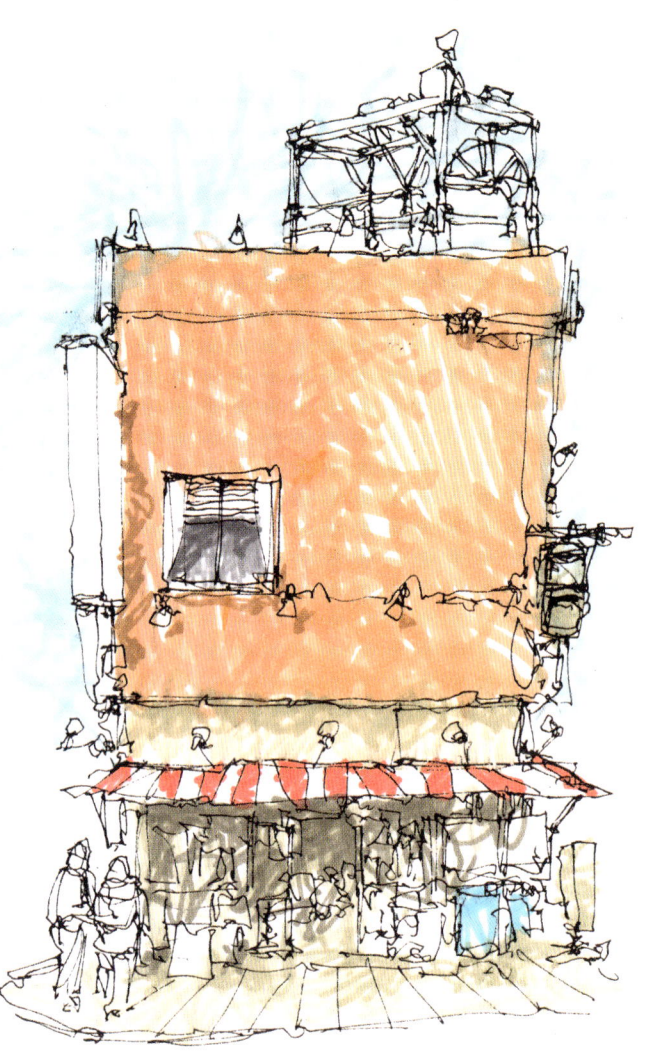

Here I colored in random directions.
See how messy it looks?

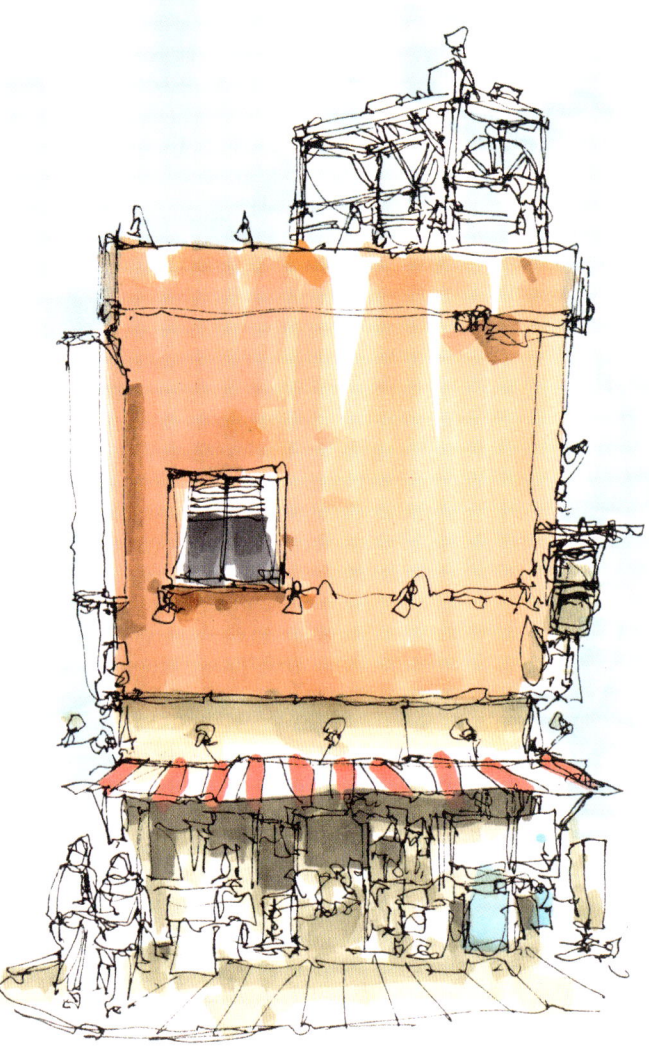

Keeping the strokes going in mostly the same
direction creates a much more pleasing effect.

STROKE DIRECTIONS MATTER

Alcohol markers are a really fast-flowing and fast-drying medium. That means that you can work quickly and efficiently in one go. No waiting for the marker to dry. But that also means you need to lay down your colors in a quick and flowing manner. Going over areas that you previously covered might lead to some nasty striping and crisscross effects. This means that you need to plan out strokes. Not in a too-conscious way, but you can't just start "coloring in" sections like in coloring books. Of course, if that is what you aim for, that's no problem. But if you want your sketches to be dynamic and breathe life, your brushstrokes will matter . . . a lot!

*Scan to watch
a tutorial.*

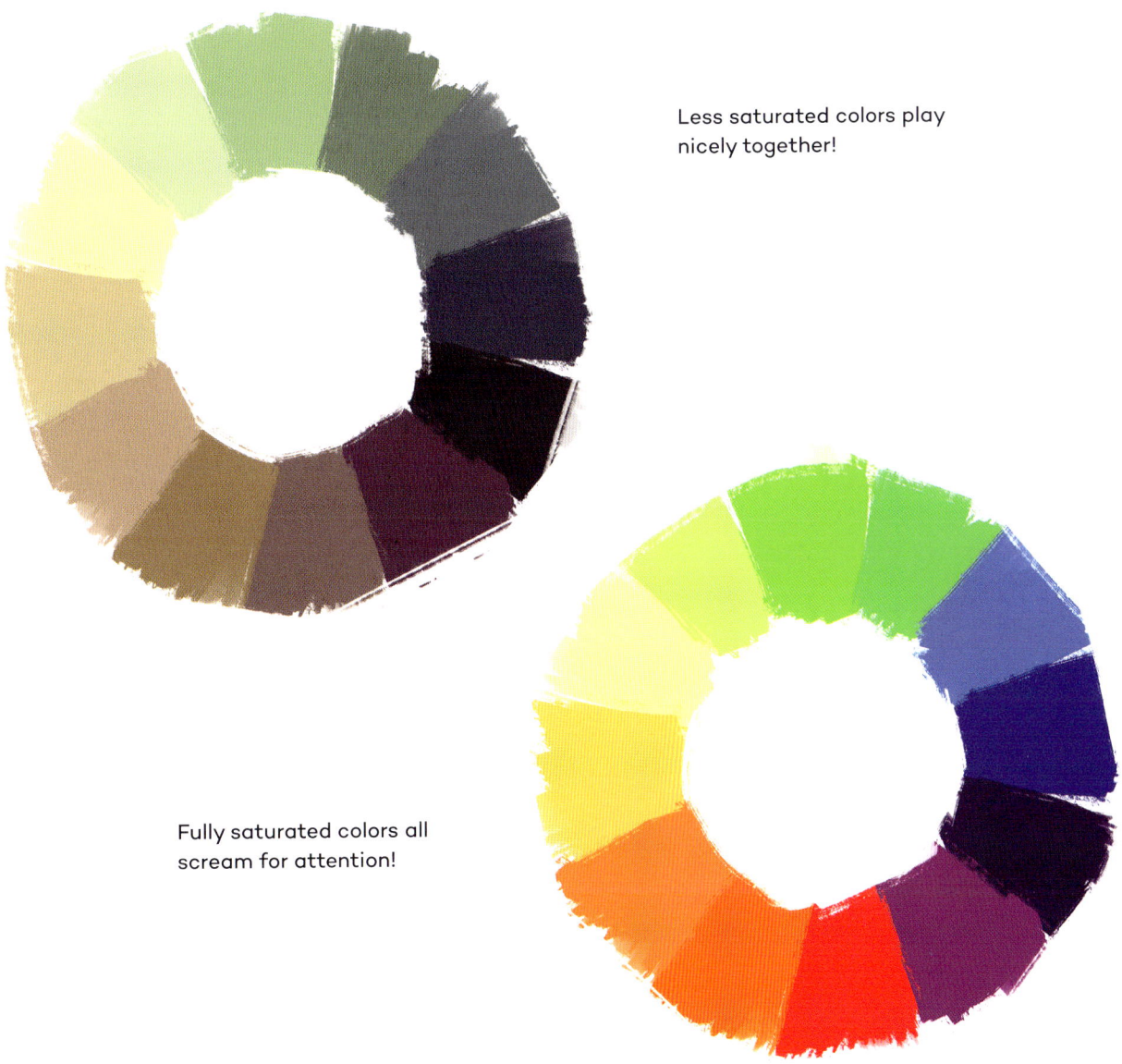

Less saturated colors play nicely together!

Fully saturated colors all scream for attention!

CHOOSING COLORS

What I read a lot in the reactions when I post a sketch on Instagram is that people love my colors. That is a very nice compliment for me. Especially because when I started use markers, I didn't know what I was doing. On the computer I work in 3D and when I describe colors there, the software does a lot of the calculations to make things look right. I have worked extensively with colors in my house sketches and learned what works.

One of the secrets I discovered is the relation between the saturation of a color and the way this helps balance it with different color hues. What does that mean? I mainly use desaturated colors for most sections in my sketches. These grayish mid-range value color hues almost always start to work together really nicely. If you put their saturated counterparts next to each other, things would clash intensely. So one of the most important things to look for in your marker color palette is to shop for some desaturated earth tones, desaturated greens, and very desaturated blues. They should all be close to the grayish side. You will discover that they go together much easier. If you then pick a single more saturated color for accent, you are well on your way! The shop in my hometown Venlo where I buy my markers actually has a name for the colors I buy there: "Dirty Kiefer Colors!"

DETAILING

If you look at sketching as a process of going from simplified big forms to more details, you find that it's a way to keep from getting lost in the overwhelming amount of detail that a scene can present to you. Start with the big gesture first (blocks of houses or that main block of a single house) and become more and more concrete gradually. Detail allows you to create a more interesting and visually rich sketch. But beware of over-detailing! If you add detail on every level and in every single spot of your sketch, you run the risk of creating a chaotic jumble of details that confuses the viewer, and even you, as to why the sketch suddenly doesn't work anymore. A well-constructed sketch consists of big, medium, and small shapes. And they are distributed in a balanced way on your page. With a house that can be a large facade (big shape), subdivided by a series of floors (medium shapes), and windows, doors, and signs of flowerpots hanging on the wall (small shapes). And to take that street example again, you have the big chunks of that street (big shape), subdivided into single houses (medium shapes), and finally doors, windows, and people shopping in that street (small shapes). By grouping these big, medium, and small shapes, you create a sense of balance that gives your sketch a pleasant and interesting feel.

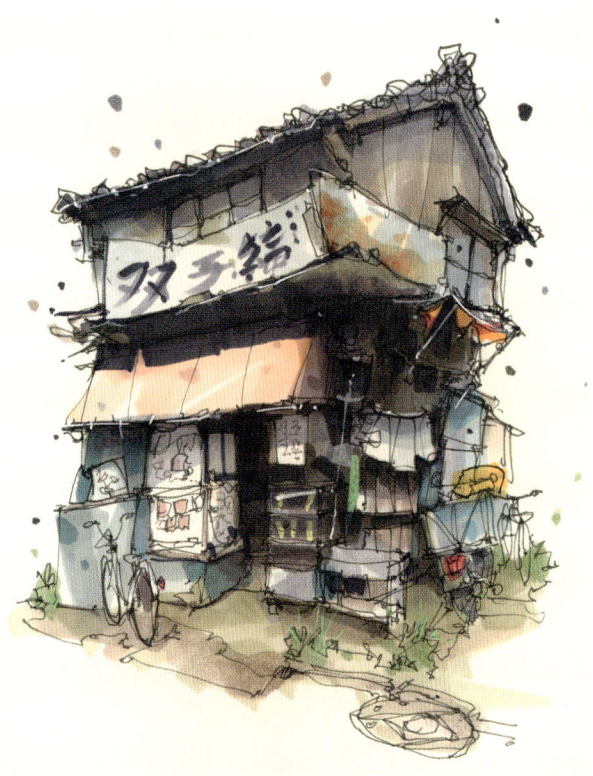 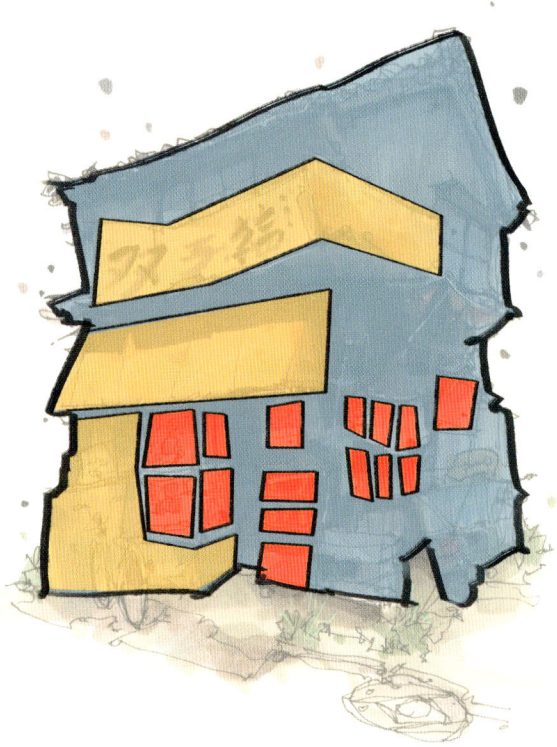

Sketch and schematic detail distribution.

LET THERE BE WHITE

Now, how can we achieve a sense of detail? Since we have worked with a transparent marker medium, we gradually went from light to dark. So, trying to avoid overwriting small details, we could very carefully paint around the intended detail, but that always results in an "avoidance" look. That's where the addition of a white acrylic pen comes in very handy. The white is opaque and can be painted over dark areas. Perfect! So have a look at your sketch and see where you would like to add detail. The first urge could be: "Wow, I can make lines here and here and here." But that will inevitably result in a sketch with white "spaghetti" all over it screaming: "Look at me!!!" So be mindful as to where you would like to draw the viewer's eye. Is there an interesting section of a building? Or do you want to draw attention to how crowded a shopping street is? That's where to place some white lines and leave the rest untouched (by white lines).

Scan to watch a tutorial.

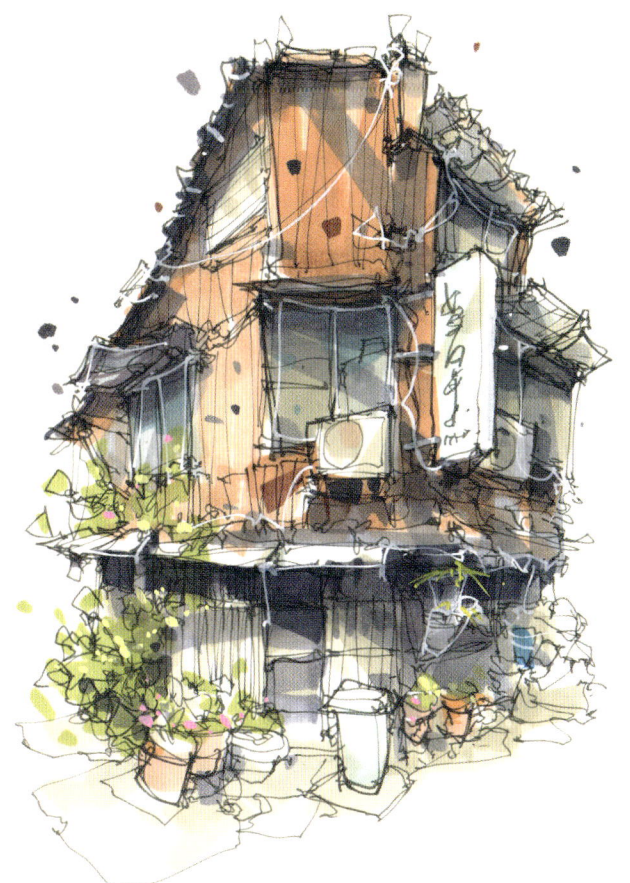

Adding details with a white paint pen draws the eye to certain areas.

> **TIP** White acrylic pen comes in very handy. The white is opaque and can be painted over dark areas. So see where you would like to add detail.

INTEGRATION

Adding these white lines is great for suggesting detail back over darker areas (white lines over light areas isn't nearly as useful). But what you will discover when you have finished with the rough white line stage is that it also tends to flatten your sketch. With that I mean that if you have carefully built up volume in your subject with light to dark shades of value, putting fully white lines on top of that will tear that illusion of depth apart. So you will need to do some integration housekeeping to pull this back together again and integrate the whites more into your sketch. When you think about it, this is quite logical. In the shaded areas of a house, there might be lighter lines present, like window frames, for instance. But they are never fully white (the lightest value possible). They will probably be in a gray zone. And that is where this integration stage will solve the problem. You can brush a medium value gray value or color over those white lines and in that way darken down the whites. This way, you will see that become much more a part of the total picture. For this phase, you need to check that your white lines have dried out fully. Going over them with a marker when they haven't yet dried enough will smear the white and you can get a dirty mess. It can happen, but here, a little patience can prevent a lot of hassle afterward.

Before use, always shake these pens vigorously with the cap securely tightened! And check if they don't have a "runny nose." The pen can release

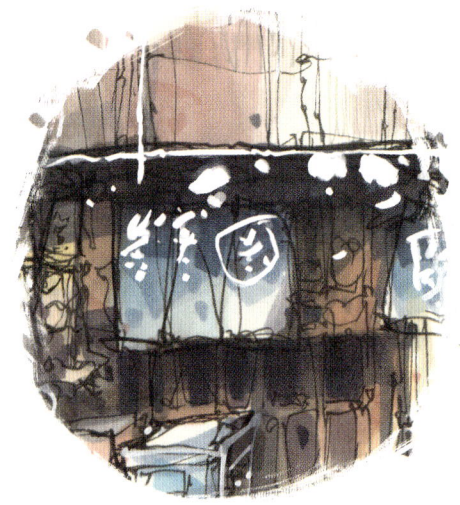

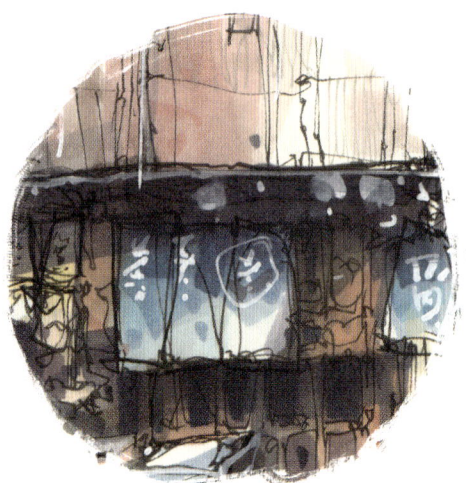

a gush of liquid and ruin your work. That still happens to me on occasion, and it takes a lot of correcting to get rid of these stains. For that reason, I always have a set of paper tissues on standby to clean up both the blobs on the page, but also to wipe the pen with before I actually start the white line process. And if you look at the "bleed sheet" in the photographs, you also see that I regularly test out the lines on that scrap paper before committing lines to my sketch.

Scan to watch
a tutorial.

← White sticking out versus white integrated into the sketch.

ACCENT LINES

As a final pass in my sketches, I will see where lines can be used to enforce depth even more. Since fineliners are of a fixed width for me, this stage has evolved to taking place at the end and not before coloring. The reason is that the thicker lines do tend to smear a little more. So, applying them after coloring is done keeps the sketch clean.

→ The thicker lines in the foreground building enhance depth perception.

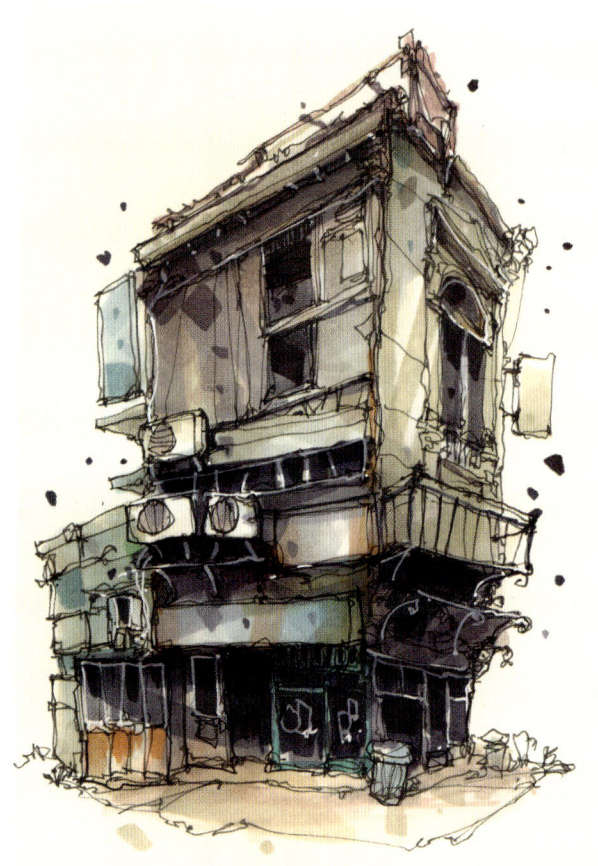

Scan to watch
a tutorial.

HOW TO MAKE A SKETCH MORE INTERESTING

Just as in films where you have set dressing, your main subject can benefit from items that help tell the story of your house. The first place to start looking to add elements is on the ground. No house (on Earth) floats in space. It's rooted to the ground. And it is that contact plane where you can start adding detail. Be careful not to overdo it. Keep in mind that the house is the main subject, and "stuff" around the main subject is there to serve the bigger story. With ground contact, you can think of elements like tufts of grass here and there, or a tossed away can, or a set of stones.

Apart from these little details on the contact plane or line, you can enhance your sketch with some larger shapes (or medium shapes, to refer to that design principle), like flowery bushes, crates, or a carelessly parked bicycle against the wall. In many of my Japanese house sketches, you will see items like air-conditioning units and satellite dishes mounted against the walls. And on the roofs, there are lots of opportunities for placing items like old antennas or an extra air unit.

Keep in mind what the purpose of your sketch is. Do you want to stay close to the real thing, keeping the additions modest and believable (no medieval houses had satellite dishes or air conditioners)? But if you go for a more loosely inspired interpretation, you can have a lot of fun adding these storytelling elements.

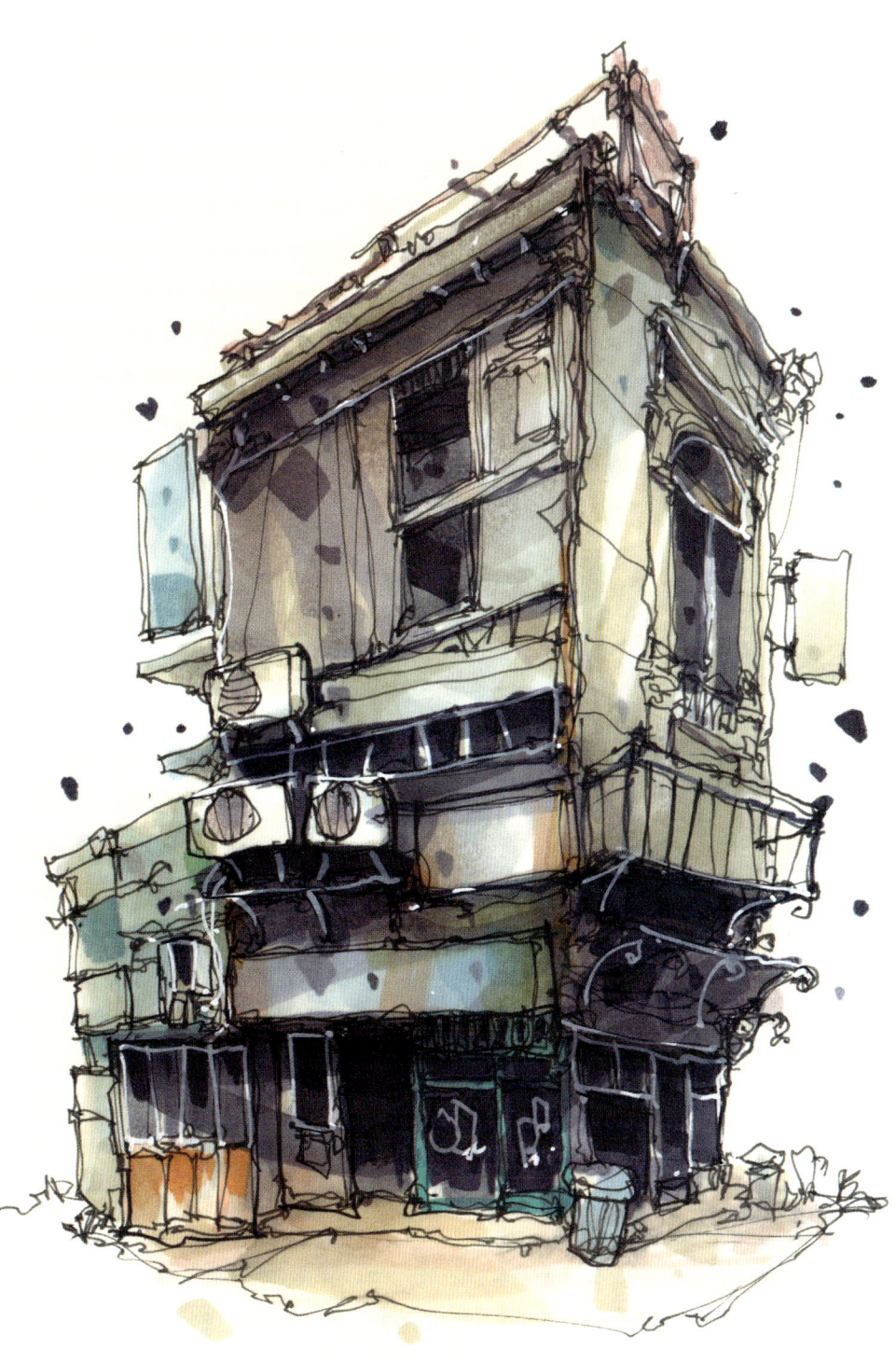

↑ Ground elements like grass and, yes, even air conditioning units in abundance, add life to this building.

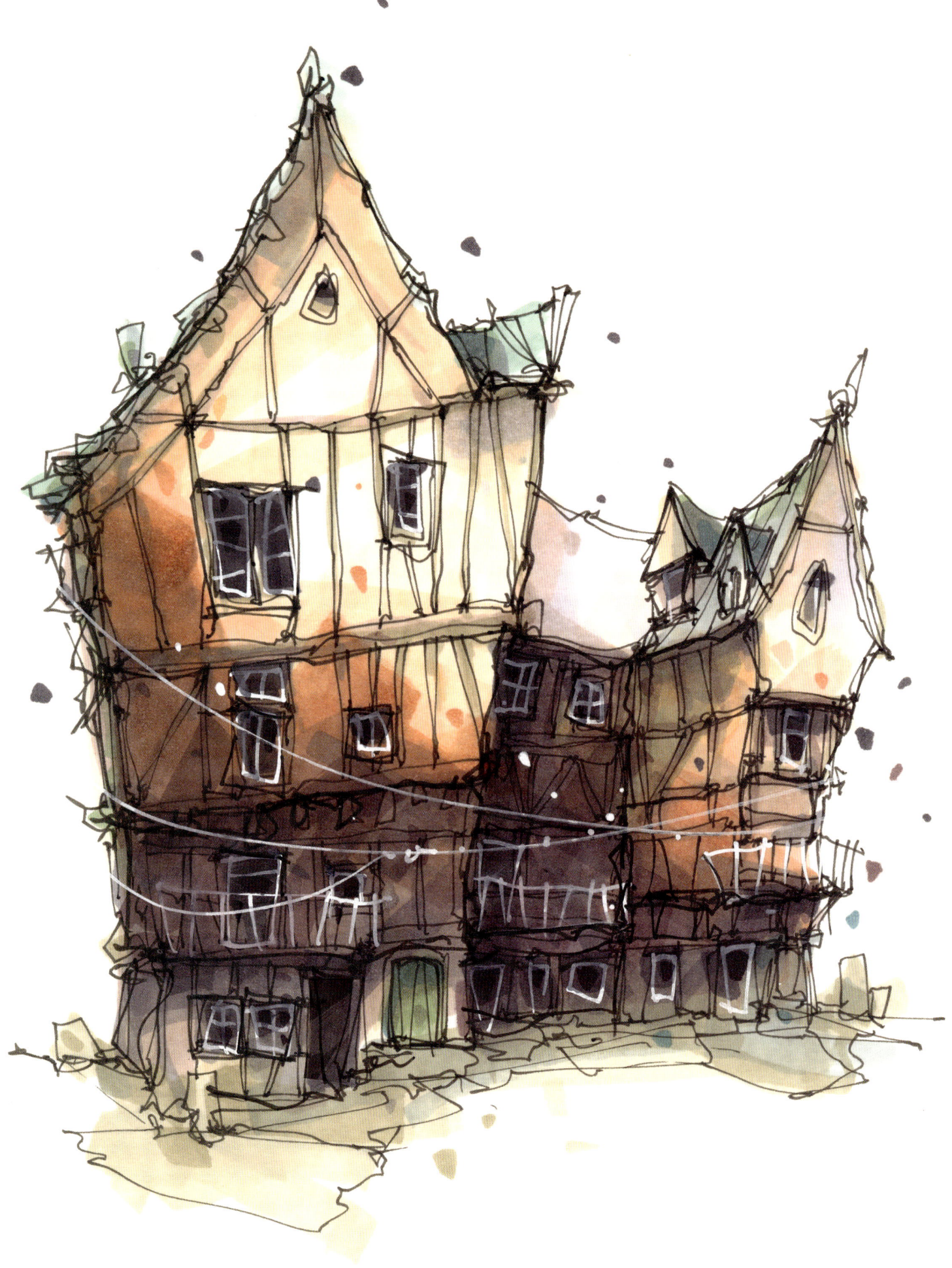

3

THE PROJECTS

It's time for some concrete examples of what I have tried
to illustrate (pun intended) in the previous two chapters!
In this chapter, I will show you several case studies of
how I handled a certain sketch from the original
source photo to the final, fully colored sketch.

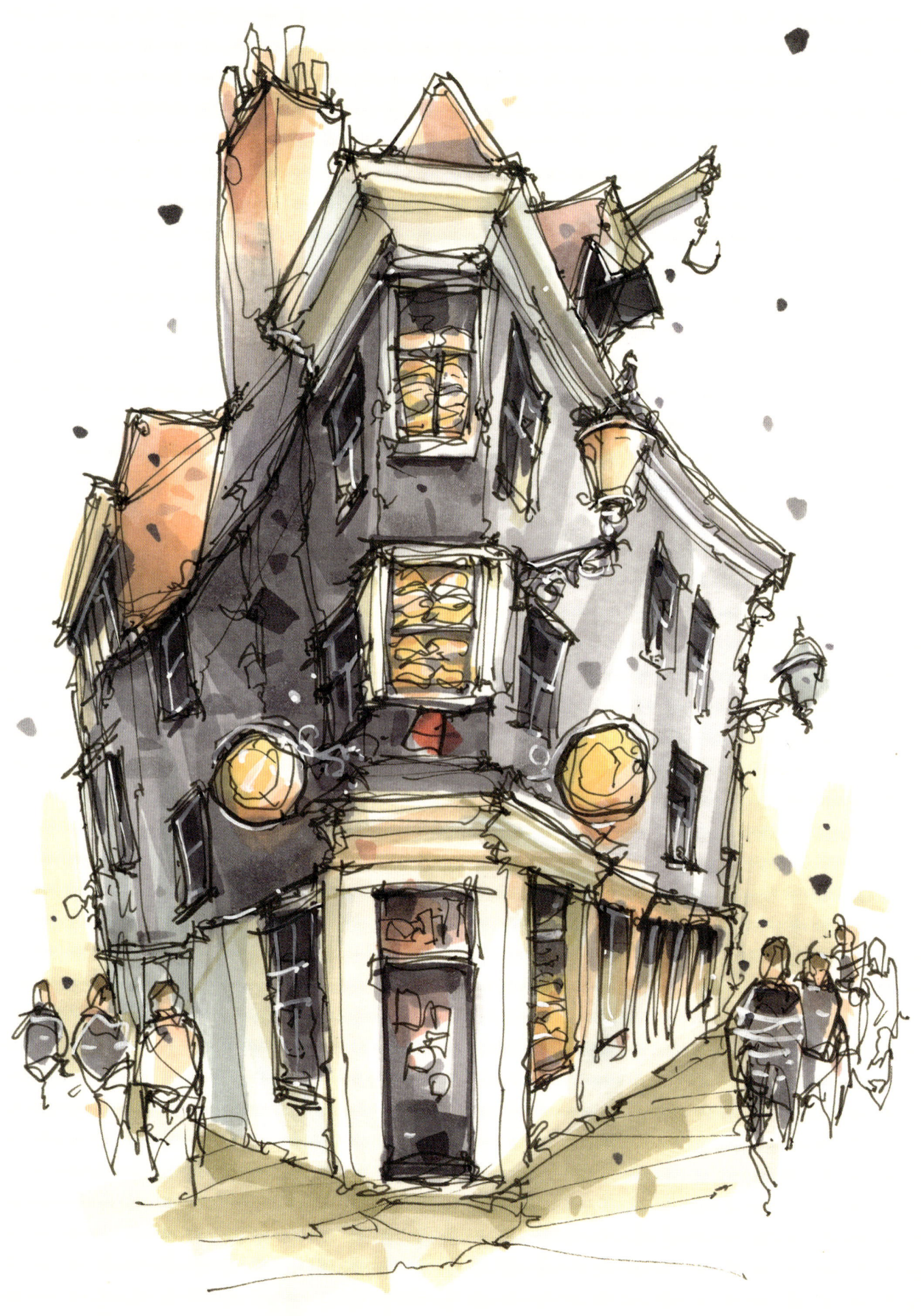

Cheese Shop // Amsterdam, Netherlands

Let's visit the wonderful city of Amsterdam with its amazingly diverse architectural styles, from hyper-modern office buildings to structures from the golden age of Rembrandt. Here's a corner store with a very interesting wedge shape. Notice how one skinny corner is turned into the entrance for the store with the wheels of cheese visible in the windows above.

MARKER COLORS

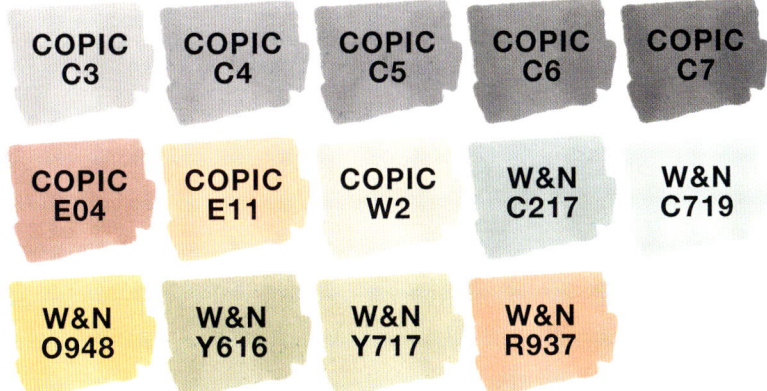

COPIC C3 · COPIC C4 · COPIC C5 · COPIC C6 · COPIC C7

COPIC E04 · COPIC E11 · COPIC W2 · W&N C217 · W&N C719

W&N O948 · W&N Y616 · W&N Y717 · W&N R937

REFERENCE PHOTO

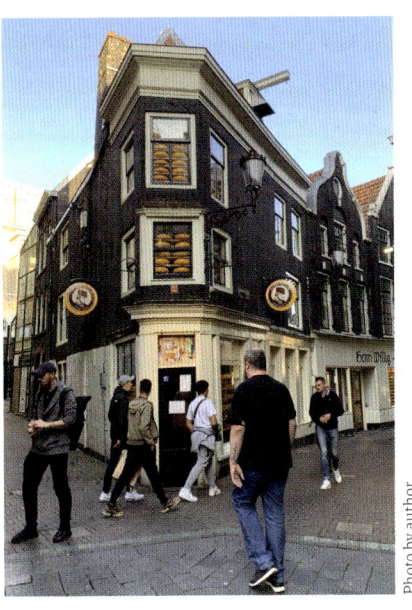

Photo by author

PERSPECTIVE

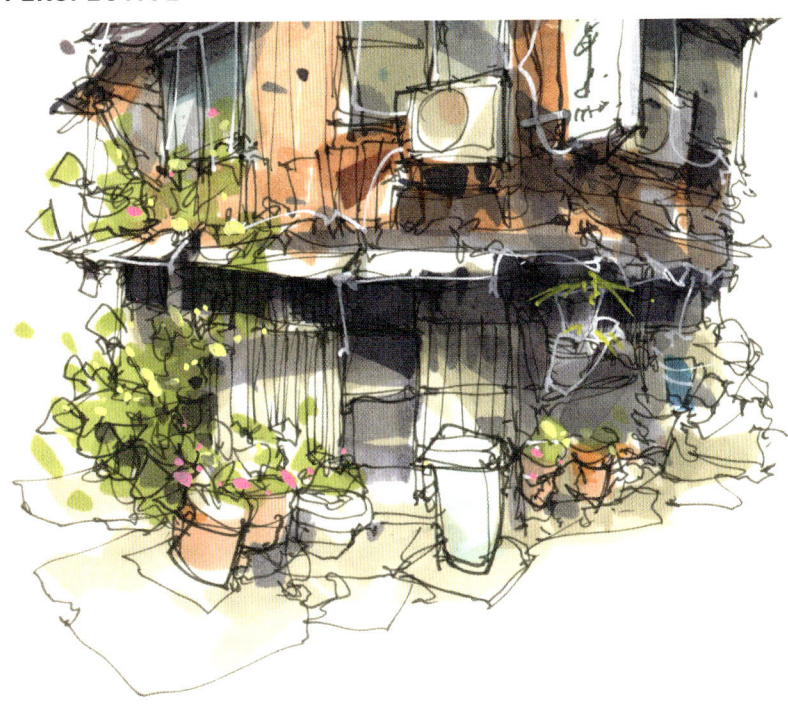

SILHOUETTE

THE PROCESS

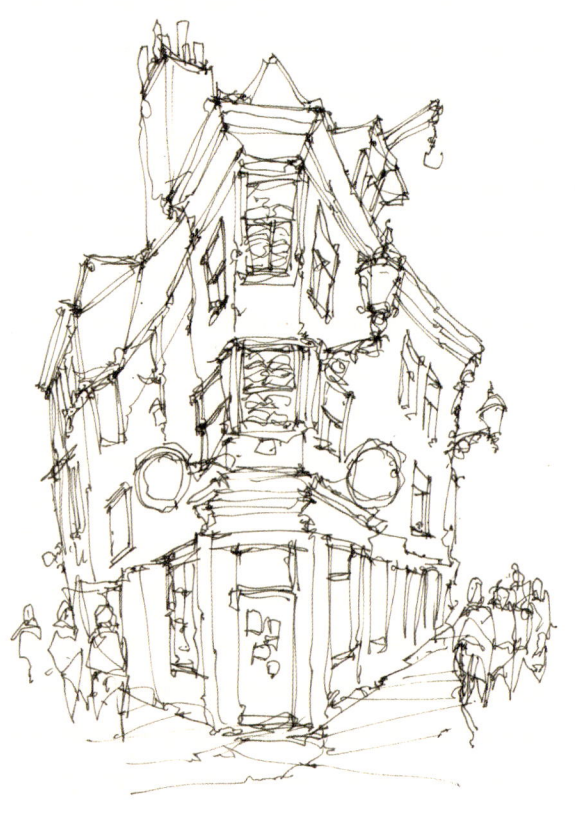

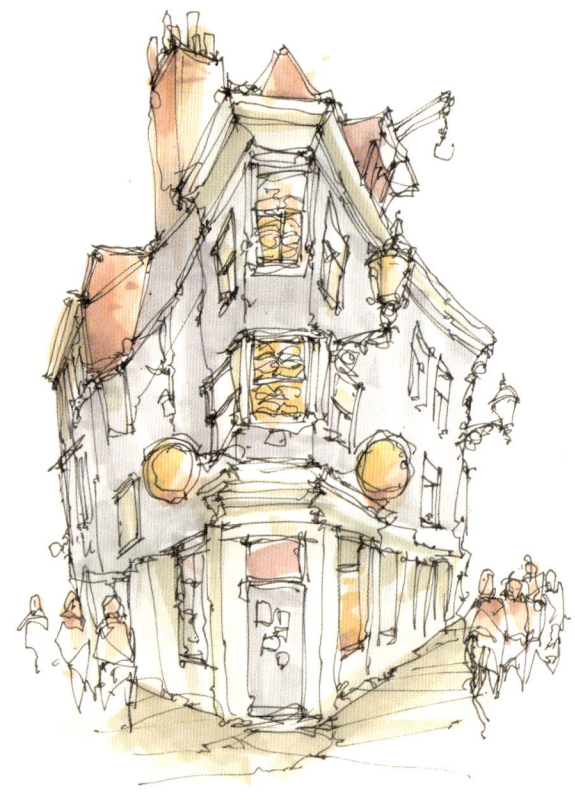

STAGE 1

After you have analyzed your subject, it's time to travel around the major features, including some recognizable landmarks, like floors or rooflines.

After you have your main lines in place, you can move around more freely and confidently sketch in the rest of the features, such as windows, doors, and details. Don't try to sketch material qualities like the lines in wood or shadows. This will all be handled by the coloring process.

STAGE 2

The first layer of colors: Apply the lightest shades and keep some areas even page-white. Use this first pass to establish some of the light and dark value play that you're later going to accentuate.

Add some secondary hues (like the pale earth tones and blues) and slightly darker values that reinforce your first color statement.

Colors used: C3, C4, C6, W2, E04, E11, Y717, C719, O948

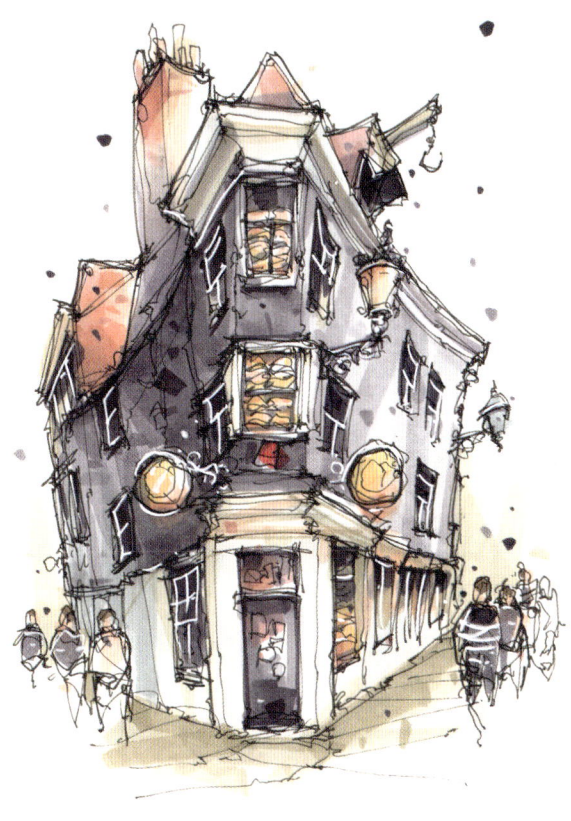

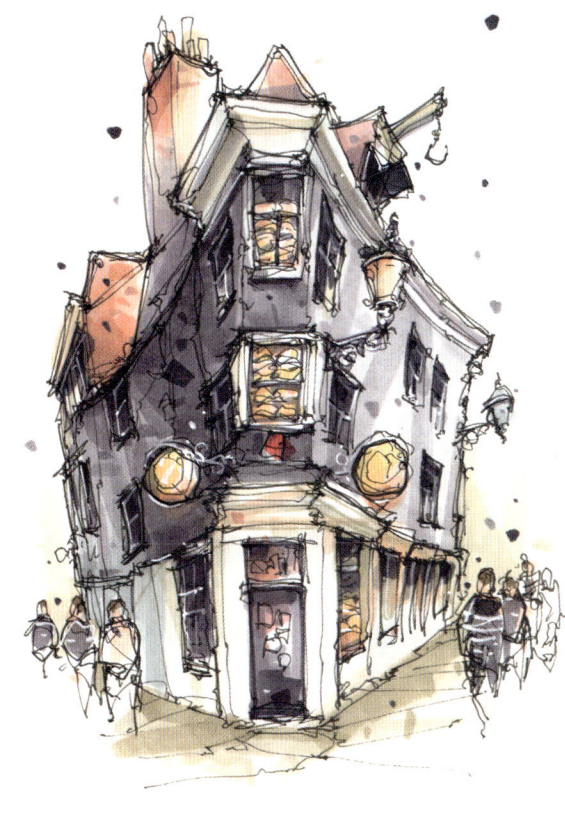

STAGE 3

Continuing the coloring process with really strong accents. Here you add the darkest values to areas like the windows and cast shadows under the roof sections. This brings out a powerful volume in your sketch.

Now it's time to add accents. For that you can use a white acrylic marker of your choice. Apply full white lines and dashes where you think they will add to the character of the sketch.

Colors used: C5, C7, Y616, R937, C217

STAGE 4

In this last but vital step, you will take a 60 to 70% cool gray marker and "touch back" some of the whites to integrate them into their surrounding values. This also adds even more dimensionality to your work. Now the only thing left is to see where you could add some thicker accent lines. This is something I borrowed from technical drawing, where you add thicker lines to outline shapes or hard edges that bend away from you. But don't overdo it, because that will also flatten things out.

Color used: C7

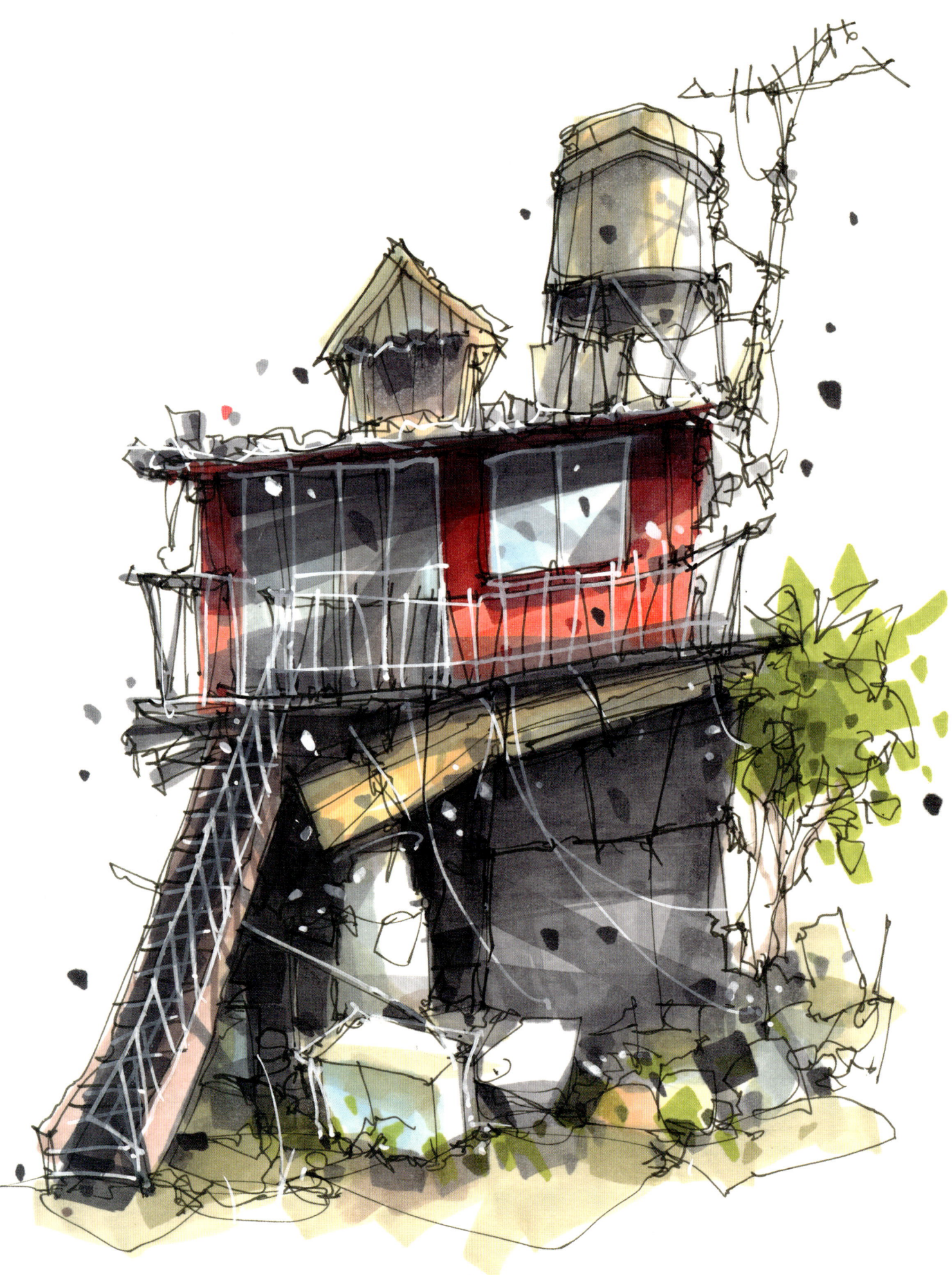

Red House with Stairs // Shizuoka, Japan

I love these backyard scenes a lot. This chaotic ramshackle place immediately spoke to me. Since I wanted to sketch it in a more vertical way, I scooted the stairs over to the right a bit more. This gave me the vertical lift I needed. I also took some extra liberties; can you spot them?

MARKER COLORS

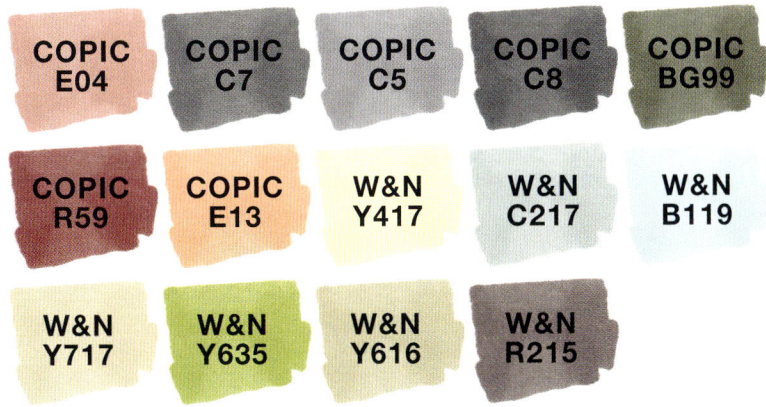

COPIC E04 · COPIC C7 · COPIC C5 · COPIC C8 · COPIC BG99

COPIC R59 · COPIC E13 · W&N Y417 · W&N C217 · W&N B119

W&N Y717 · W&N Y635 · W&N Y616 · W&N R215

REFERENCE PHOTO

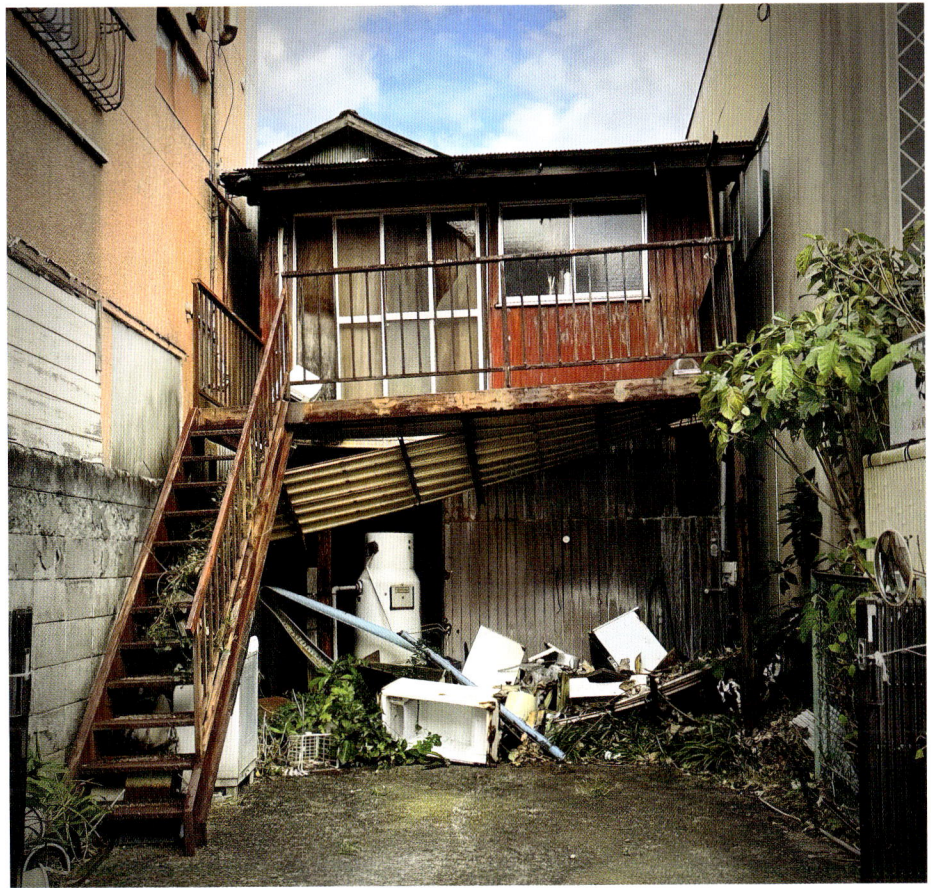

Photo by @masktnak

THE PROCESS

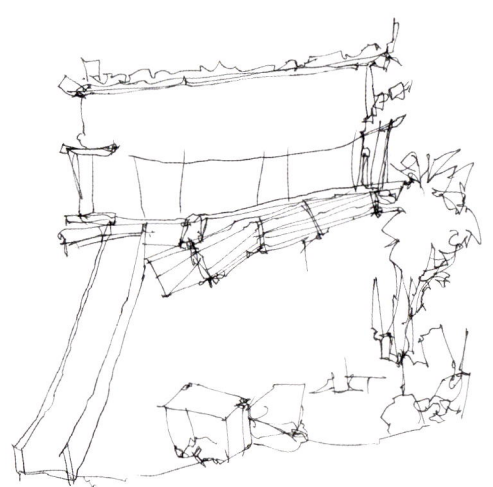

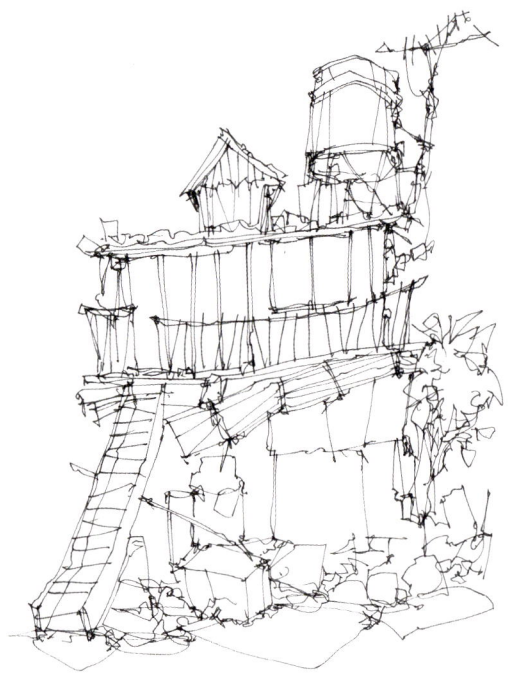

STAGE 1

There is not much perspective going on in this scene. Most of the depth is achieved with light and dark values. The areas in the recessed places and the section underneath the roof define this depth. Starting with a simple rectangle, some indicated green line contours, and that directional staircase, the main setup is ready.

STAGE 2

Now for those added extra elements. I love putting on some water towers or other rooftop elements. These can add to the story such places can tell. (That roof shed . . . what's in there?)

You can see that there are lines dancing all over. The rails are a collection of lines but not all parallel.

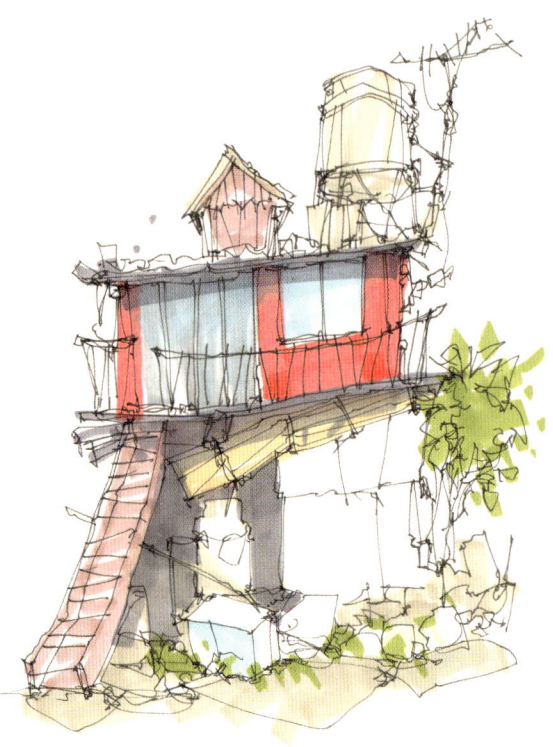

STAGE 3

The first coloring phase adds the basic colors I want this scene to have, especially that red for the house. It all still looks quite flat and saturated, but it establishes the main forms and gives me the opportunity to start pushing in the values more deeply.

Colors used: Y417, C217, B119, Y717, E04, Y635

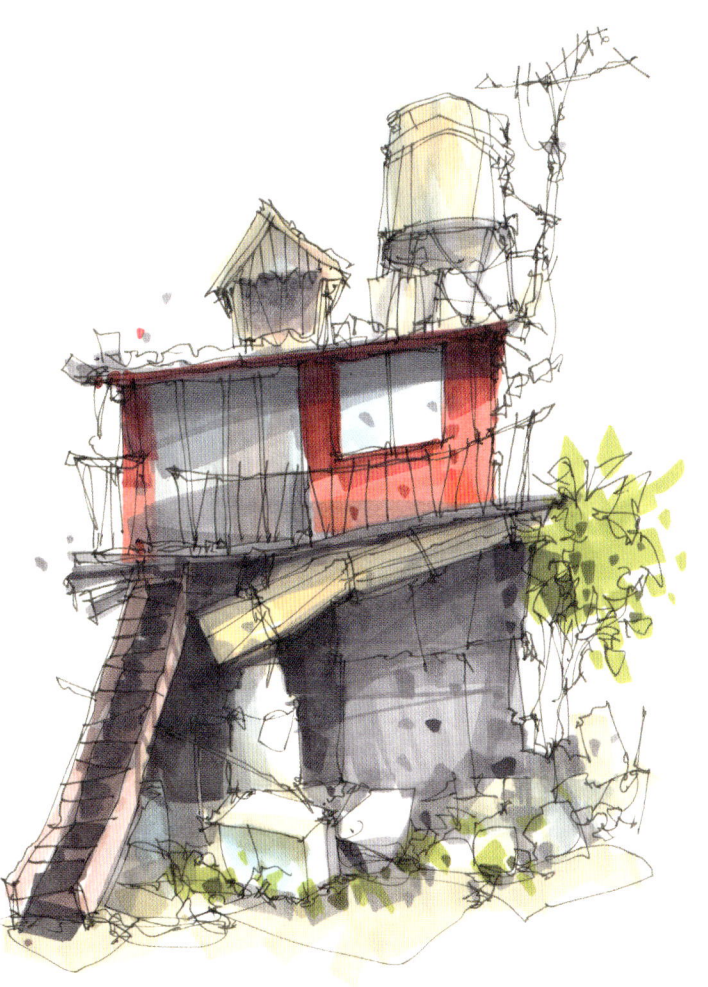

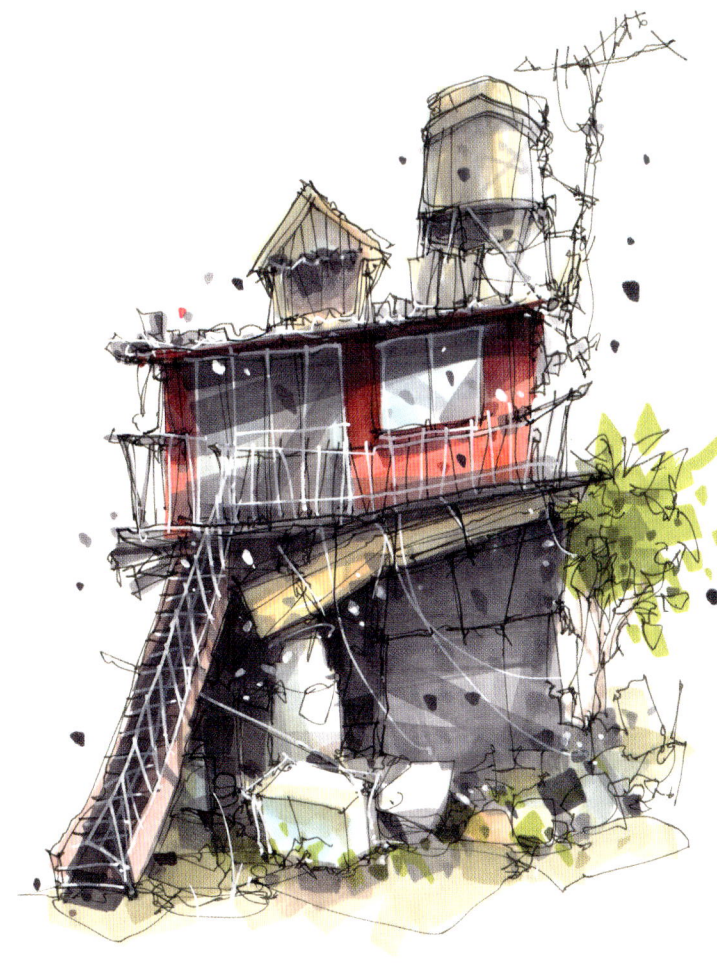

STAGE 4

Time for those deeper values. First, putting in the cast shadows underneath the roof immediately brings a very nice feel to that part of the sketch. Next, I add deep values in the recessed area behind the stairs and underneath the house. I accentuate that rolled up sheet by casting some darker shades behind it.

Color used: E13

STAGE 5

Time for the finishing touches. The white lines for trimming, rails, and cables are shown in this sketch. Again, I push them back into the sketch with a medium gray. I also add some white and darker spots here and there for some extra dust "kick up."

Colors used: C7, Y616, C5, R215, C8, BG99, R59

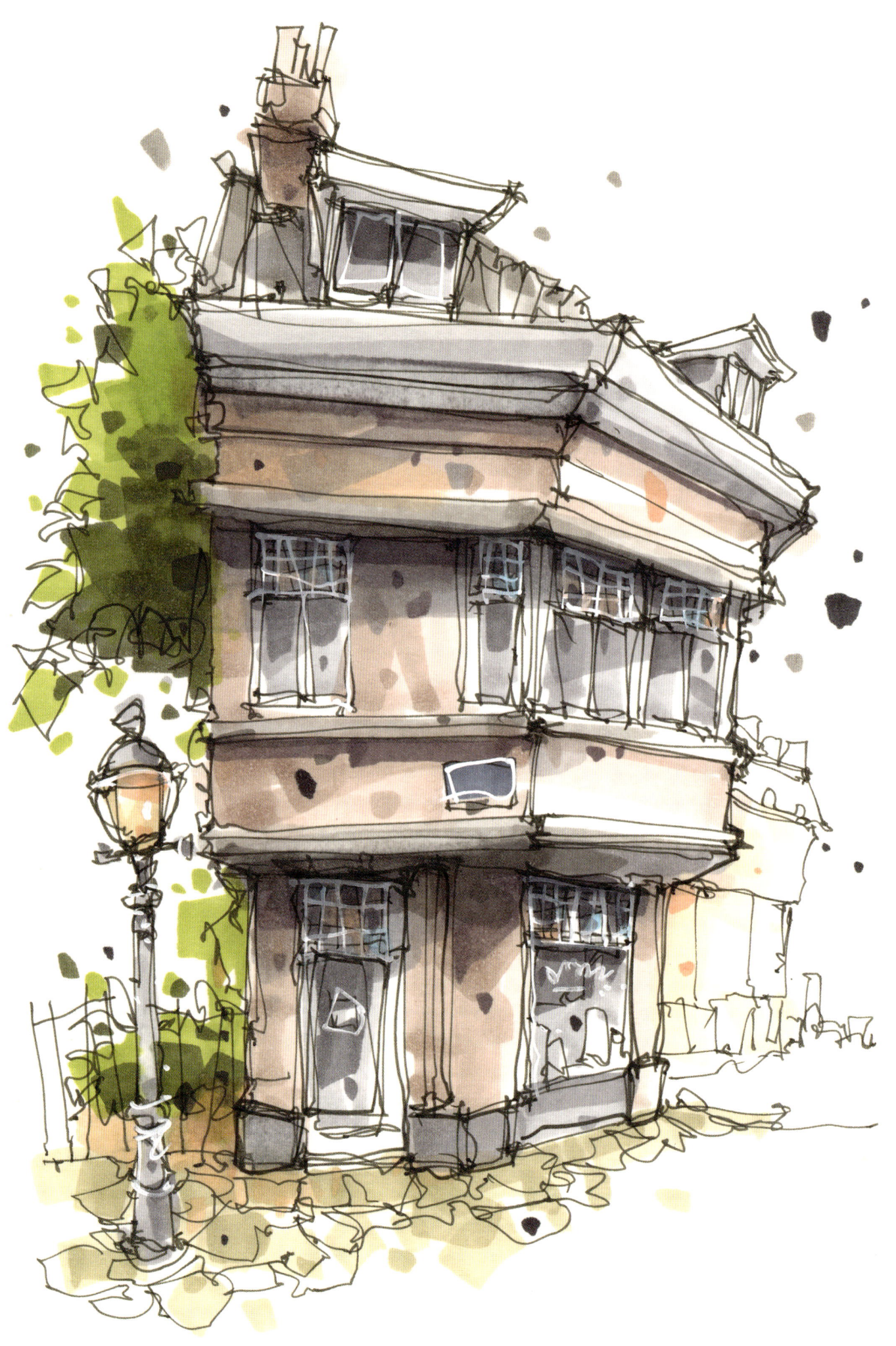

"Half" House // Maastricht, Netherlands

This house immediately caught my attention because of its straight cut-off left side. It almost looked like a gigantic saw had cut it in half. By slightly exaggerating the proportions and silhouette, I gave this building some extra punch.

MARKER COLORS

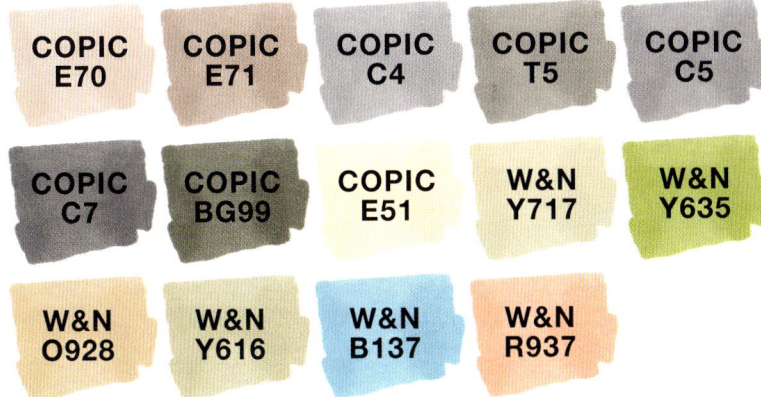

COPIC E70	COPIC E71	COPIC C4	COPIC T5	COPIC C5
COPIC C7	COPIC BG99	COPIC E51	W&N Y717	W&N Y635
W&N O928	W&N Y616	W&N B137	W&N R937	

REFERENCE PHOTO

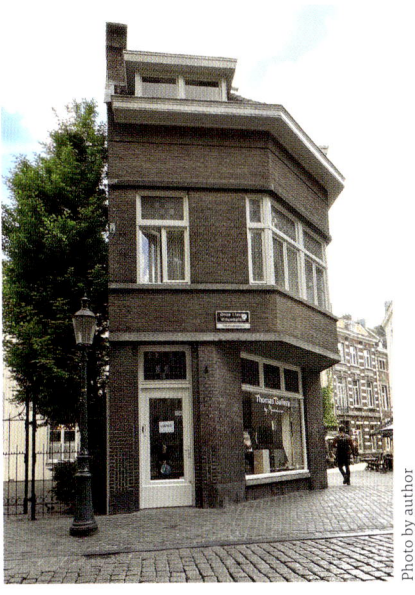

Photo by author

THE PROCESS

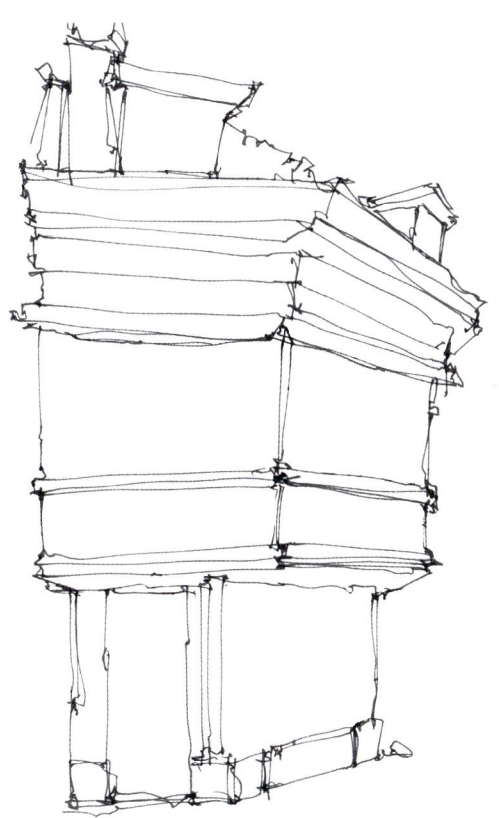

STAGE 1

There are three main sections in this building: the ground floor, the first floor, and the roof section. I sketched these in loosely and I exaggerated the gutter area a bit to add more interest there. Also observe that I slightly show more roof than would be visible normally.

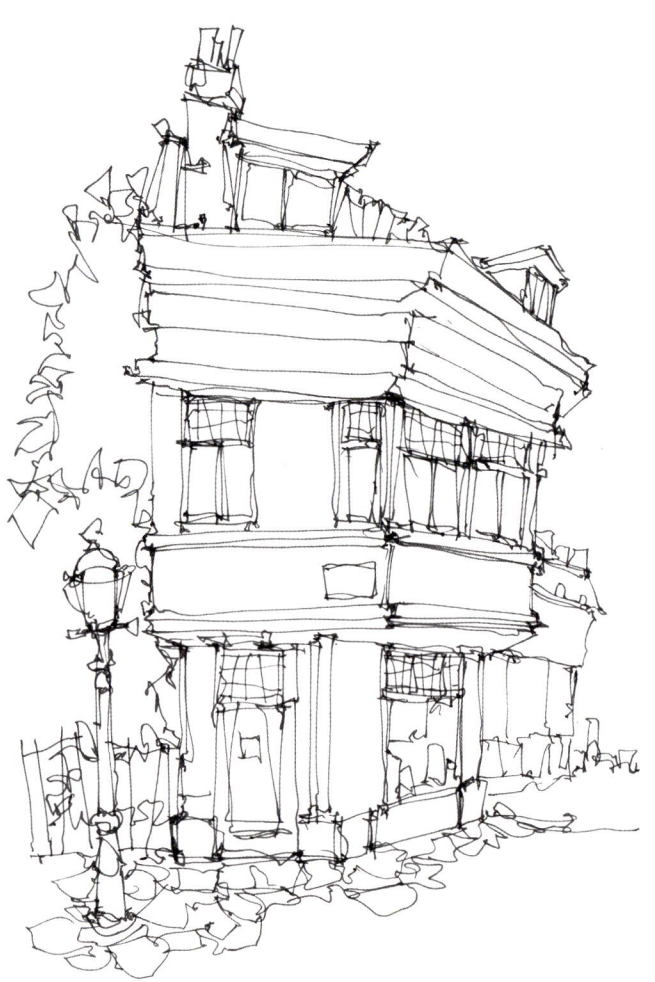

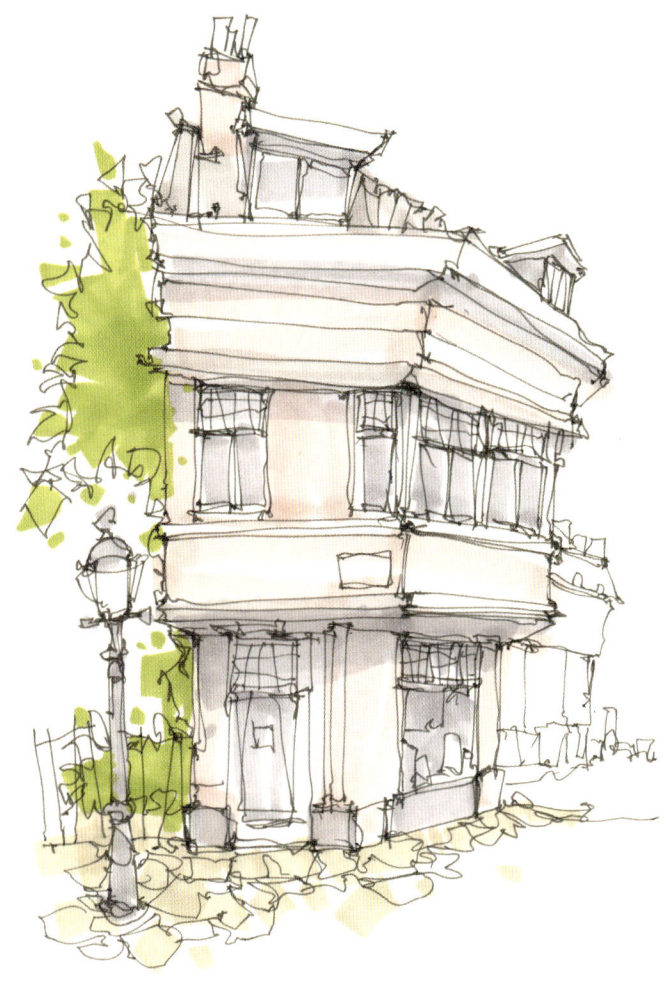

STAGE 2

Once the main divisions are in place, it becomes easier to sketch in the windows, door, and the shrubbery on the left. I also move the streetlamp slightly to give it a clearer spot in the composition. Finally, I added some background buildings for more situational interest.

STAGE 3

I wanted to shade this building a little differently from its actual colors. These dark-bricked buildings tend to quickly become very muddied when trying to replicate their colors in a sketch. So once again, starting with a light wash of colors is key. Having this first set of colors quickly establishes the silhouette too.

Colors used: Y717, Y635, E70, C4

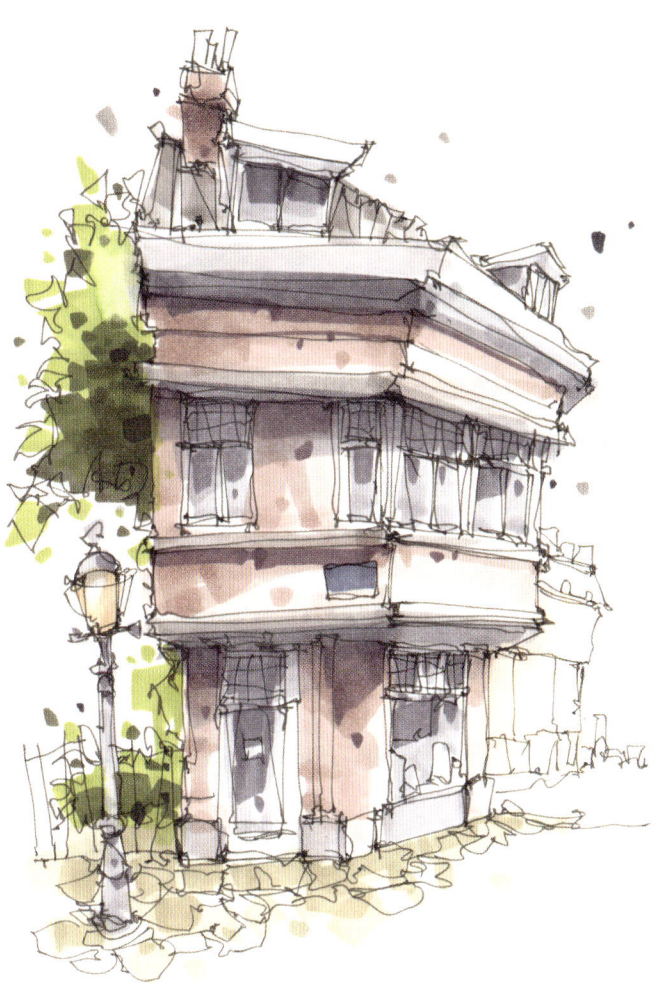

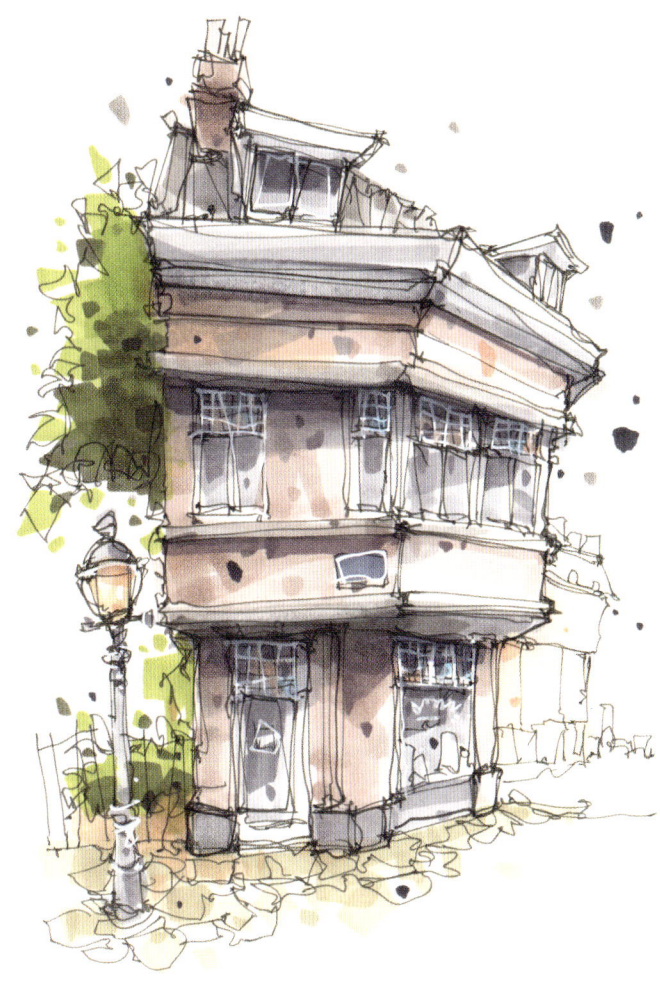

STAGE 4

It was surprisingly easy to get depth in this sketch once the first layer of colors was on paper. A slightly darker shade of the main "brick" color and starker drop shadows underneath the ledges were enough to bring out form in this building. Adding a darker green also rounded out the tree nicely.

Colors used: E71, T5, C5, C7, BG99, O928, E51, Y616

STAGE 5

In the final pass I added some warmth to the lantern and to the ground near the greens. This gives a nice warm contrast and atmosphere. A pass of white lines for window trimming (with dimming down, of course) finalized the sketch.

Colors used: B137, C7, R937, B137

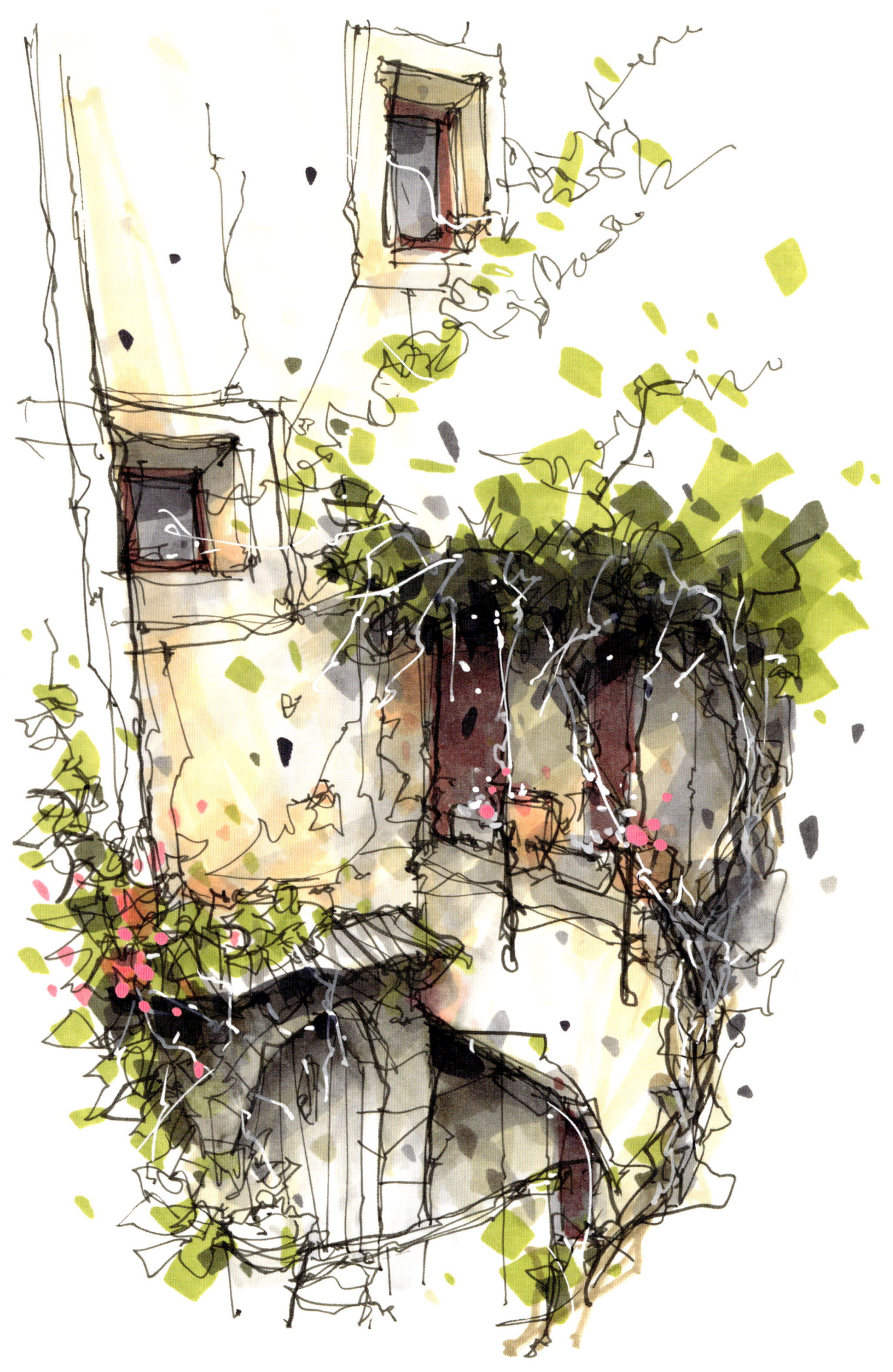

Courtyard // Entrecasteaux, France

On a trip to France, I visited one of the countless enchanting French villages where interesting sketching opportunities were present in abundance. This is a sunny inner courtyard with multiple levels that just begged to be sketched.

MARKER COLORS

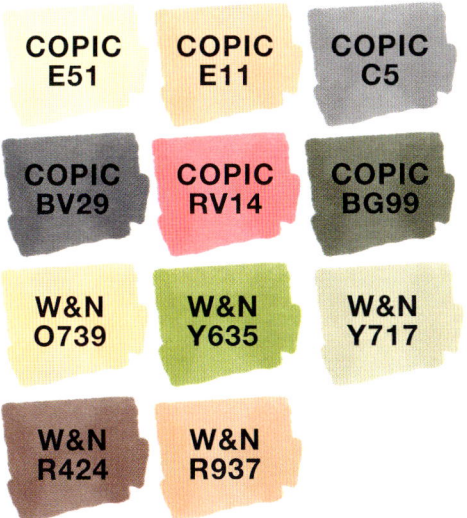

COPIC E51   COPIC E11   COPIC C5

COPIC BV29   COPIC RV14   COPIC BG99

W&N O739   W&N Y635   W&N Y717

W&N R424   W&N R937

REFERENCE PHOTO

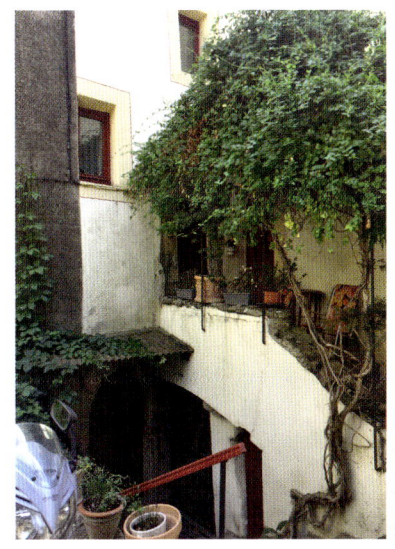

Photo by author

PERSPECTIVE

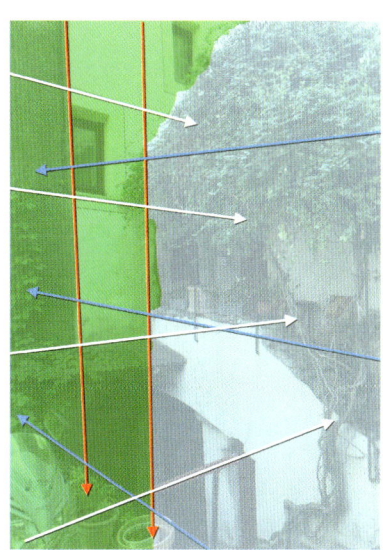

THE PROCESS

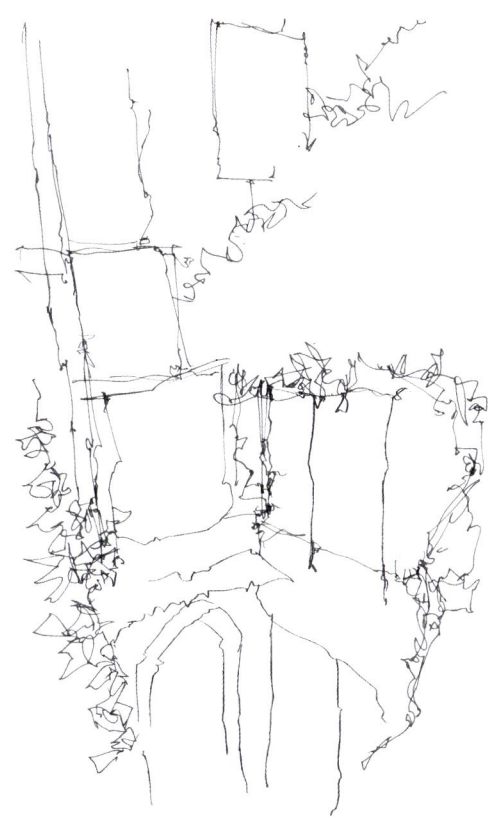

STAGE 1

Here you have a typical three-point perspective. You are looking slightly down into the yard. There are some distinctive levels apparent with the window, the overgrown hallway, and that subterrace way down. These sections are sketched in with a minimum of lines. Always remember that coloring will take care of a large chunk of depth and contrast.

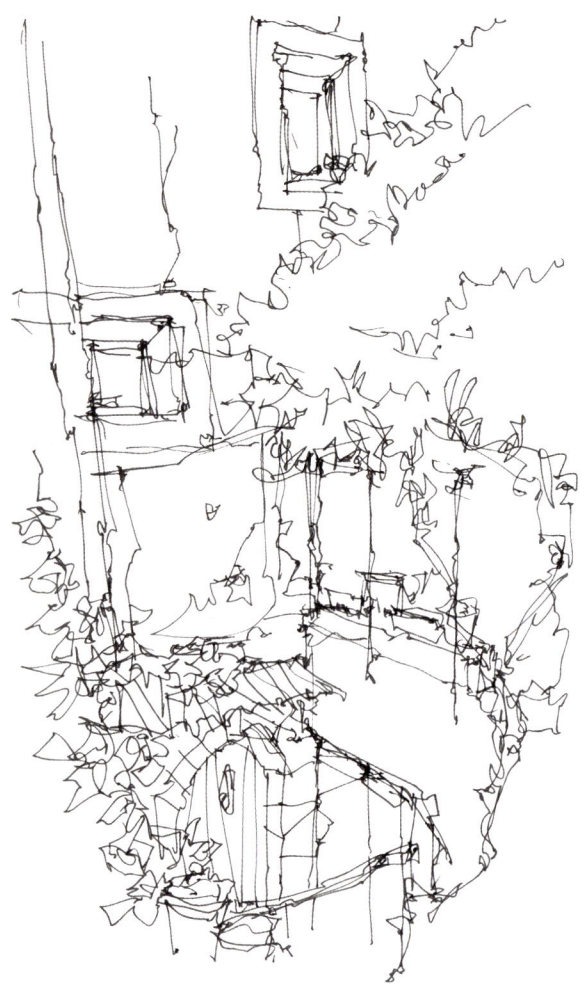

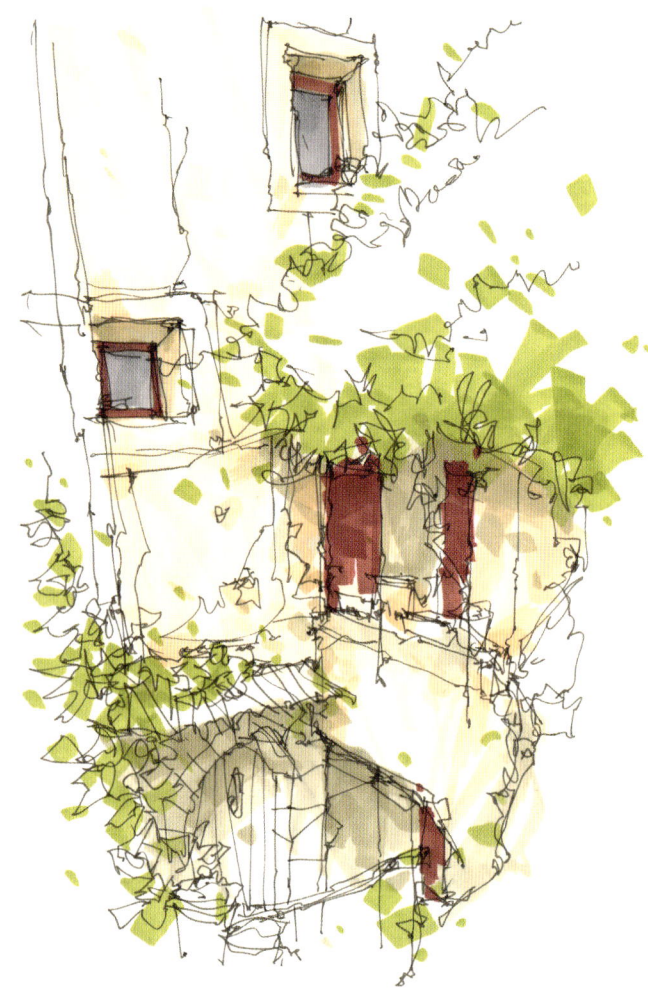

STAGE 2

With the main features in place, it's time to define objects like windows, roof covers over that door below, and some more definition into the leaves and shrubbery that overhangs that open hallway. To keep the focus on the building, I don't sketch to the outer edges, but I already plan to leave most of the organic growth page-white.

STAGE 3

To achieve volume in the suggested body of leaves, I paint the shadow side of these growth areas with the base color. Same for the doors and windows. I quickly indicate some plastered structure with a very light warm tone. Enough to quickly establish volume in the sketch.

Colors used: E51, O739, Y635, Y717, R424

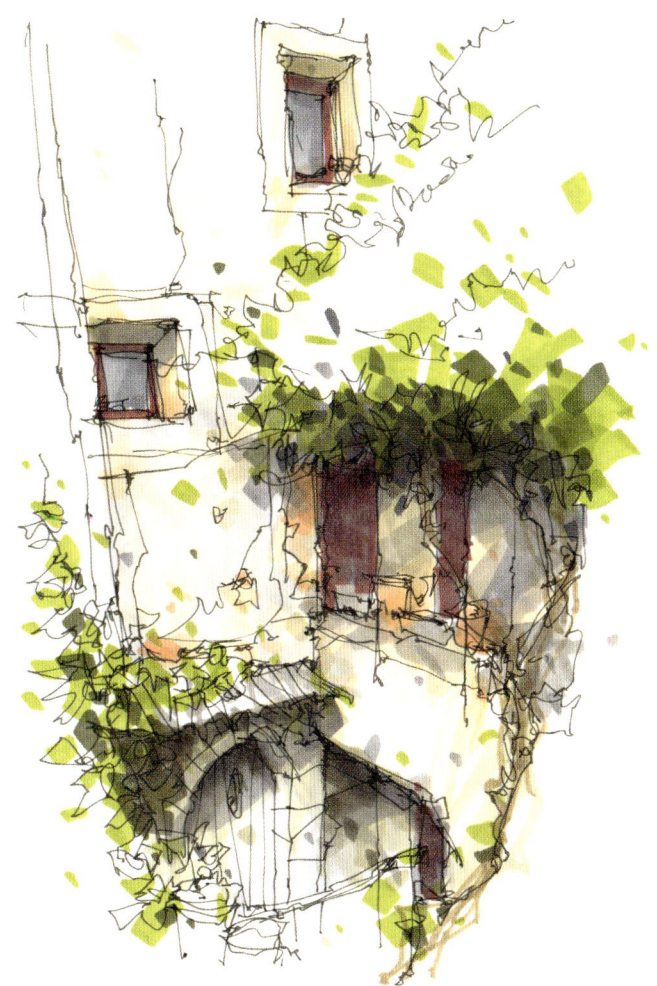

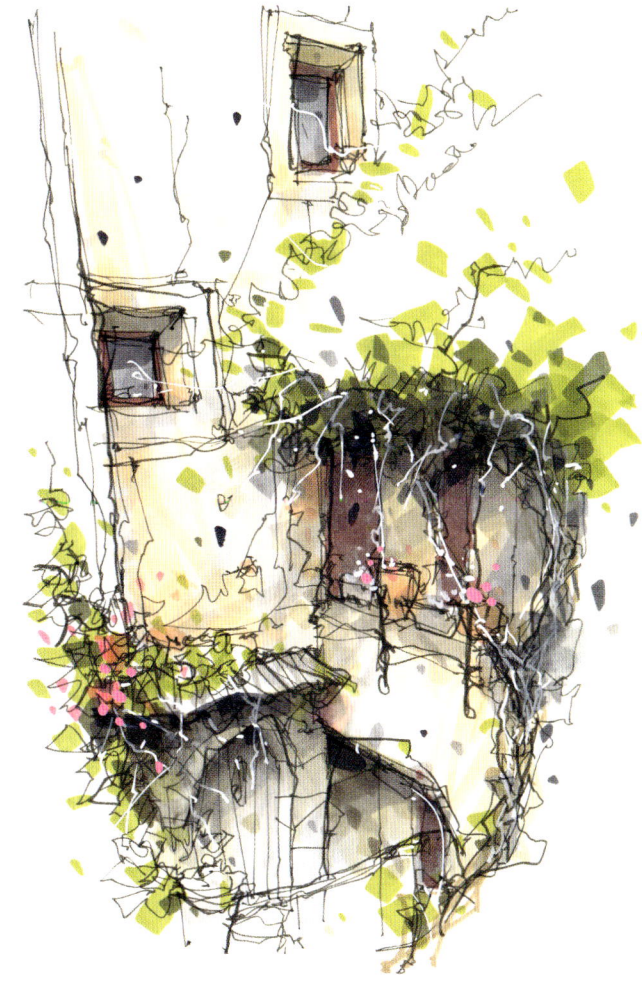

STAGE 4

Time to deepen the sketch with the darkest darks to punch out the depth even more. I have added some very dark reds and a cool gray in the deepest recessed parts of the building, which adds to the feeling of looking down into this place, further amplified by that three-point perspective.

Colors used: BG99, E11, R937, C5

STAGE 5

The finalizing stage is again to add some bright highlights, with a colored acrylic pen in this case. I used a pink Uni Posca to suggest flowers. Not literally, but just dots of bright specs. I also added some light branchy lines. Finally pushing back, I added the brightest bits with a dark gray marker.

Colors used: RV14, BV29

Sandwich Shop // Amsterdam, Netherlands

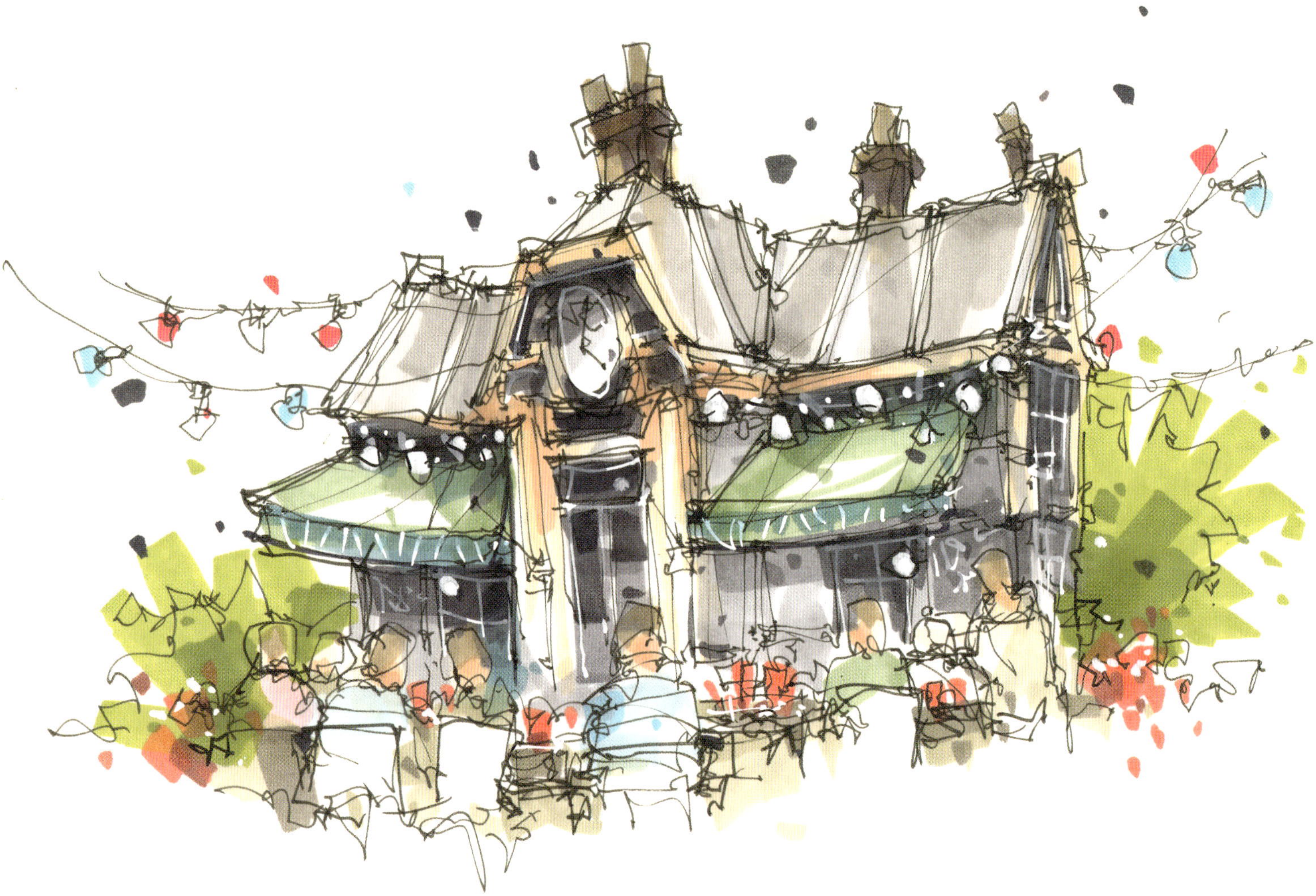

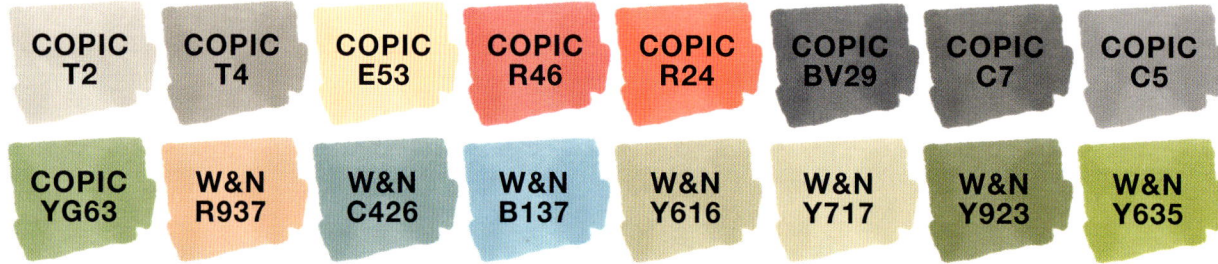

Amsterdam has such an abundance of quaint and peculiar buildings. And this coffee and sandwich shop is certainly one of them. It looks a bit like a kiosk from the 1900s. And that is exactly what inspired me to sketch this building.

MARKER COLORS

COPIC T2	COPIC T4	COPIC E53	COPIC R46	COPIC R24	COPIC BV29	COPIC C7	COPIC C5
COPIC YG63	W&N R937	W&N C426	W&N B137	W&N Y616	W&N Y717	W&N Y923	W&N Y635

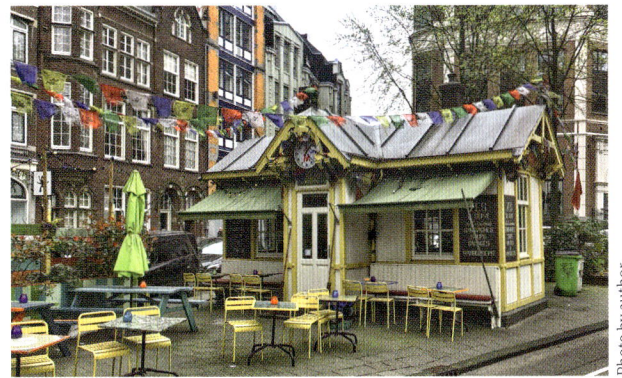

Photo by author

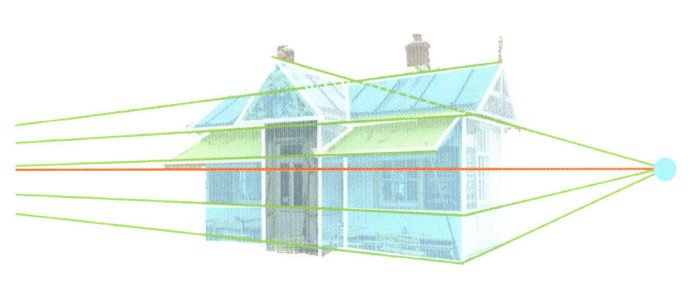

THE PROCESS

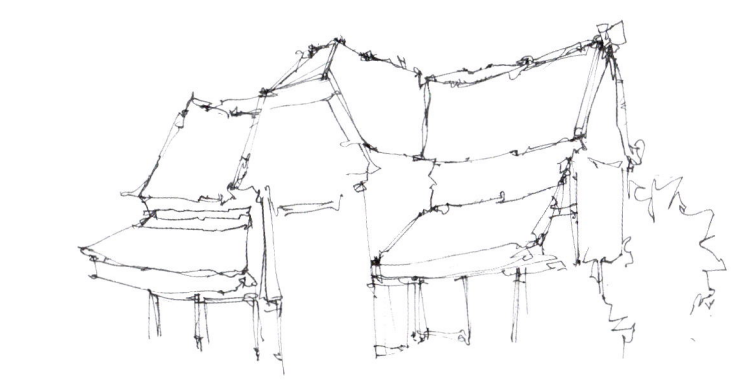

STAGE 1

First up is a quick basic setup of lines. Since I don't use construction lines, I "scan" the main features of the building, keeping in mind the general perspective directions of the place. You basically see two intersecting blocks as a main structure for this building.

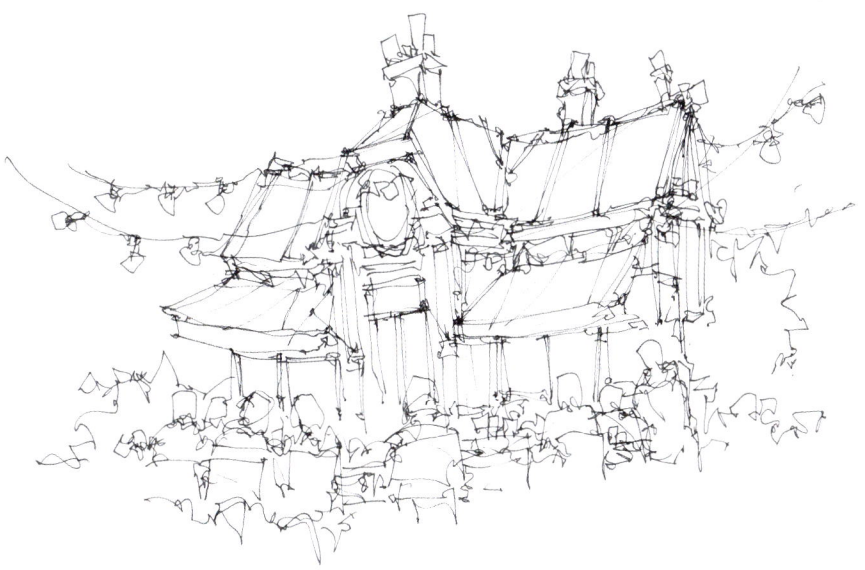

STAGE 2

Once the main areas are blocked in, it becomes much easier to "write in" the details. In this stage I add the chimneys (always a nice thing to add!), and I have also added people to this sketch because I have seen this place in summer many times, and people add a lot of liveliness to this sketch.

STAGE 3

Time to block in the first colors. Starting with some of the light ones and one medium dark, to quickly get a feel for the volume of this building. This helps to very quickly get a sense of depth, but also a sense of organization of the different parts of the place.

Colors used: BV29, T2, T4, YG63, C426

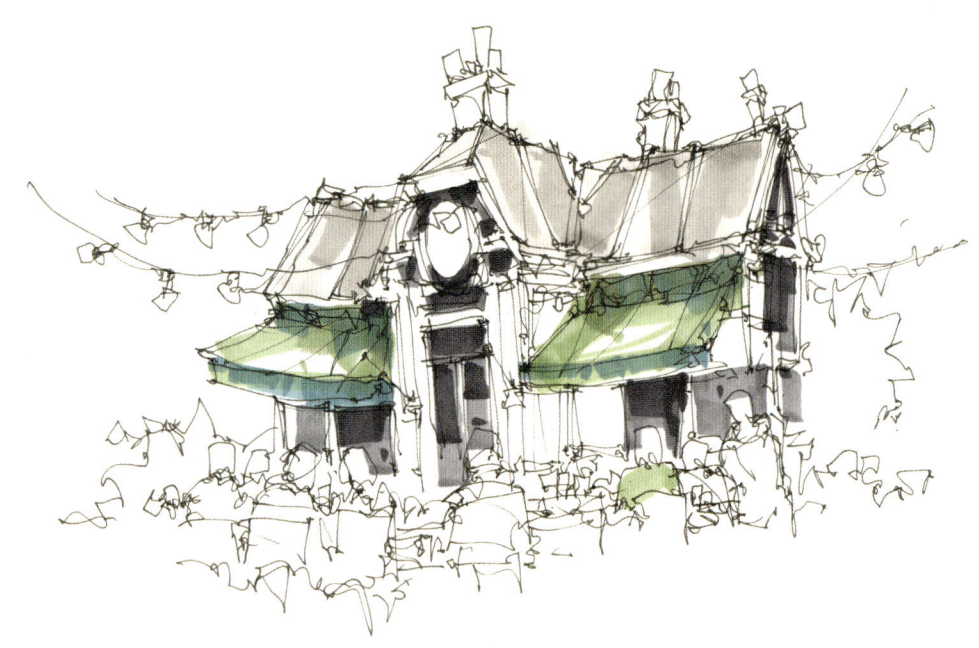

STAGE 4

Now that the first layers of color are applied, you can start to add the rest of the colors, knowing that your sketch is already structurally sound. I have added a warm yellow to the light sections and some warmer greens for the shrubbery. I top it off with some vibrant colors for the "people."

Colors used: E53, R46, R24, R937, B137, Y616, Y717, C7, C5, Y923, Y635

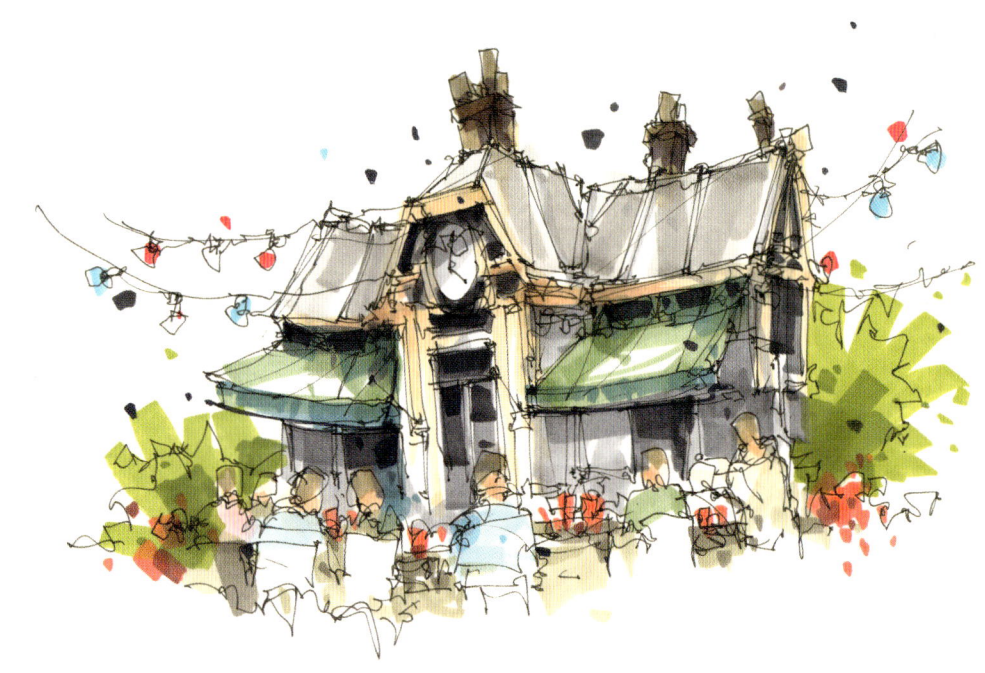

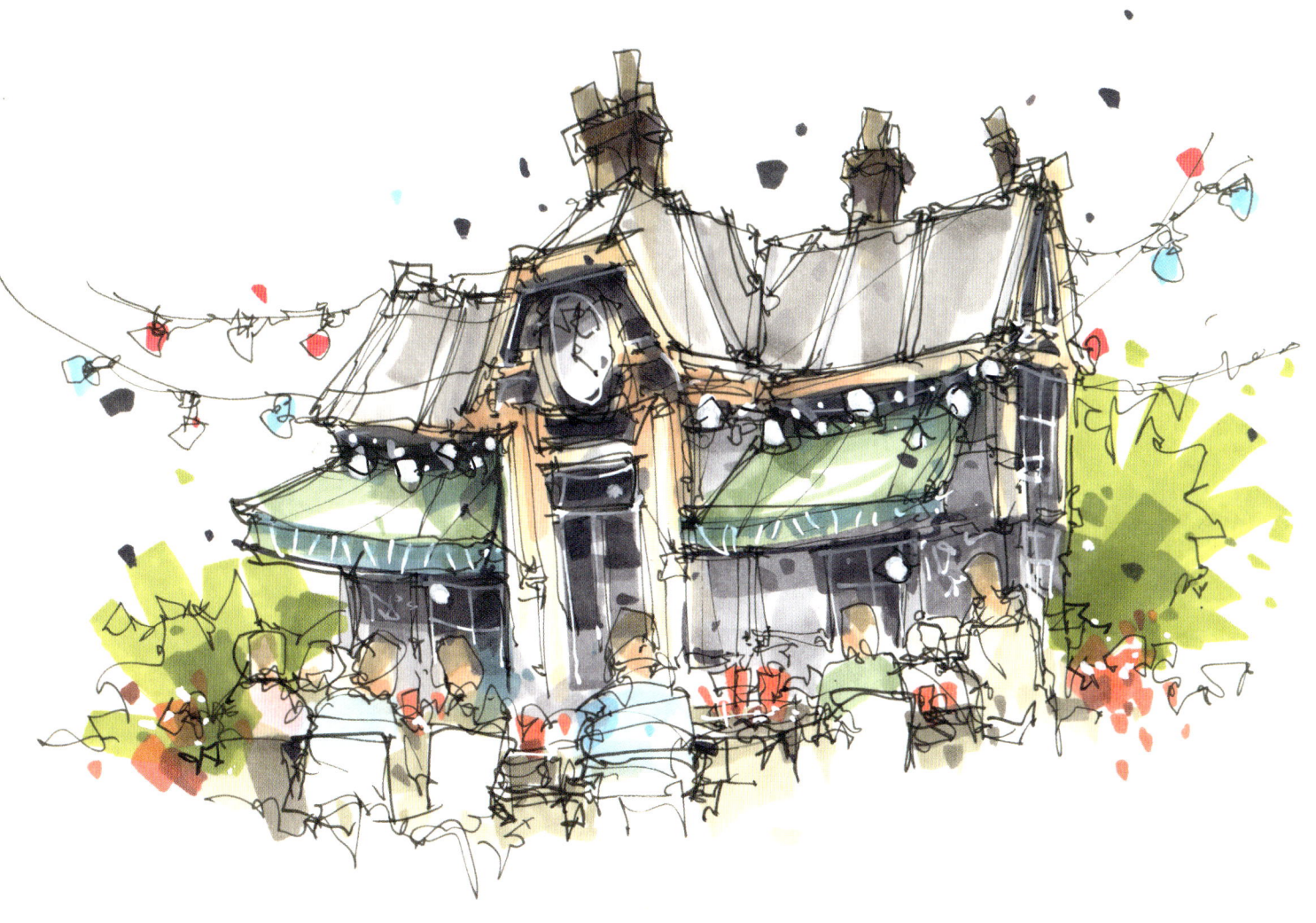

STAGE 5

Time for the detailing stage of the coloring process. A white acrylic pen (Uni Posca) was used for the white dots and lines. When these are dry (they are water based, so they take a bit longer to dry), I push some of the white back with a medium gray marker.

Colors used: C7

Cottage with Porch // Washington State, United States

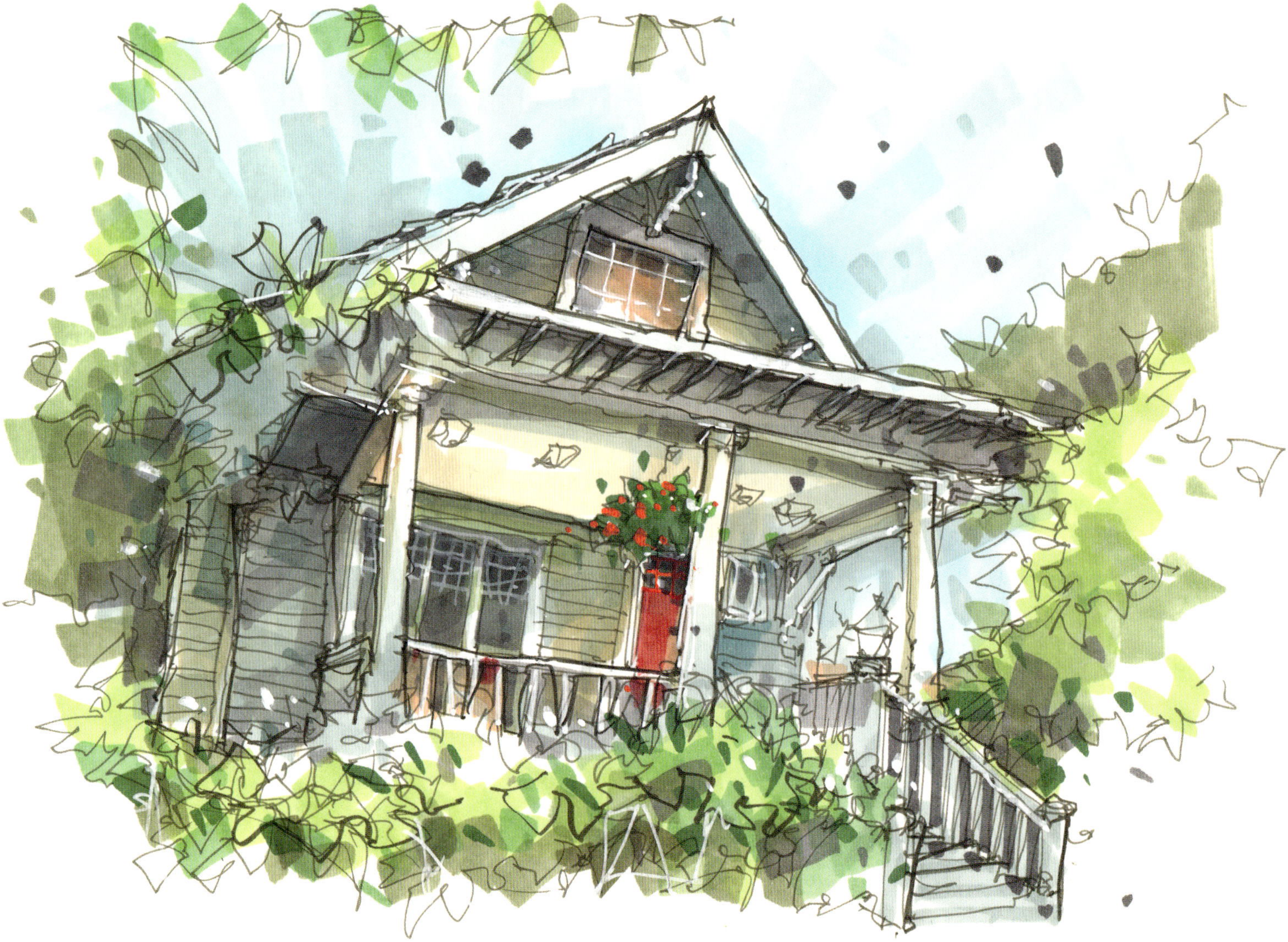

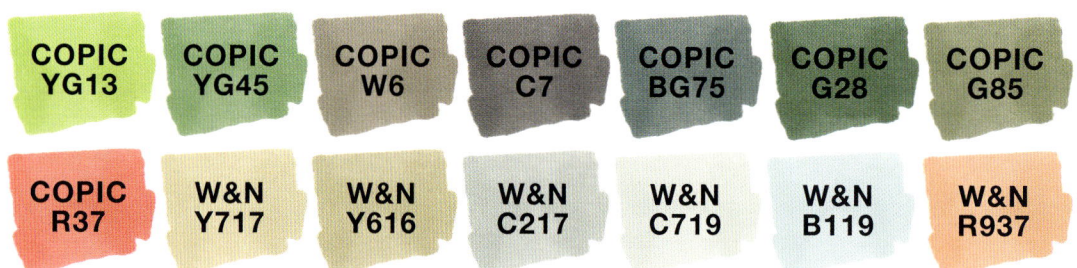

A wonderful porch area and lush greenery make this classic American house a very cozy place to sketch.

MARKER COLORS

COPIC YG13	COPIC YG45	COPIC W6	COPIC C7	COPIC BG75	COPIC G28	COPIC G85
COPIC R37	W&N Y717	W&N Y616	W&N C217	W&N C719	W&N B119	W&N R937

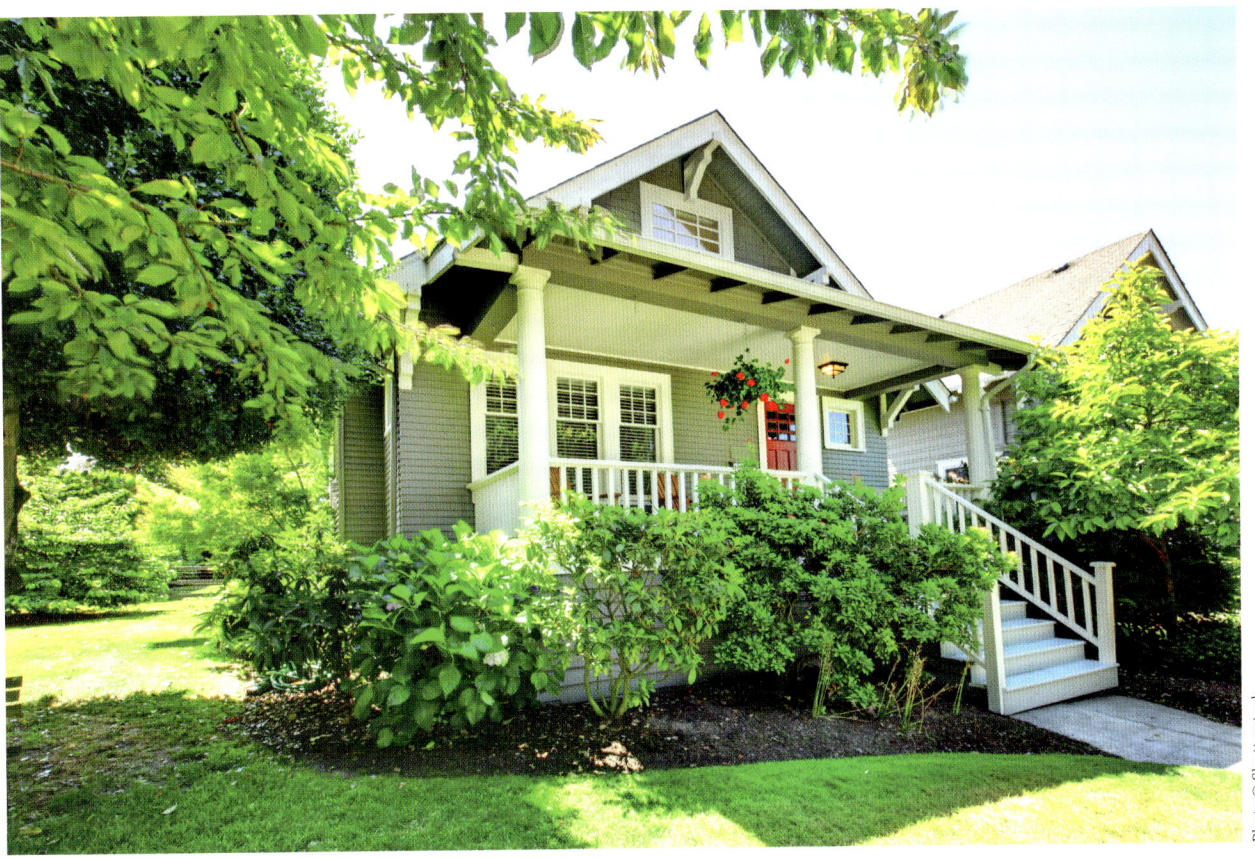

Photo © Shutterstock

THE PROCESS

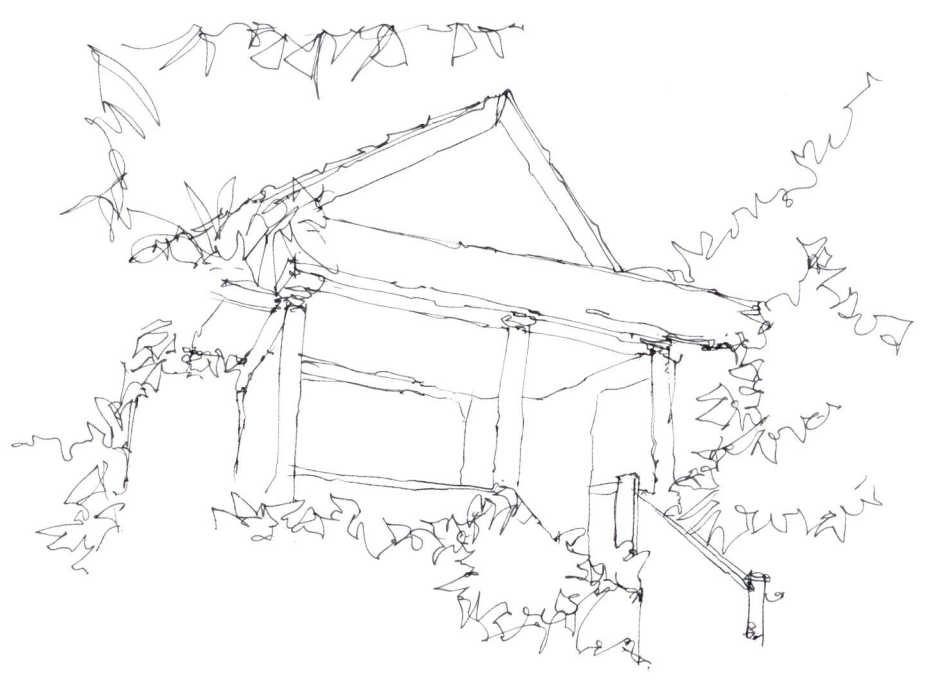

STAGE 1

Though this isn't really a fully fledged house sketch, I wanted to play out the porch area and that roof sticking out over it. This one also has a more dynamic three-point perspective that is nice to sketch. So, I started again with the main features following the perspective lines and some silhouetted shrubs.

STAGE 2

In this stage, the details are sketched in, and you can see how things quickly start to look complicated. But since the basic lines are already in place, sketching in this detail is actually not that hard at all.

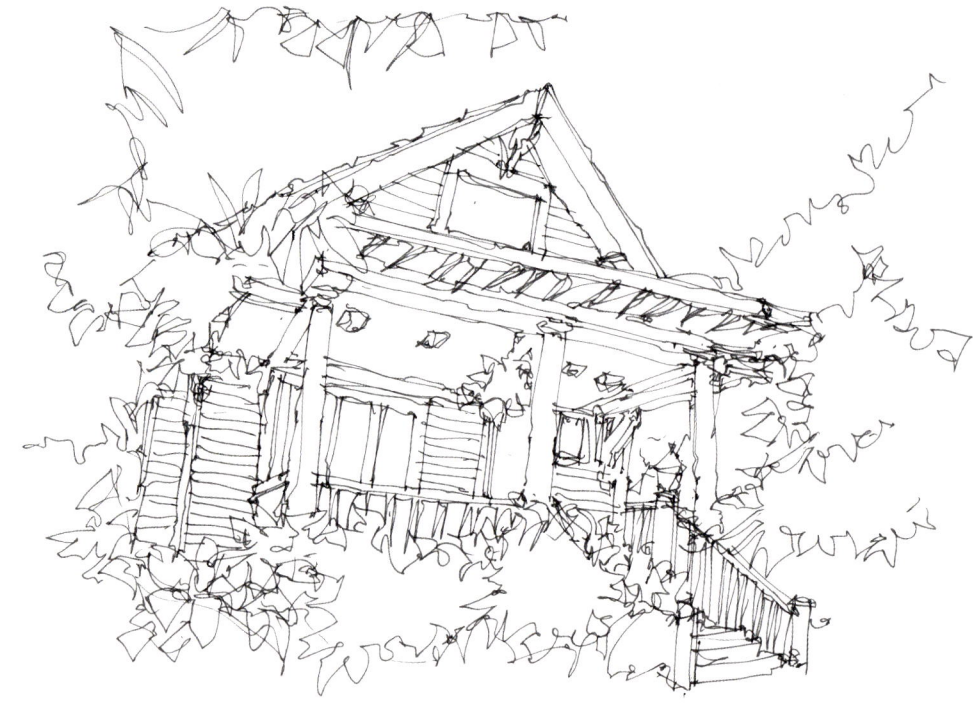

STAGE 3

Since this is a light house, I carefully start layering some basic light shades. There is a lot of green spilling into the white boarding, so I add some grayish greens there, keeping in mind not to go too dark too quickly. I also added a vibrant green to suggest some backlighting.

Colors used: Y717, Y616, YG13, C217, C719

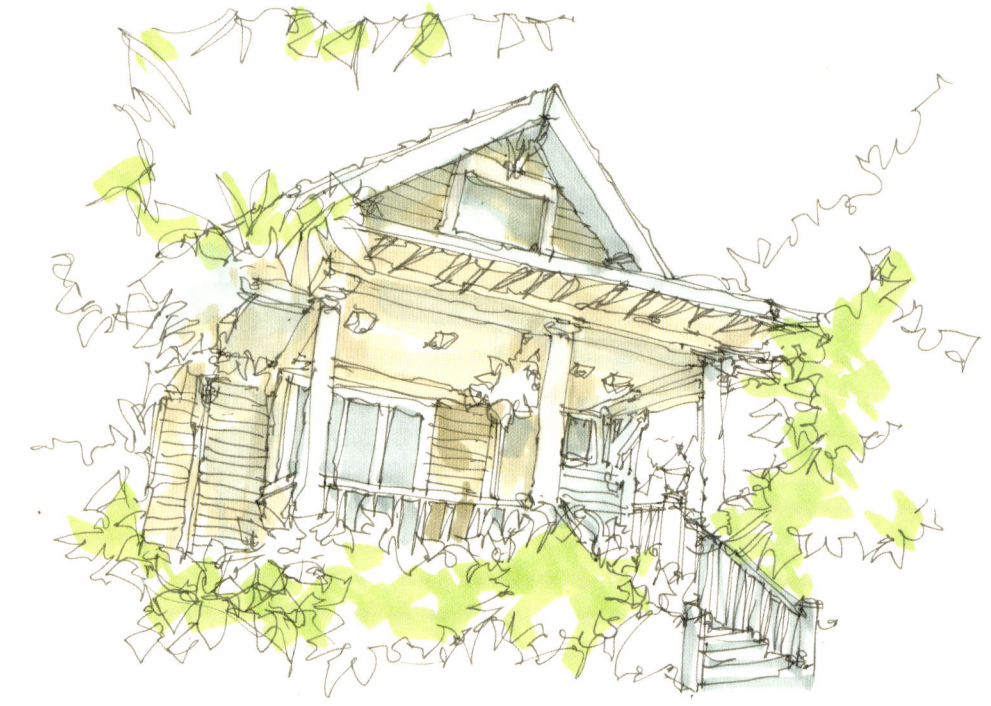

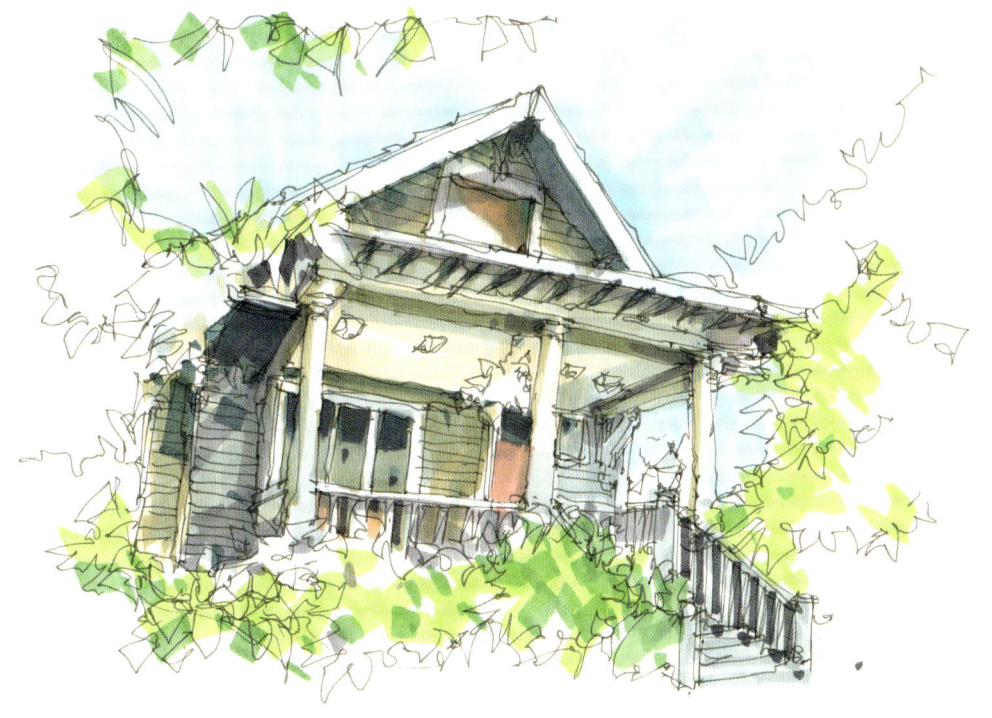

STAGE 4

Accentuating the dynamic perspective, I decided to add an outward-radiating sky coloring. This also accentuates the lightness of the building, which on a white background, is invisible. A darker color value for the surroundings can quickly lighten up your built structure again.

Colors used: Y616, YG45, B119, R937, W6, C7, BG75

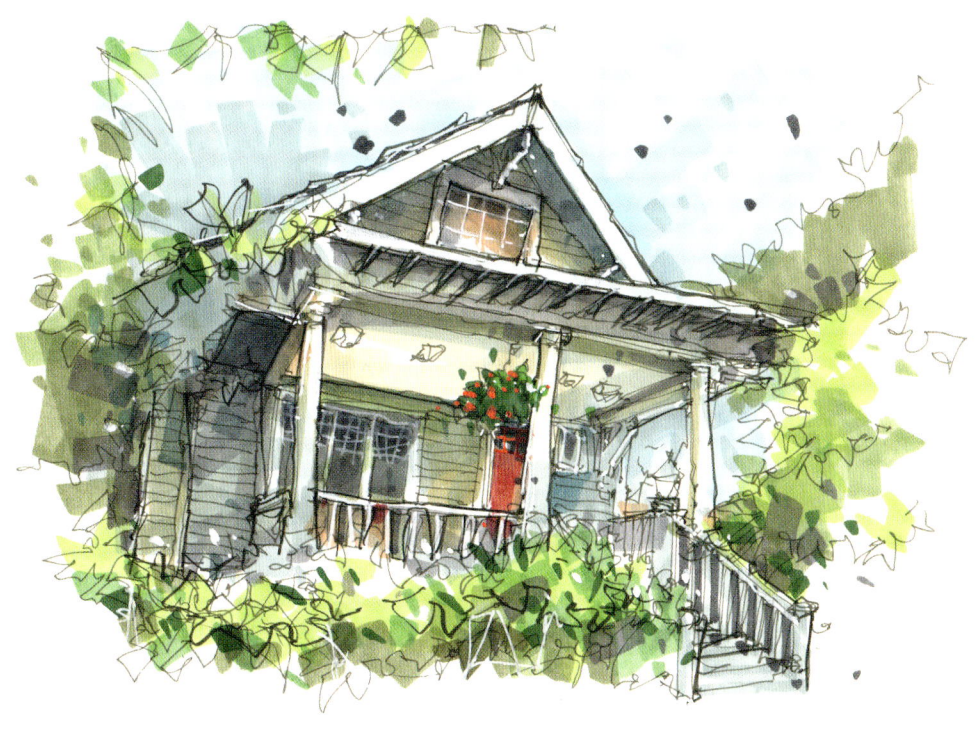

STAGE 5

Adding the final details— white lines, flowers, and deeper shading—complete this cozy cottage.

Colors used: C7, G28, C217, G85, R37

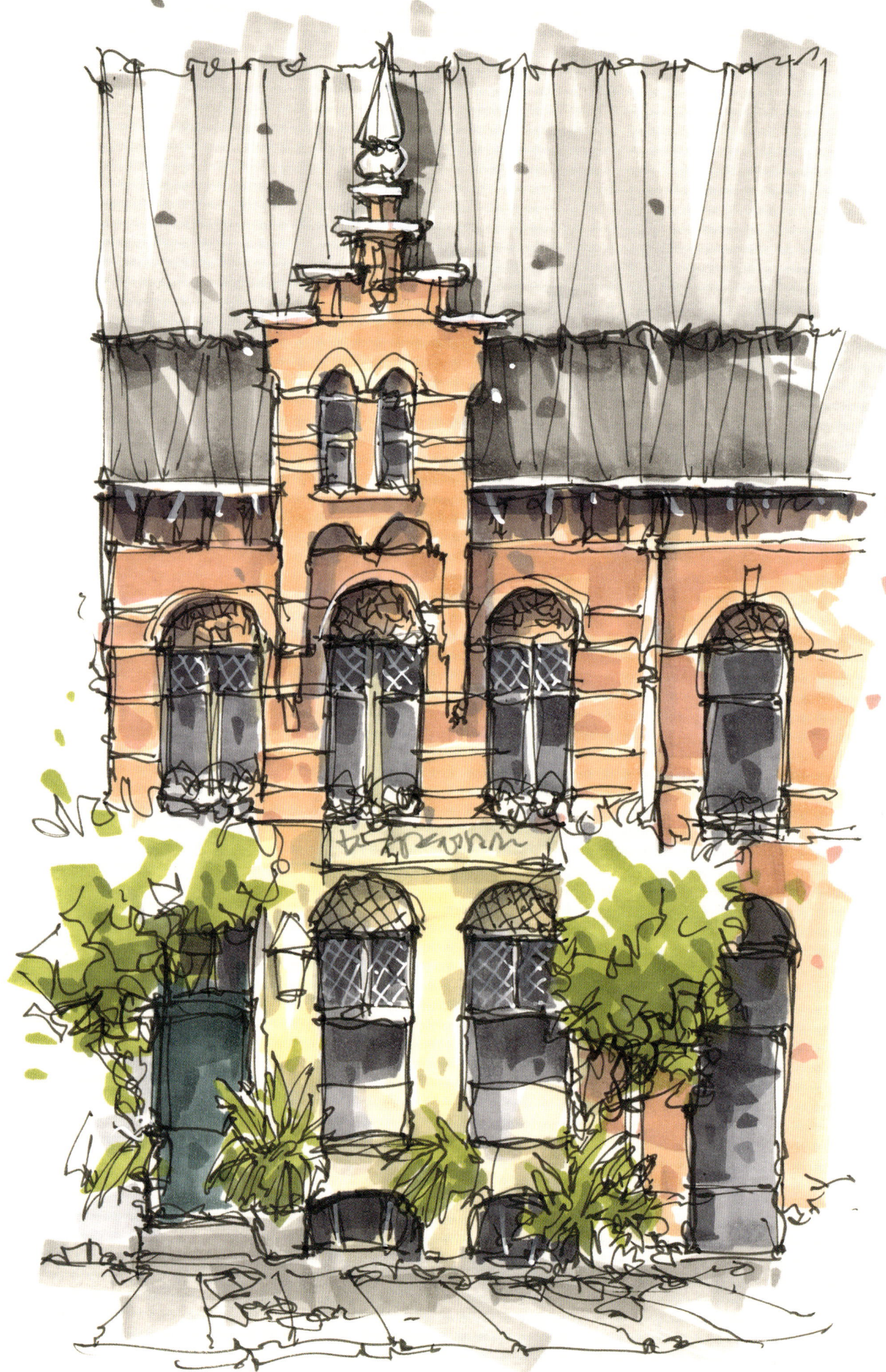

Façade with Foliage // Venlo, Netherlands

Walking around in your own town and looking up and around, it will amaze you how many hidden jewels surround you. My hometown of Venlo has lots of these wonderful structures. The nice thing about sketching façades is that you don't have to worry about perspective at all. One thing though—usually you don't see the whole roof structure. So here I have cheated perspective and added the missing section.

MARKER COLORS

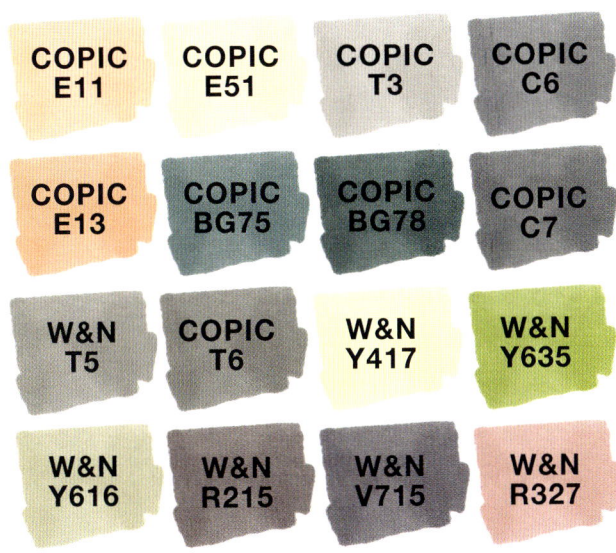

COPIC E11 | COPIC E51 | COPIC T3 | COPIC C6
COPIC E13 | COPIC BG75 | COPIC BG78 | COPIC C7
W&N T5 | COPIC T6 | W&N Y417 | W&N Y635
W&N Y616 | W&N R215 | W&N V715 | W&N R327

REFERENCE PHOTO

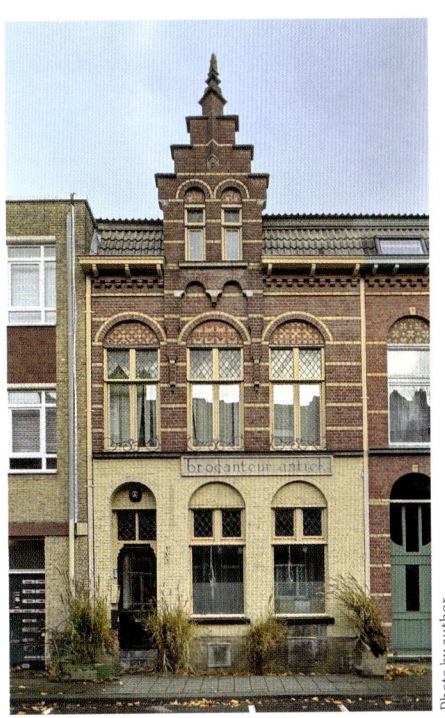

Photo by author

THE PROCESS

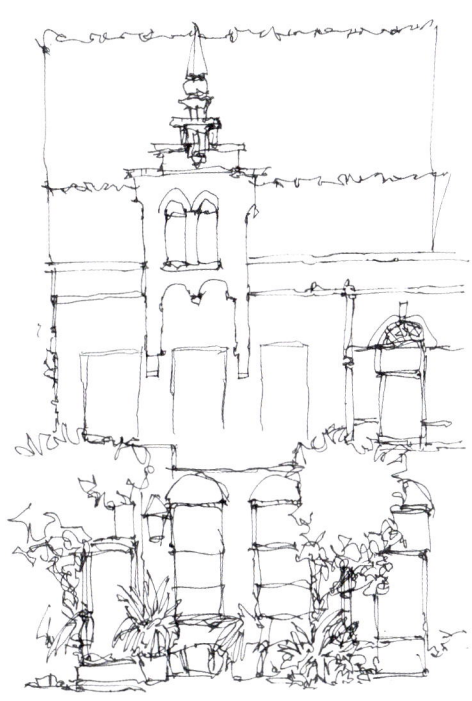

STAGE 1

A crucial thing in sketching façades is trying to see the main structure and not getting overwhelmed by all the "noisy" details. Simplify as much as possible and use that as a jumping-off point for more detailed sketching, where necessary. In this case, I started with the ground level, first floor, and attic.

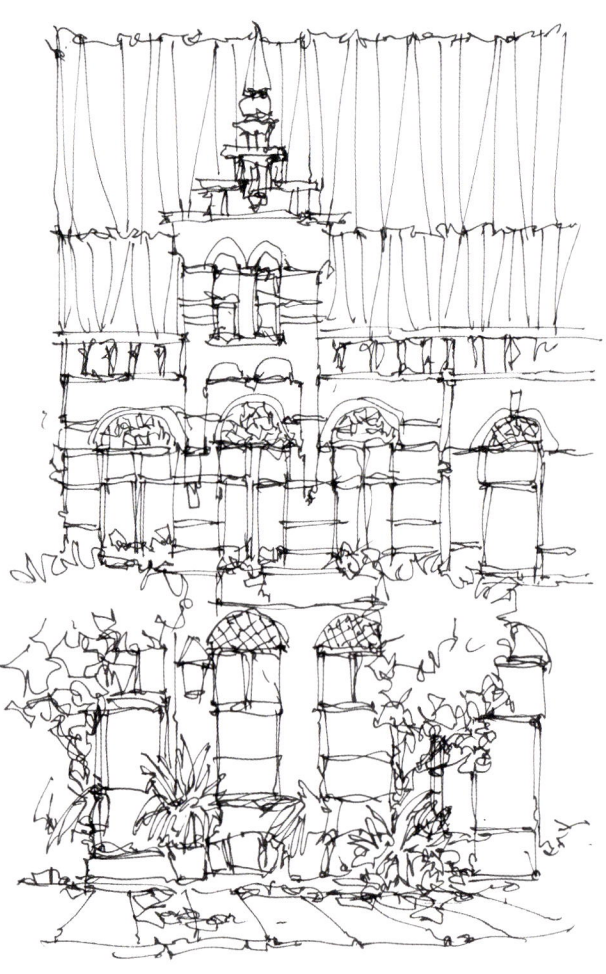

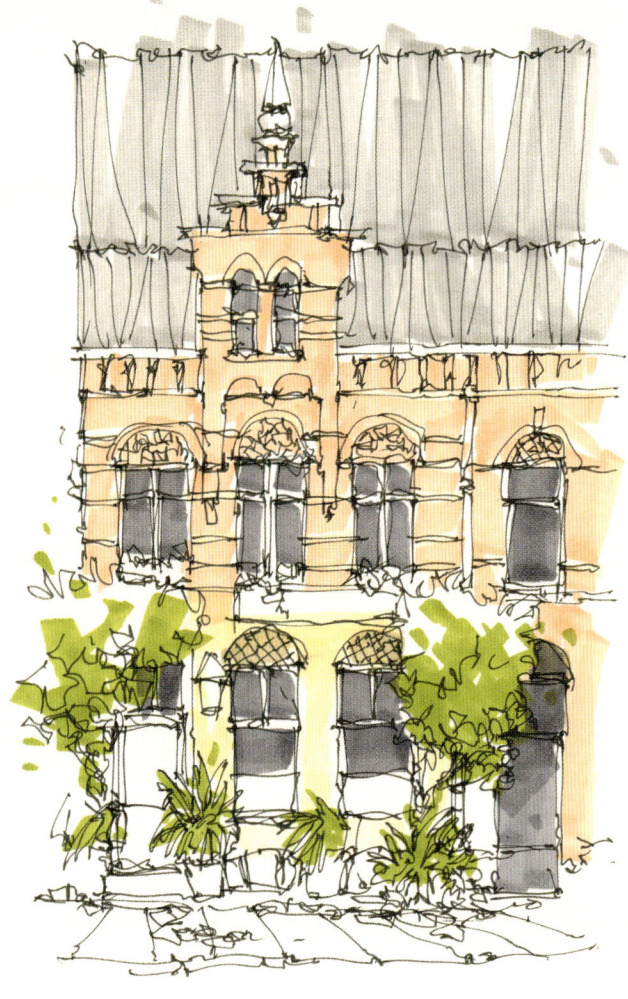

STAGE 2

Once the main structural elements have been laid down, it becomes much easier to fill in the more detailed sections. Always keep in mind to place detailed areas not all over the place, but in areas where you want the viewer to look. Especially with richly detailed brick-work, things could become overwhelming very quickly.

STAGE 3

The coloring of this sketch is not that complicated. I list lots of shades, but it could be done with fewer. Starting off with a main reddish wash, a light green and a medium dark for the windows quickly gives a basic setup. Note the purposely left white areas in the shrubs.

Colors used: E11, Y417, E51, T3, Y635, C6

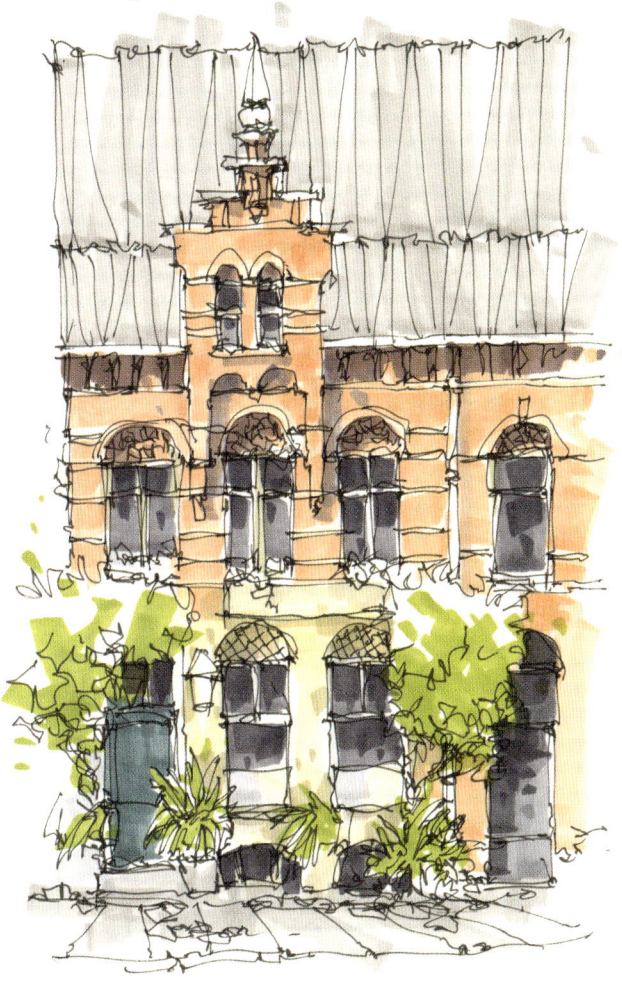

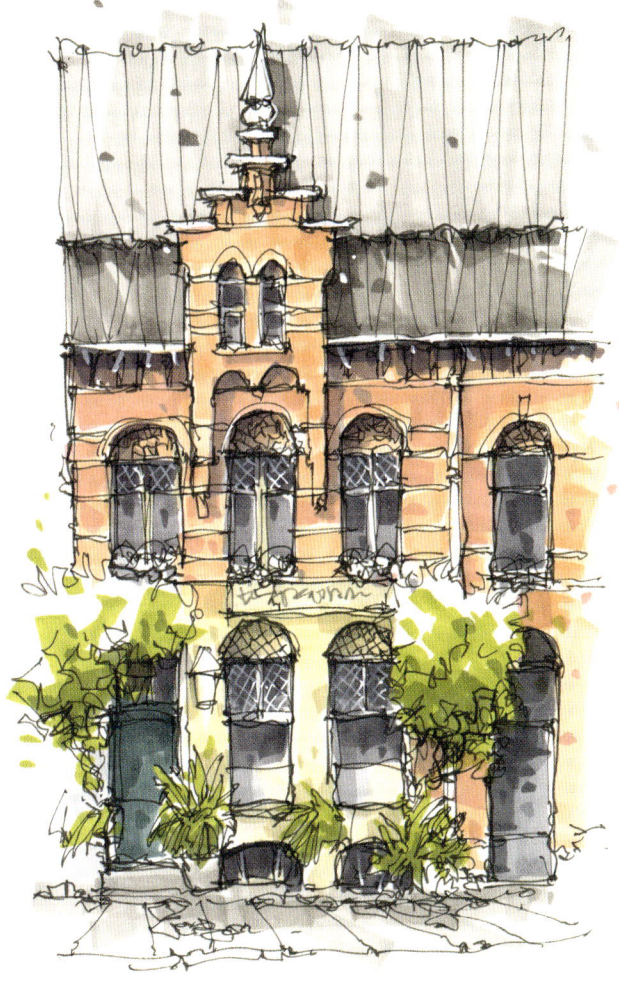

STAGE 4

As soon as the darker shades are applied within the recesses, this façade starts to get some very nice depth. It's great to see how a medium-value purple works so wonderfully as a shadow color for the reds. I use this combination regularly. I punch in some darker gray values in the windows as well.

Colors used: E13, BG75, Y616, R215, C7

STAGE 5

The darkest values are a nice foundation to start applying the white accents. I added these to the roof ledge and the stained-glass windows, mainly. After these have dried, it's time for the final touches of pushing back the whites and also adding some heavier lines in areas to accentuate the arches and protruded sections more.

Colors used: V715, T5, T6, BG78, R327

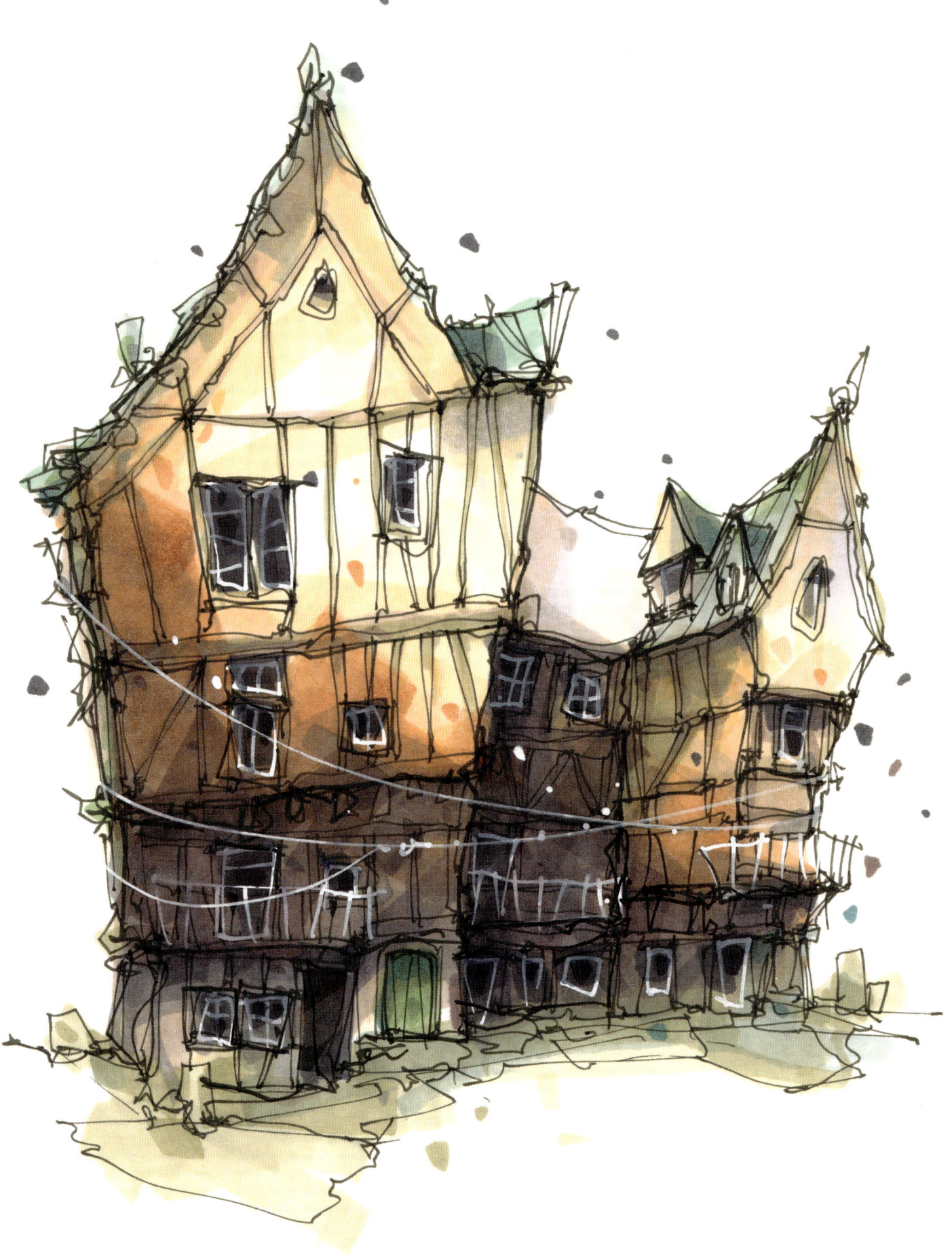

Half-Timbered Houses // Rouen, France

On this sketch, I have done some major remodeling. I wanted to exaggerate the depth perspective as well as change the lighting on the group to a much warmer one, to make it more dynamic and less gloomy in mood.

MARKER COLORS

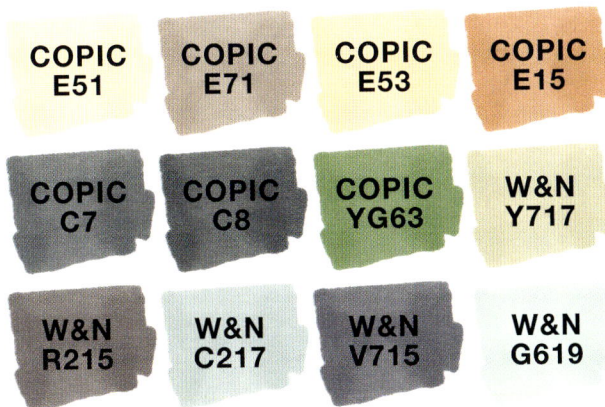

COPIC E51 · COPIC E71 · COPIC E53 · COPIC E15

COPIC C7 · COPIC C8 · COPIC YG63 · W&N Y717

W&N R215 · W&N C217 · W&N V715 · W&N G619

REFERENCE PHOTO

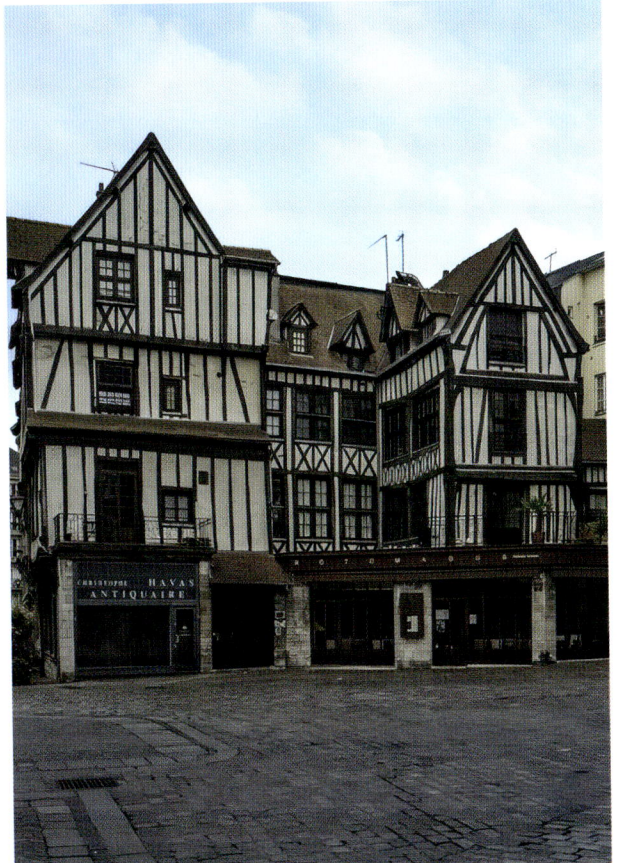

Photo by @manuuu_manuuu_manuuu

EXAGGERATION

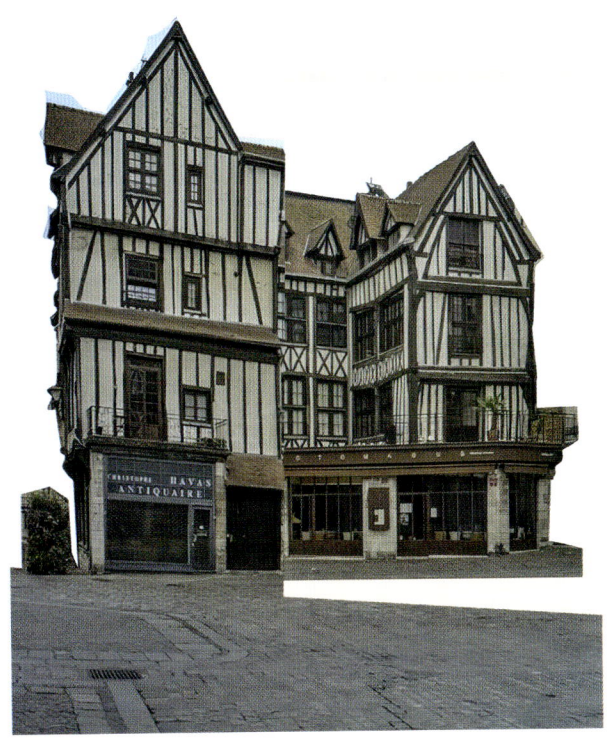

THE PROCESS

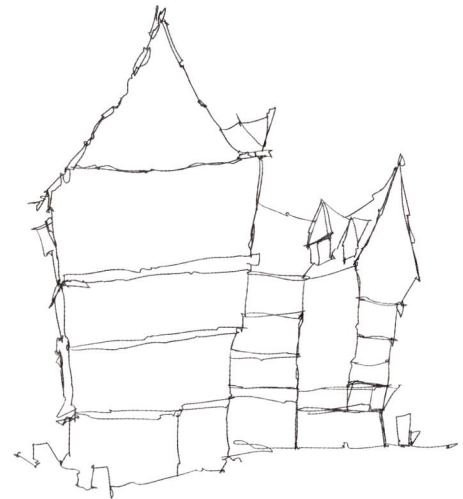

STAGE 1

Identify the main blocks of the building group and traveling these group outlines to get the main structure down. You see that here depth is suggested more by small versus big, than constructing a perspective with vanishing points. I used the subdivisions as the main organizing element.

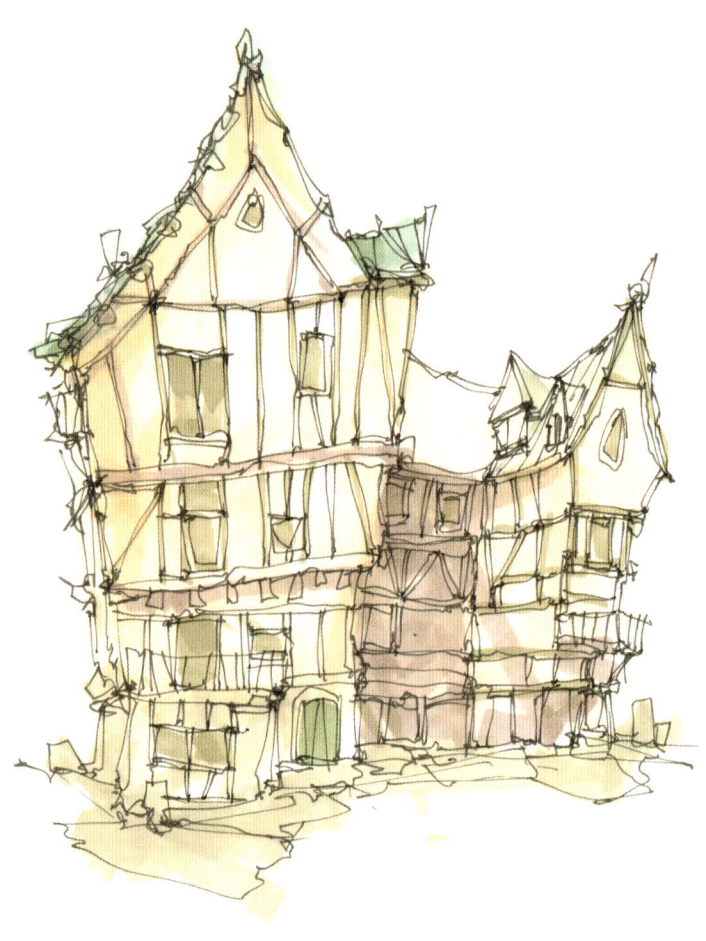

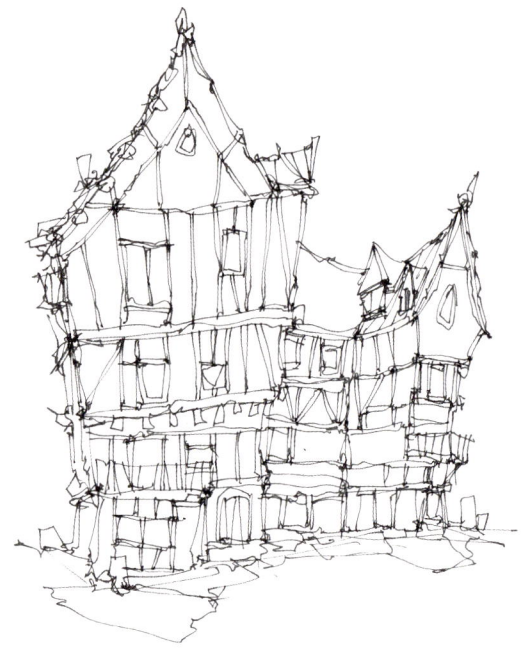

STAGE 3

The first set of colors are very light. Since the buildings are mostly white plaster. I "haze in" these light colors. I still place them in sections that help me quickly establish the dimension (i.e., I mostly place them in areas of shadow).

Colors used: E51, G619, Y717, E71

STAGE 2

Since these half-timbered houses mainly consist of linear beams, having the base structure down makes it easy to fill in the rest. I make a conscious effort not to "align" these beams. This helps create a more organic rhythm throughout the sketch. Keeping everything light also prepares for a balanced coloring stage.

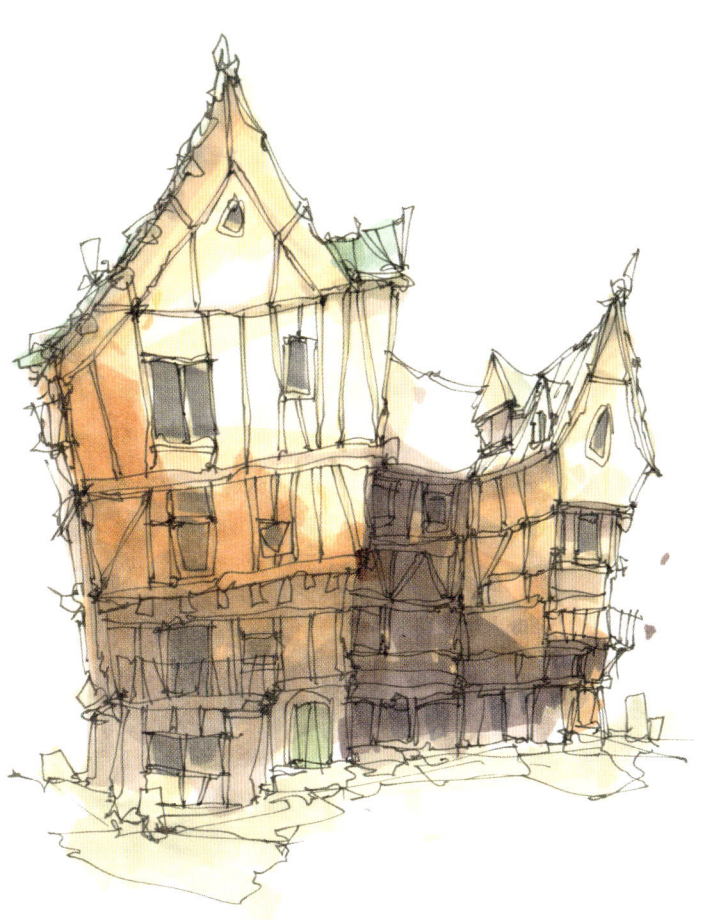

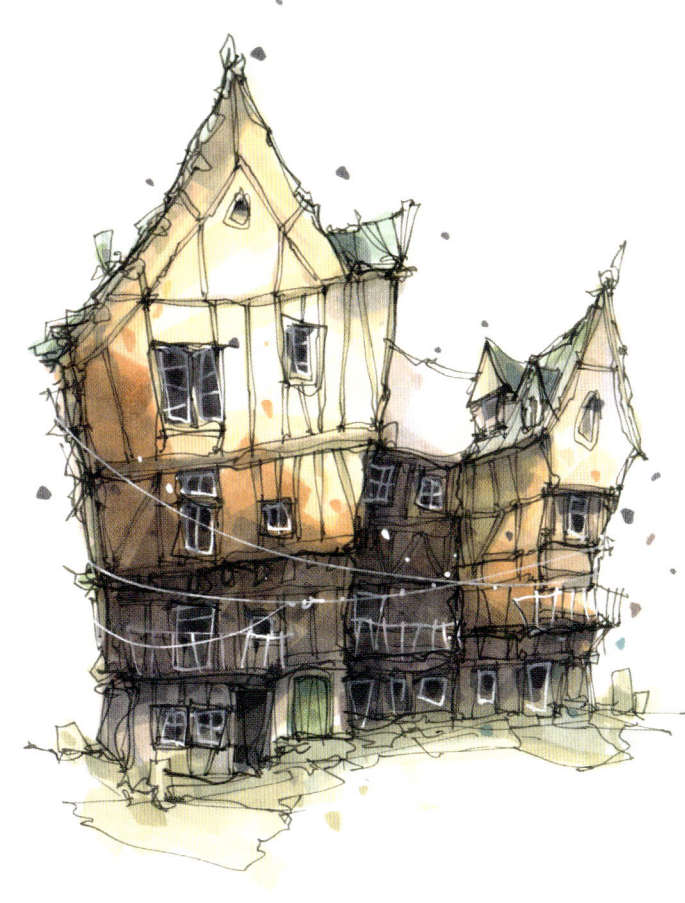

STAGE 4

Next up, I intensify the colors I use to push in more darks. Observe how the colors I use are mostly warm ochres and yellows with just a slight shift to a purple. I wanted to simulate a sundown that casts shadows from neighboring buildings onto these houses.

Colors used: YG63, E53, E15, R215, C7

STAGE 5

In the final stage, I push in the dark values. These are the deepest shadow areas, as well as the windows and doors. Having the lower portion and the recessed section of the building in the shade also helps when I add the lighter white accent lines on top. These immediately jump-start depth and detailing.

Colors used: C217, C7, C8, V715

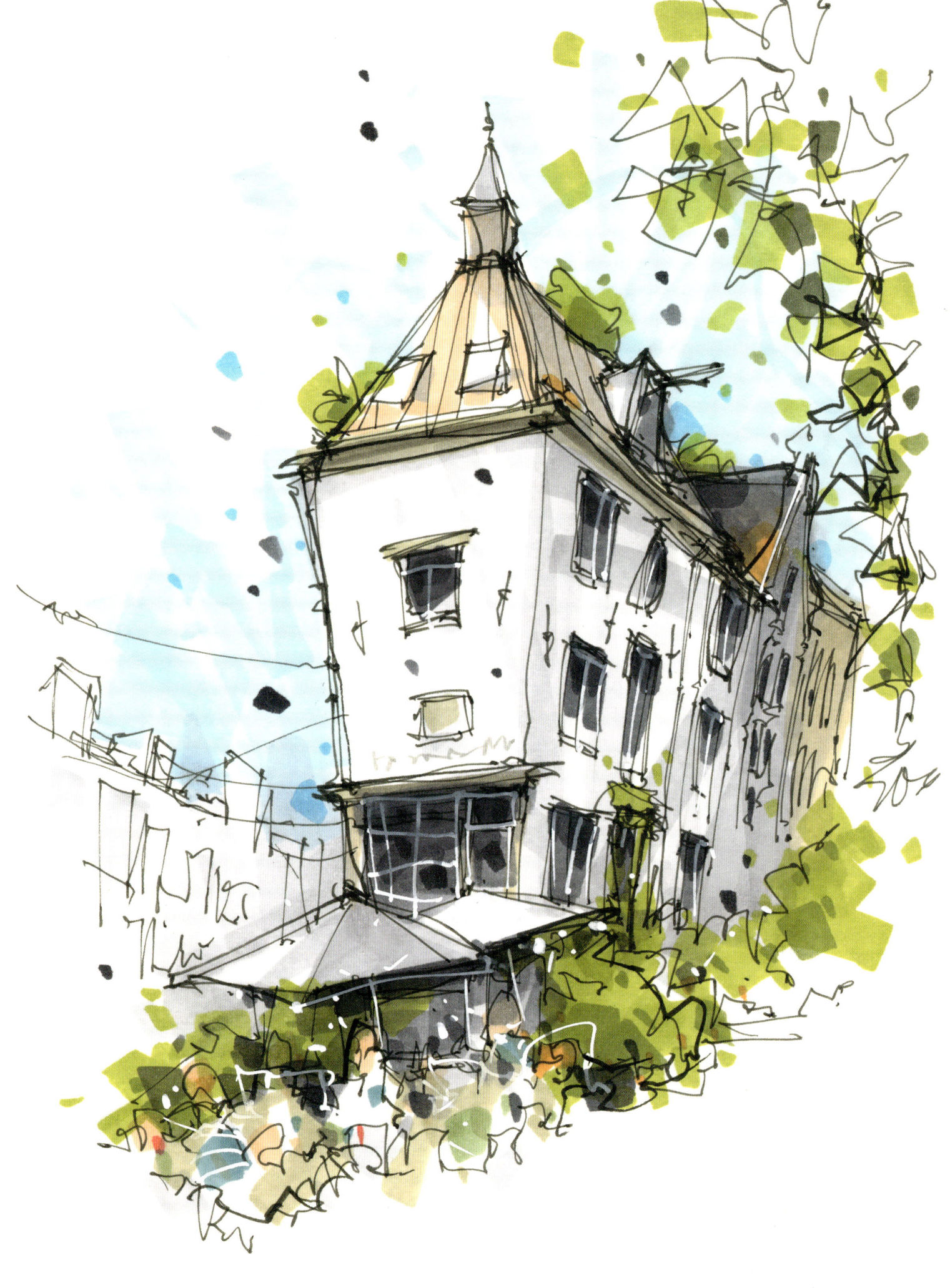

Corner Café // Amsterdam, Netherlands

Returning to Amsterdam, I found this wonderful corner street café with a nice, crowded terrace. The weather was not too great, but that is something that can be perfectly remedied in a sketch.

MARKER COLORS

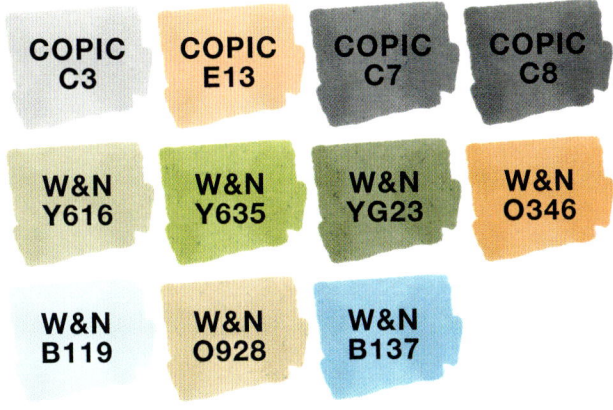

COPIC C3
COPIC E13
COPIC C7
COPIC C8

W&N Y616
W&N Y635
W&N YG23
W&N O346

W&N B119
W&N O928
W&N B137

REFERENCE PHOTO

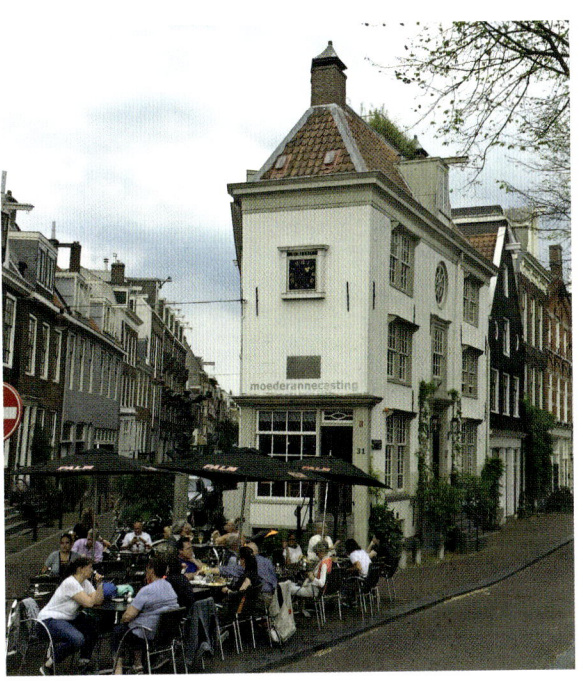

THE PROCESS

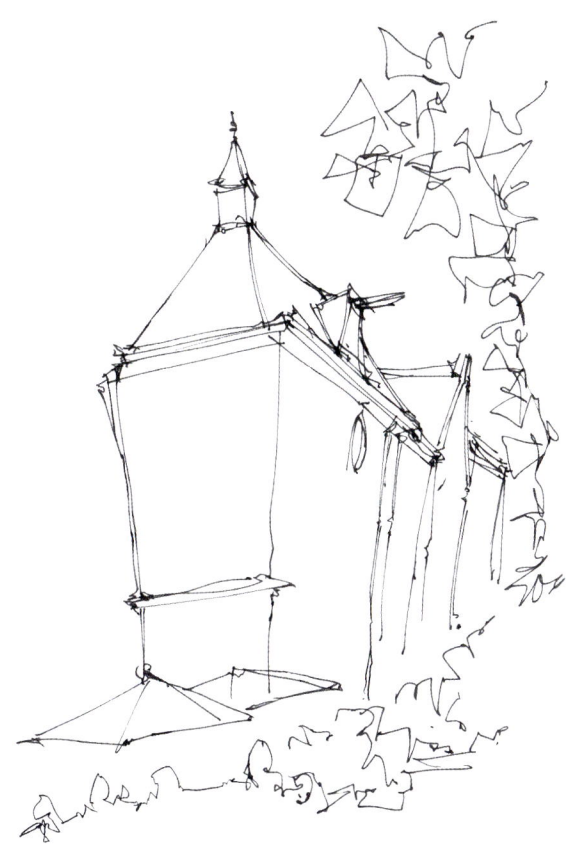

STAGE 1

Start with some basic forms. It's not really a rectangular block, but close enough to serve as a basis. The roof can be treated as a wedged shape with that small protruded attic window. I also added some triangles serving as umbrellas, and a wavy line to suggest silhouettes of people.

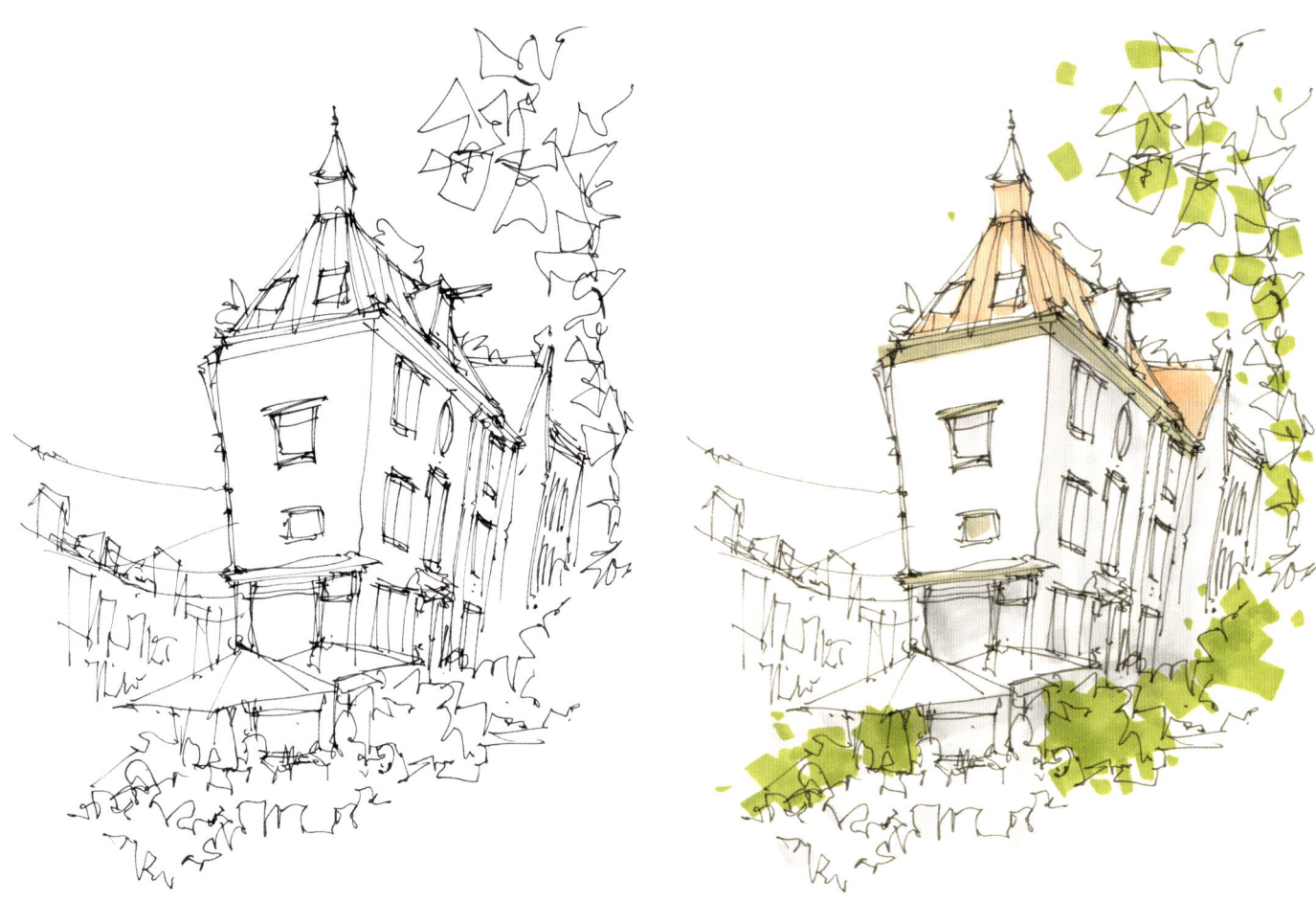

STAGE 2

Quickly fleshing out the linework with roof and window details, I generally use long irregular lines to indicate roof tiles. This can be applied in both a horizontal or vertical way. There's not always a need to go full detail. I also added a very simplified row of buildings on the left.

STAGE 3

Coloring white structures can be very tricky. But I made use of the page-white once again. I added a very light shade of cool gray as a shadow side to start up the basic volume of this building. Even in this basic state, you can see things taking shape.

Colors used: C3, Y616, E13, Y635

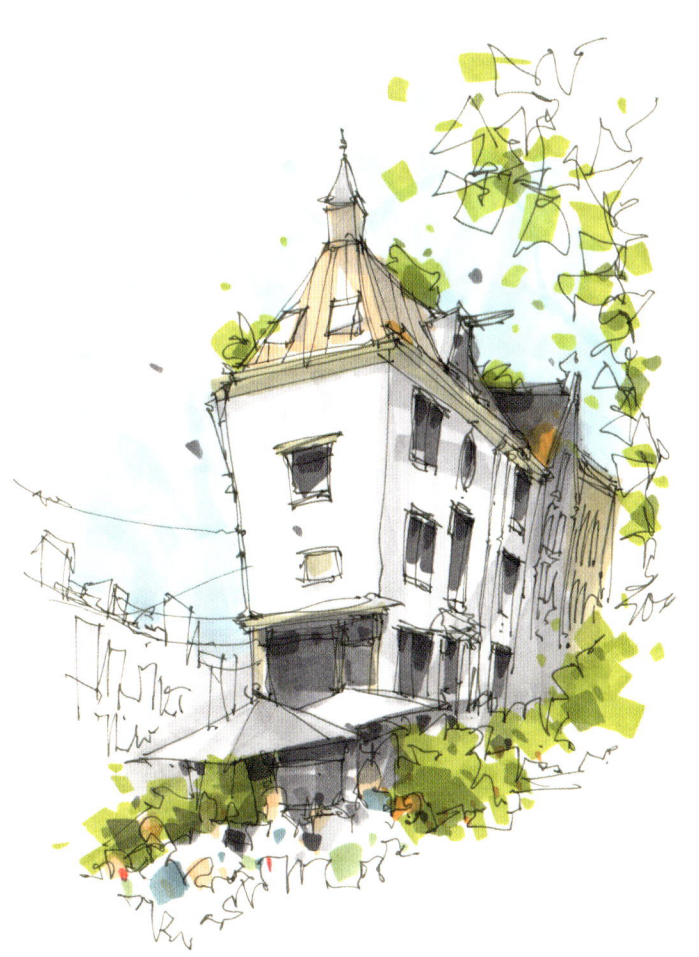

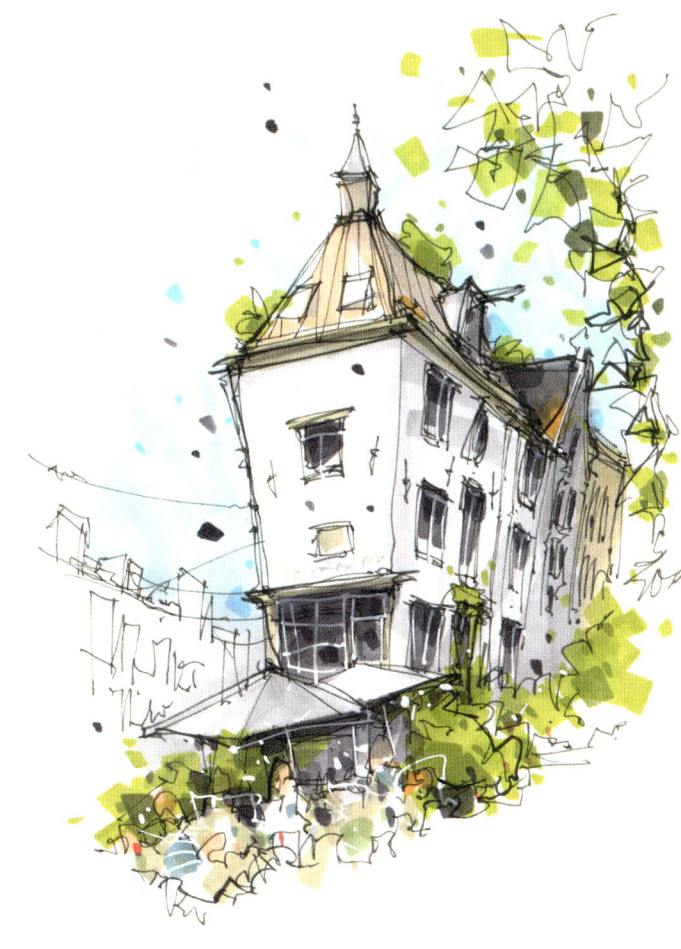

STAGE 4

One way to express more light in the building is to make the surroundings darker. In this case, a blue indication of sky does that very nicely. Also, deepening the values in the windows and the shade underneath the umbrellas help sell this feeling of white.

Colors used: YG23, C7, O346, B119, O928

STAGE 5

I played a little more with wavy whites and some bright dashes of color in the final stage to give more vibrance to this scene than what is visible in the photograph. This is something to keep in mind when sketching. It does not need to faithfully represent what you see. Make it yours!

Colors used: B137, C8

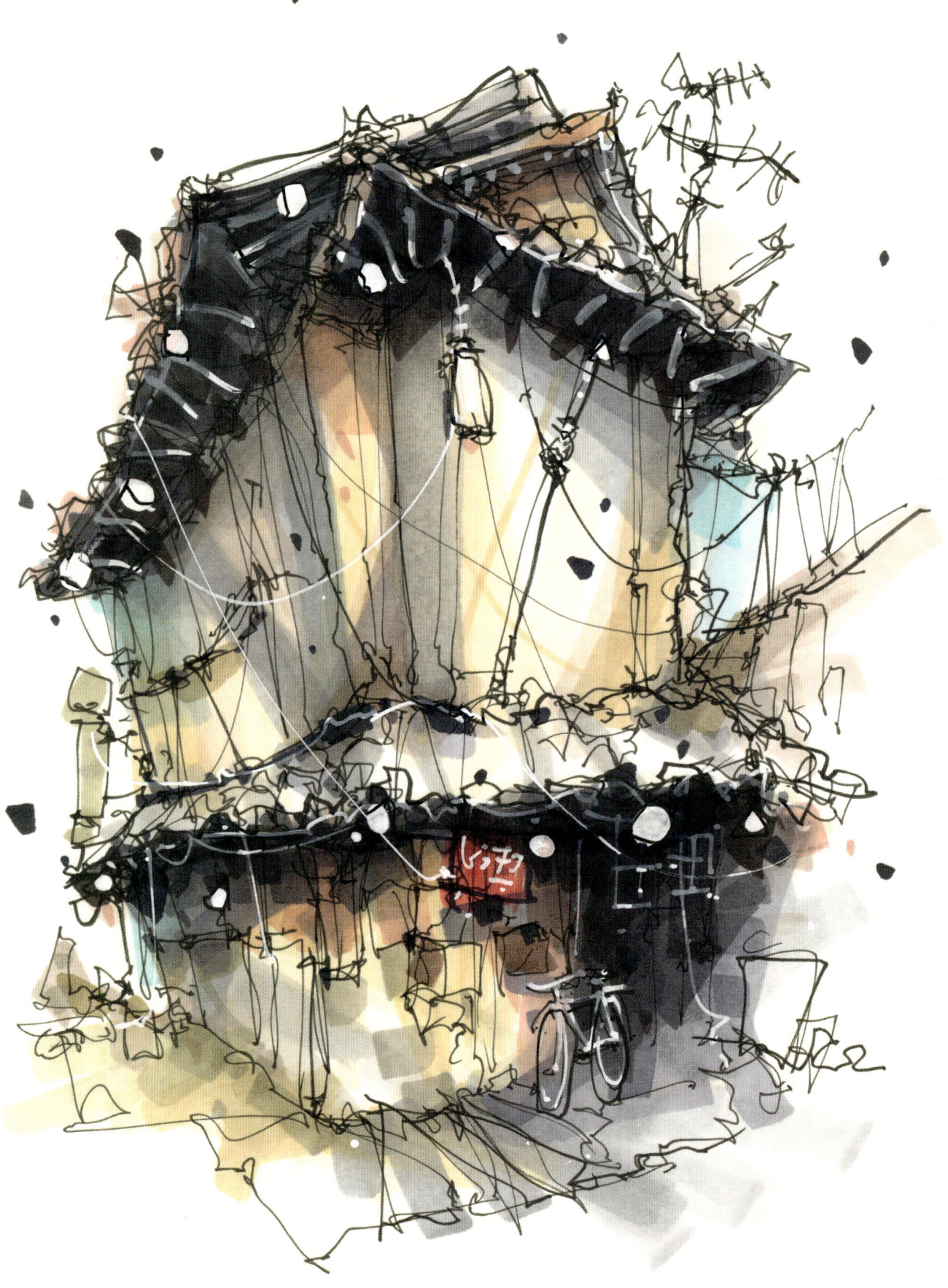

Wooden Shop // Tokyo, Japan

This project highlights a wonderfully chaotic store built out of wooden panels and lots of debris that in itself already makes this incredibly inspiring to sketch. I loved the sectioned floors (remember the anatomy of a building?), and I wanted to exaggerate that first floor a little more and made it more vertical than the original. I also changed the roofing structure and the protruding area a little more to let this building make more sense with some of its structure removed. This accommodated my sketch better.

MARKER COLORS

COPIC C3	COPIC C4	COPIC C5	COPIC C6	COPIC C7
COPIC E04	COPIC E11	COPIC W2	COPIC E41	COPIC E70
COPIC E71	COPIC E13	COPIC B02	COPIC R46	COPIC T10
W&N C217	W&N C719	W&N O948	W&N Y616	W&N Y717
W&N R937				

REFERENCE PHOTO

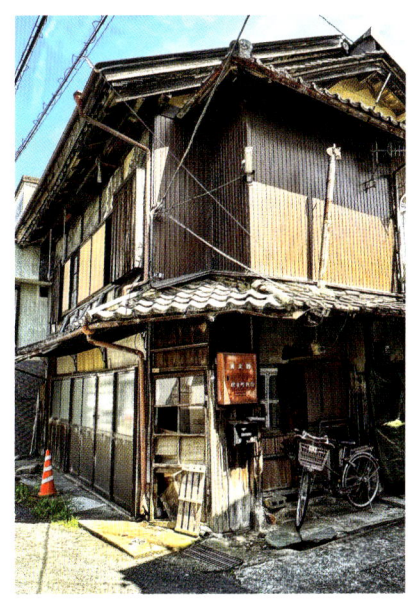

Photo by @daco_go

PERSPECTIVE

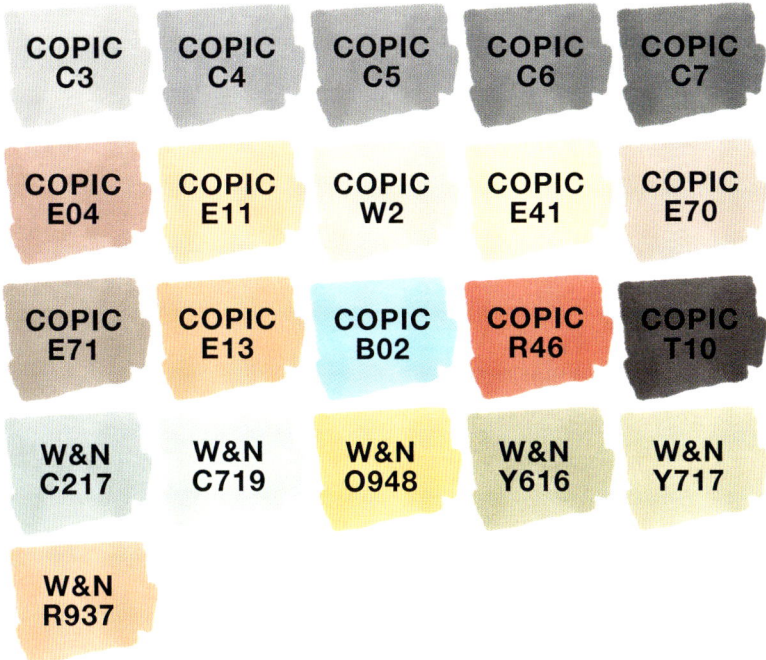

SILHOUETTE

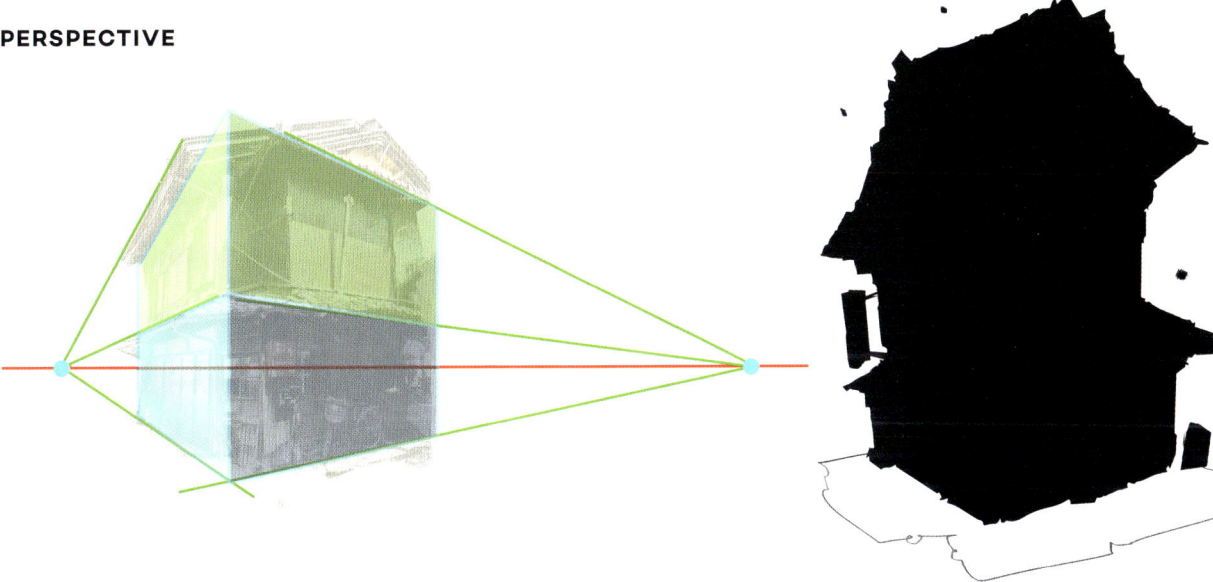

THE PROCESS

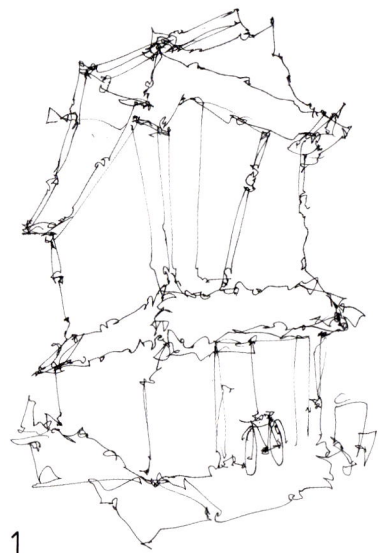

STAGE 1

To simplify the rather complex bustle of shapes and forms, I start to sketch the basic landmarks for quick orientation during the rest of sketching. It's always a good idea to look at things like roof lines and major façade edges.

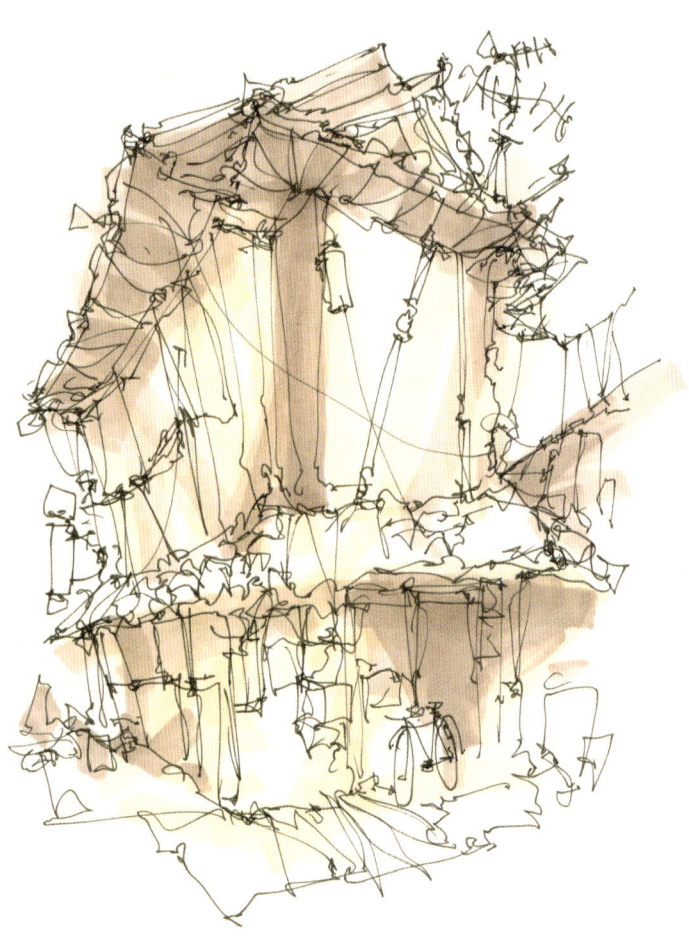

STAGE 3

The first stage of coloring with the lightest earthy colors and values quickly lays in the volume. You can see that even with only a minimum of colors, and even very light ones, the form of the building quickly becomes visible.

Colors used: E41, E70, E71

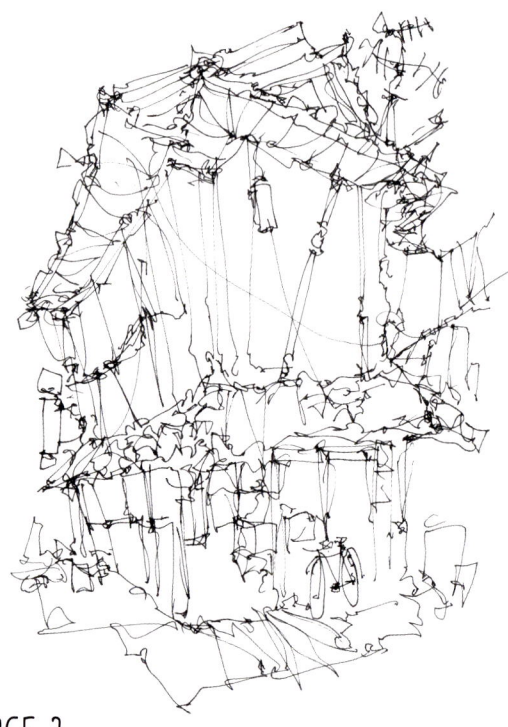

STAGE 2

Complete all the primary sketching with details like windows, doors, openings, roofing tiles, and entourage detail (stone tiles and rubble). What looks like a complex sketch is actually based on that simple primary line work in stage 1.

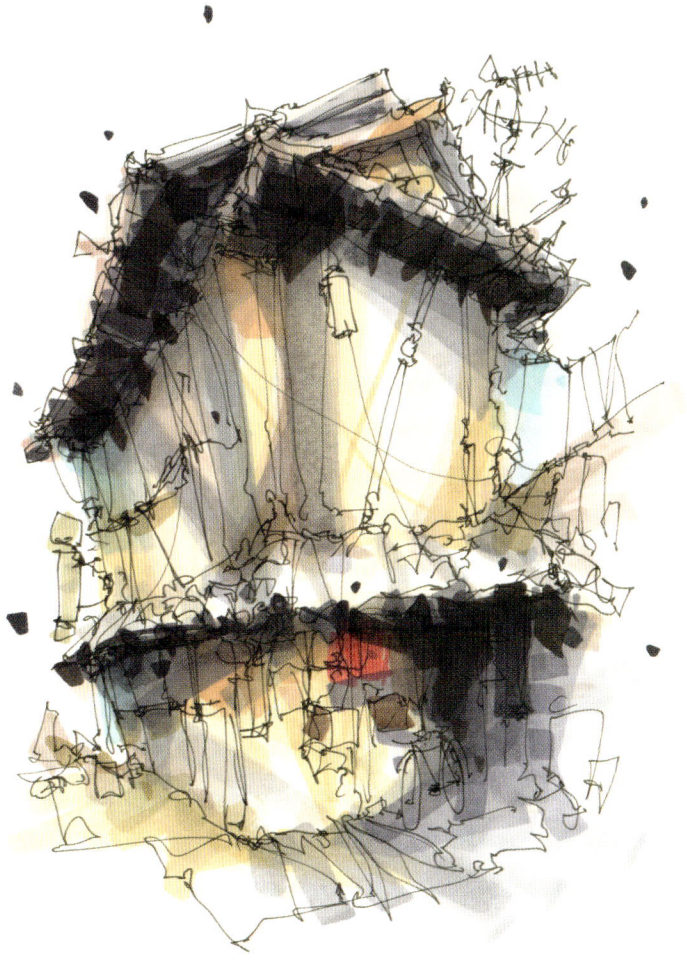

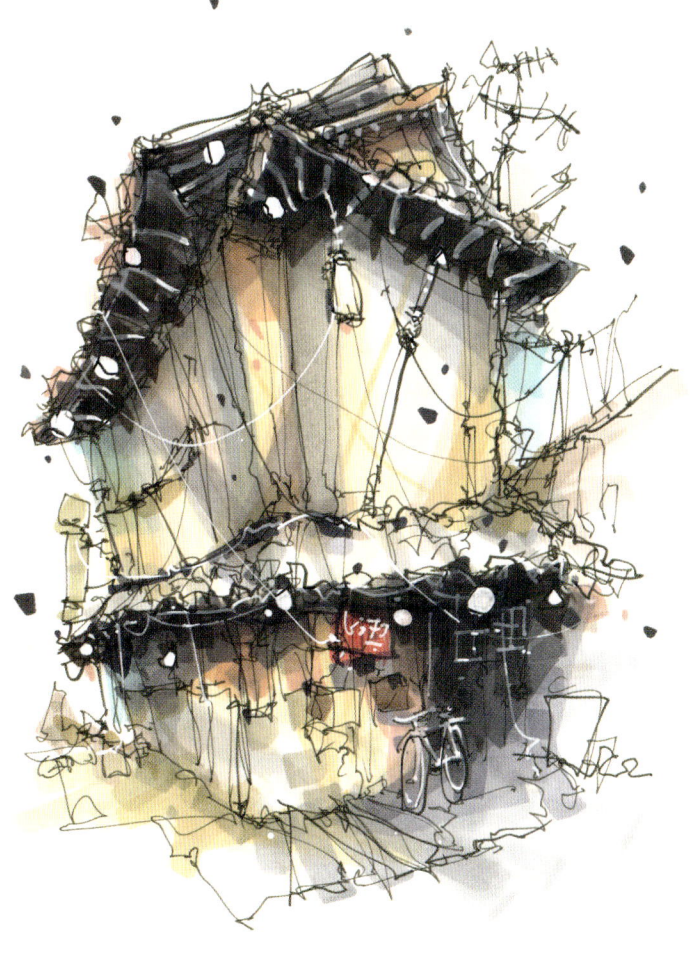

STAGE 4

As you can see in the reference, the strongest values are the cast shadows from the roof sections. And when these really dark values are applied, the building immediately starts to pop. To prevent these shadow shapes from becoming too solid, I will add some detail back in the next and final stage.

Colors used: E04, C217, E13, Y717, Y616, C3, C4, C5, B02, C6, C7, R46, R937, T10 , E11, W2, C719, O948

STAGE 5

As a first pass, I add the white acrylic marker lines with a Uni Posca. These lines are going to stand out very strongly. Especially against the very dark shadows. To counter that, I push them back a little in some areas with a medium dark gray marker.

Colors used: C7, C8

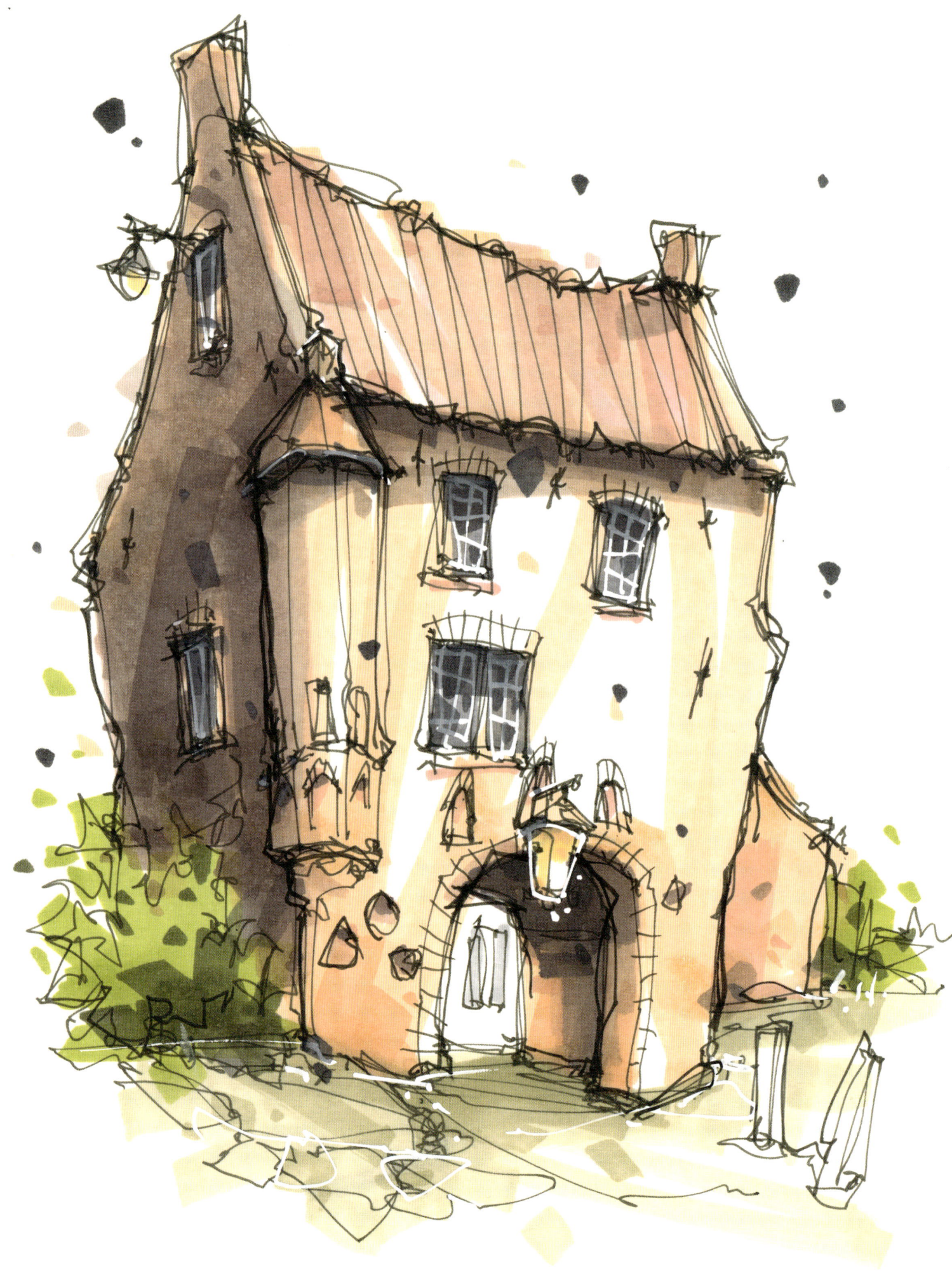

Gate House // Woudrichem, Netherlands

This looks like it used to be part of a walled, fortified town. The Netherlands is rich in some ornate red brick buildings. Especially around town entrances, they used to be more special. I love that little protruded turret, or cylindrical tower element, in this one.

MARKER COLORS

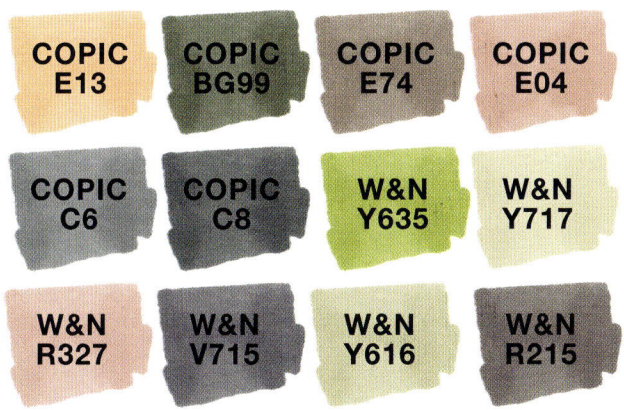

COPIC E13
COPIC BG99
COPIC E74
COPIC E04
COPIC C6
COPIC C8
W&N Y635
W&N Y717
W&N R327
W&N V715
W&N Y616
W&N R215

REFERENCE PHOTO

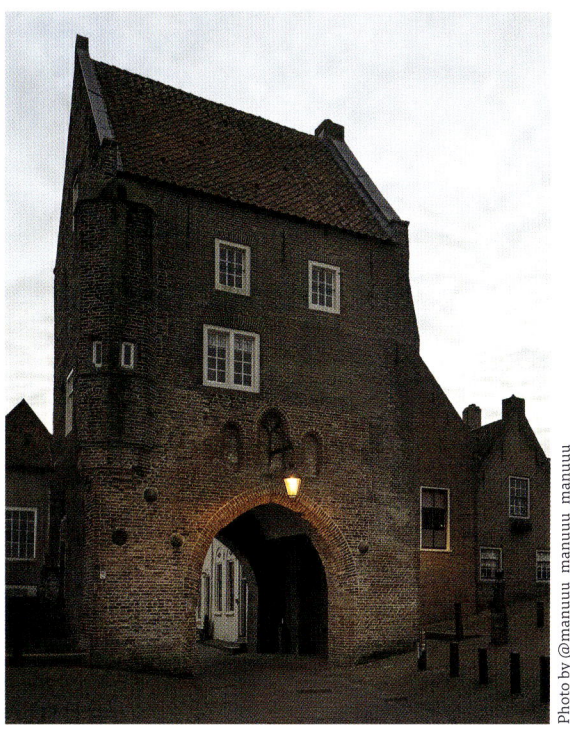

Photo by @manuuu_manuuu_manuuu

THE PROCESS

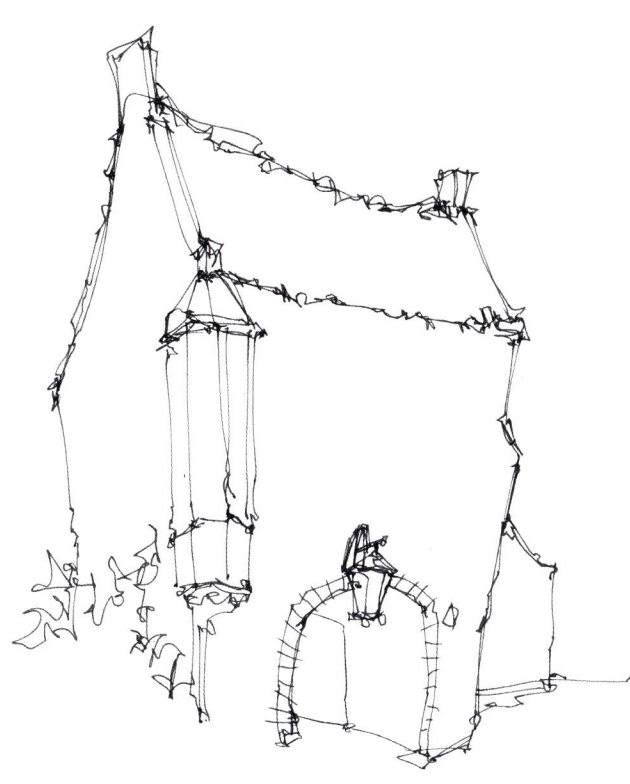

STAGE 1

The original building felt quite stiff, and I wanted to loosen that up a bit. I made it stubbier too. My first line pass concentrated on the elemental shapes: a block with a prism-like roof and the turret sticking out. I also added a quick indication of shrubs (also to cap off that left section).

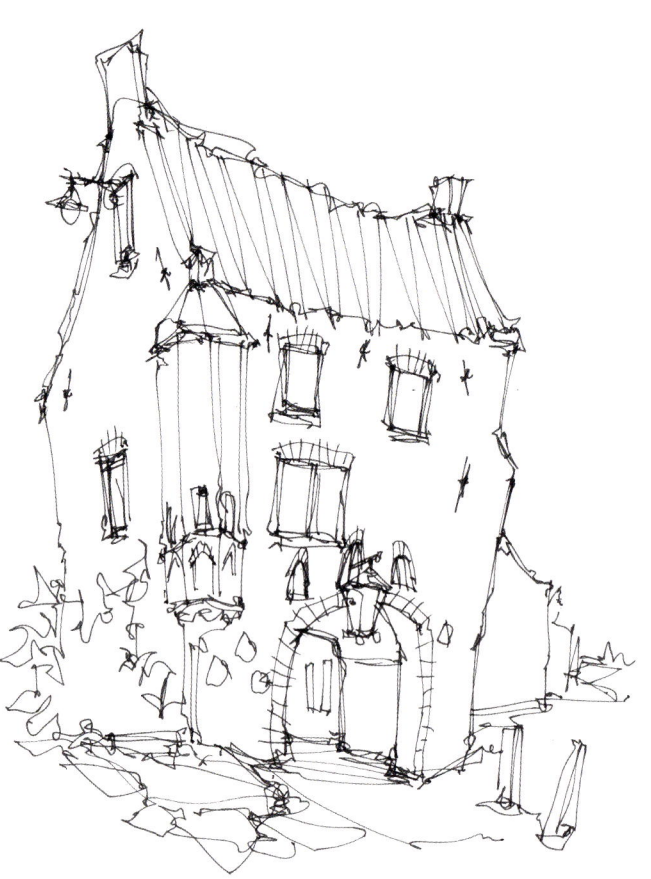

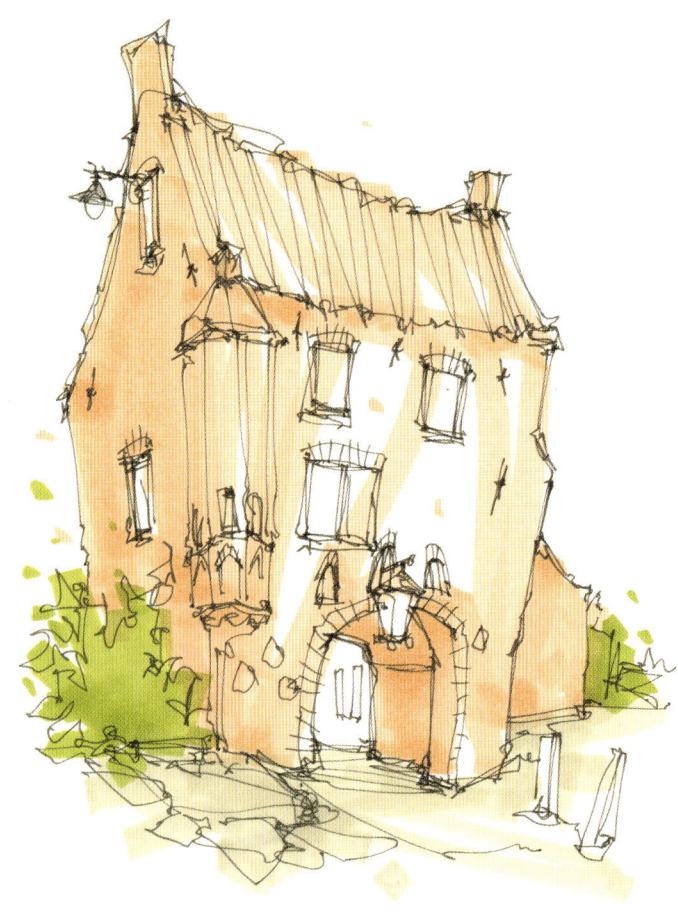

STAGE 2

Adding in details like windows, some ornamental elements, and indications of the roof tiles (again only some irregularly spaces long lines), quickly had this place standing proud. I left out some distracting background elements because I wanted to make this building a separate character. I added some lead-in elements to the right with these poles.

STAGE 3

The first stage of coloring is a medium reddish wash. Note the shards of page- white that I leave untouched on purpose. This sharding technique is something that is very important for me to let a sketch breathe. It also simulates a vibrant play of light. The greens are loosely brushed in.

Colors used: E13, Y635, Y717

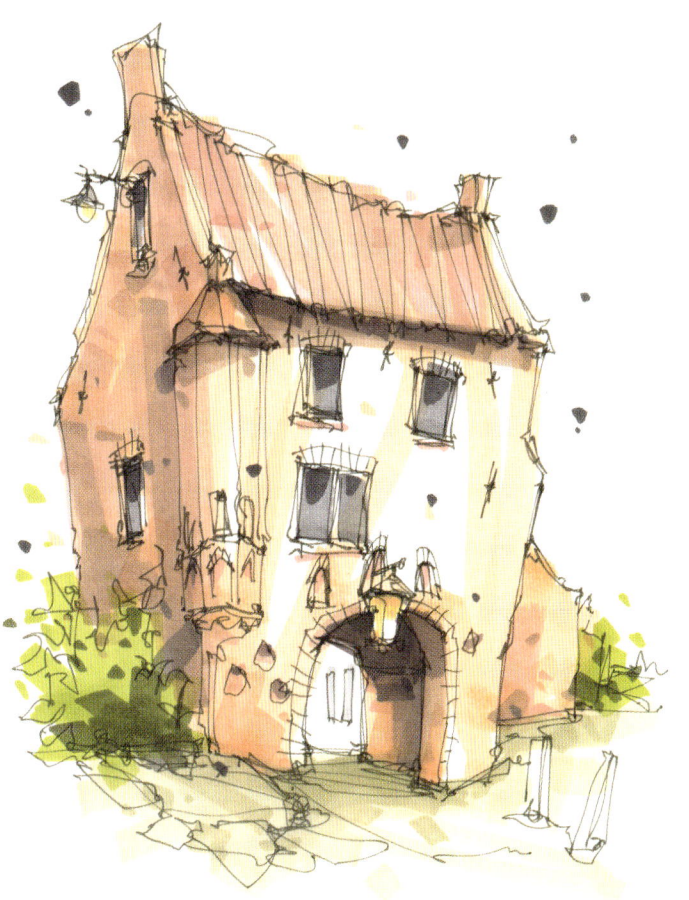

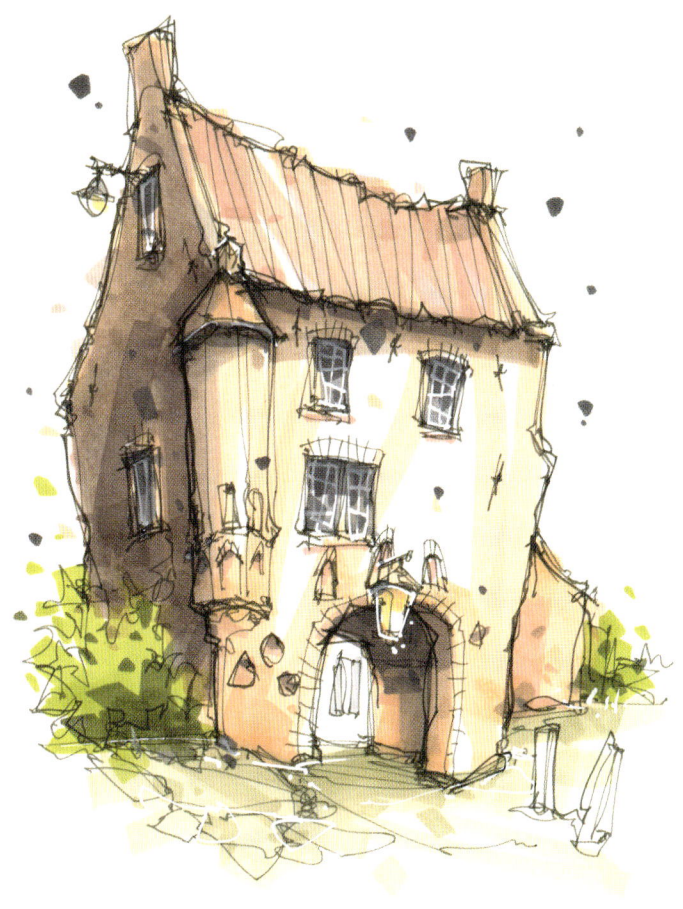

STAGE 4

As soon as those darker shades are brushed in, the building quickly becomes very dimensional. In this case, it's again that deep purple in the shadow areas that takes care of that. Treating the bottom areas of these green shrubs with a dark shade of green helps to quickly build volumes for these shrubs too.

Colors used: BG99, E74, E04, R327, V715, C6, Y616, C8

STAGE 5

In the final stage, I deepened the shadow side of this building even more. That brings out the bush on the left even more, and suggests it's been lit. The white trims of the windows are accentuated and integrated, and some final contrasting specs add some extra "life" to this peculiar building.

Colors used: E74, R215, C8

Blue Bungalow // Washington State, United States

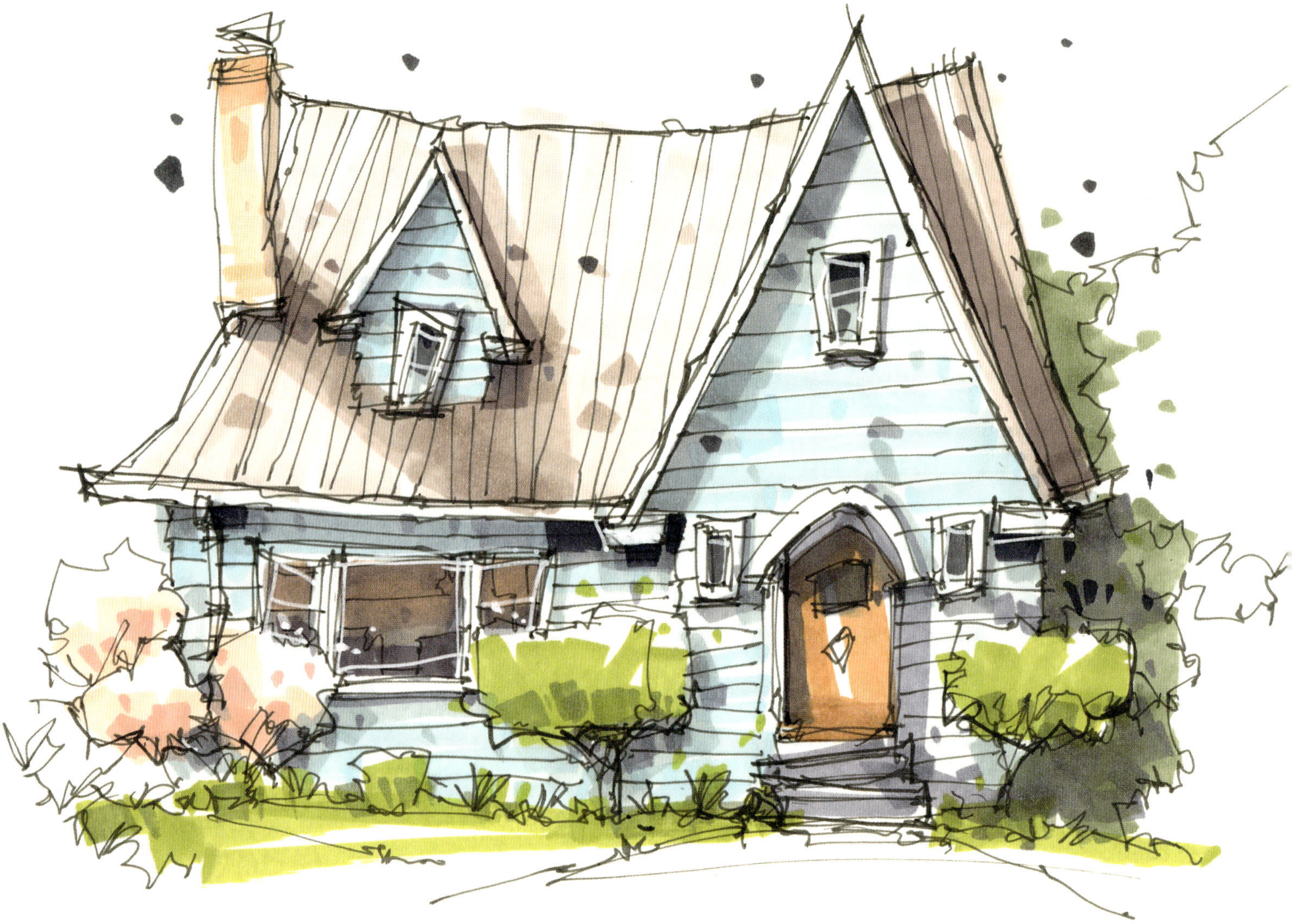

This reference photo for this sketch shows the house straight on with no perspective. Exaggerating the curves of the roof and other lines of the house save it from being a potentially boring sketch!

MARKER COLORS

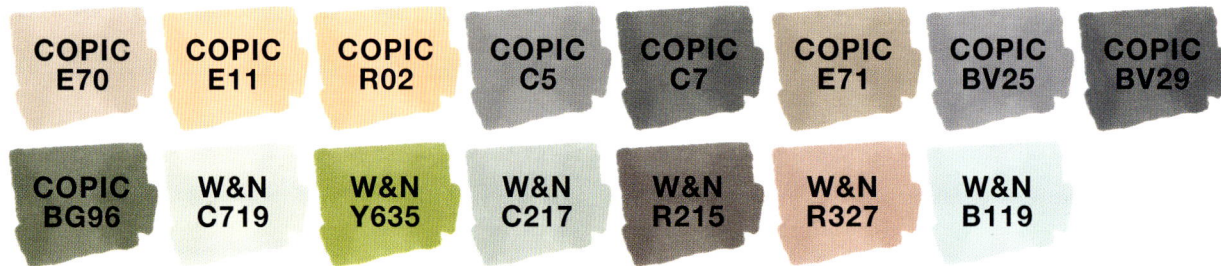

COPIC E70 · COPIC E11 · COPIC R02 · COPIC C5 · COPIC C7 · COPIC E71 · COPIC BV25 · COPIC BV29

COPIC BG96 · W&N C719 · W&N Y635 · W&N C217 · W&N R215 · W&N R327 · W&N B119

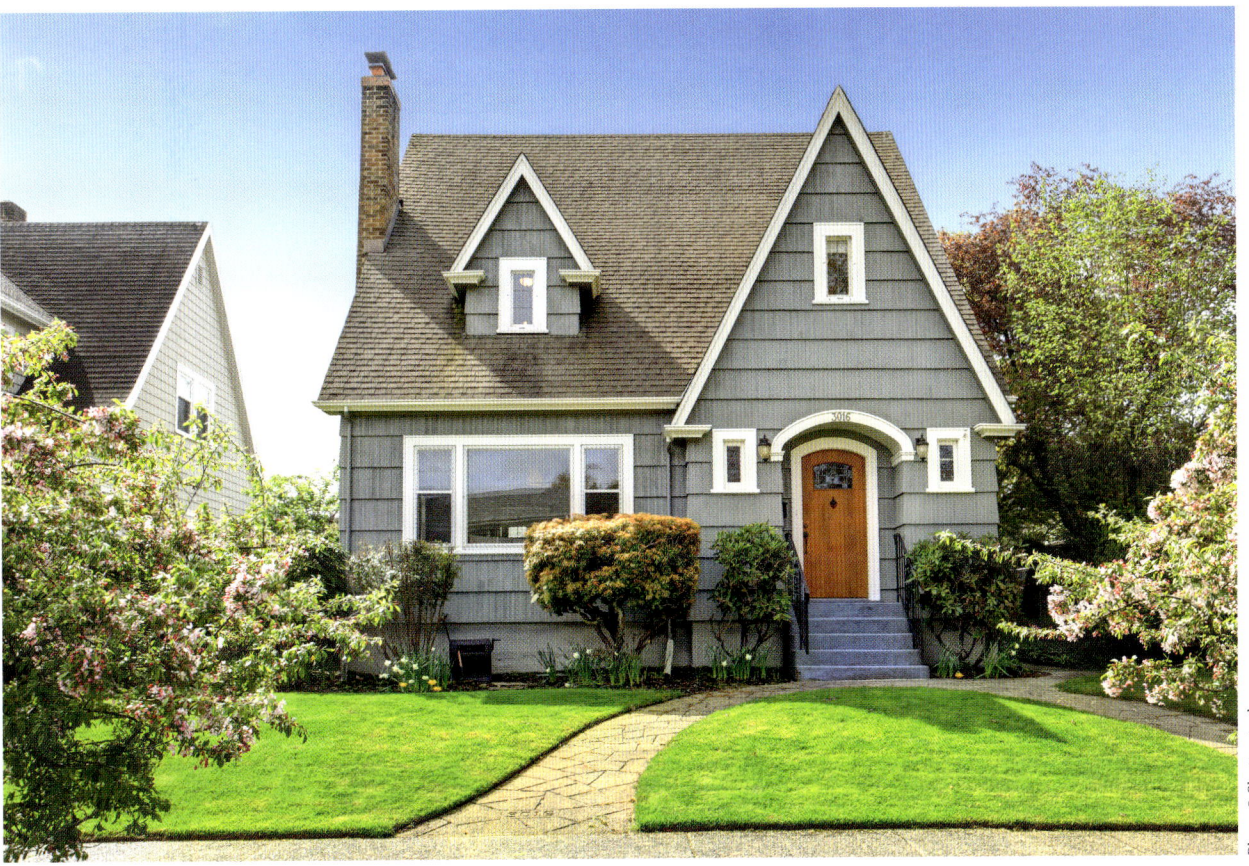

Photo © Shutterstock

THE PROCESS

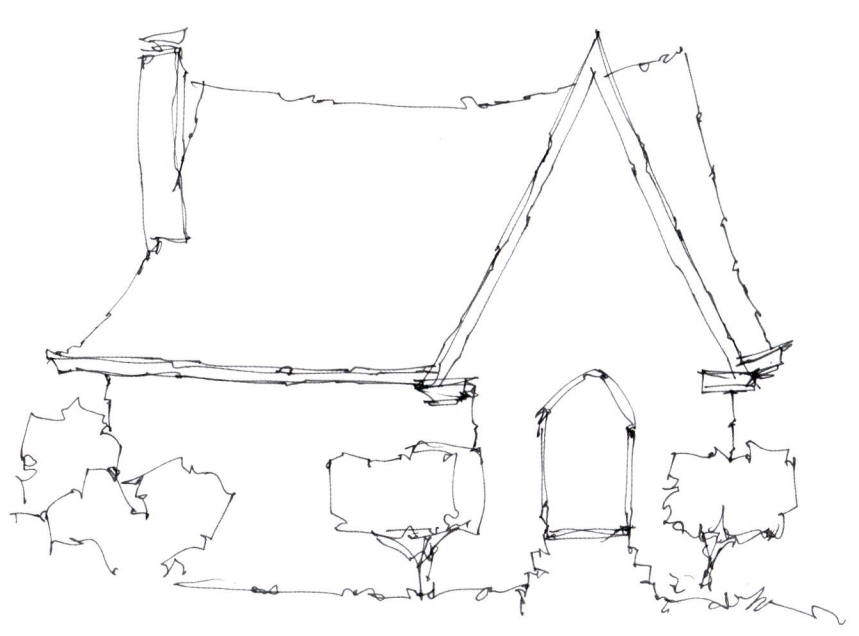

STAGE 1

This frontal facing shot make it generally very easy to start sketching the main forms. You can see these two triangle shapes and two, more or less, rectangular shapes for the ground floor and the roof (a trapezoid). I sketched this house a little more stylistically because it was fun to do.

STAGE 2

After having the main forms down, I sketched in the boarding and the roof detail. Note how I used vertically flowing down lines instead of the horizontal directions in the photograph. I wanted to have these contrasting directions between roof and side paneling. Otherwise, the two would merge into one form.

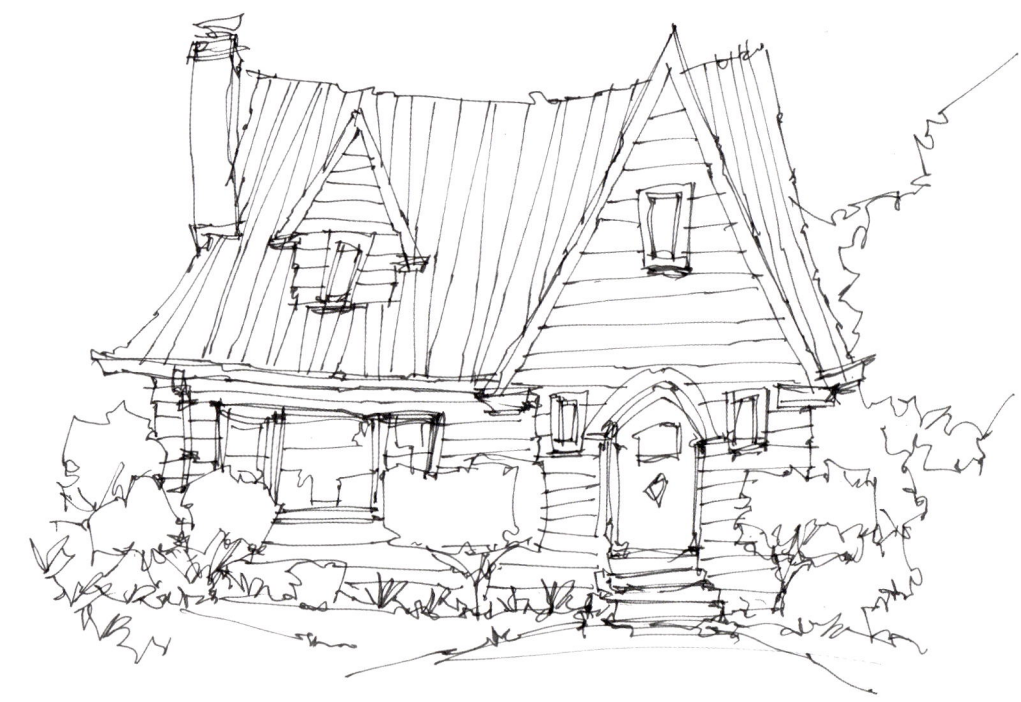

STAGE 3

The color scheme for this sketch is very light. I also wanted to deviate from the grayish color of the photograph because that looked too somber for my taste. So some very light shades with clear "sharding" in the appropriate directions for roof and side paneling sets the stage for the darker values.

Colors used: C719, E70, E11, R02, Y635

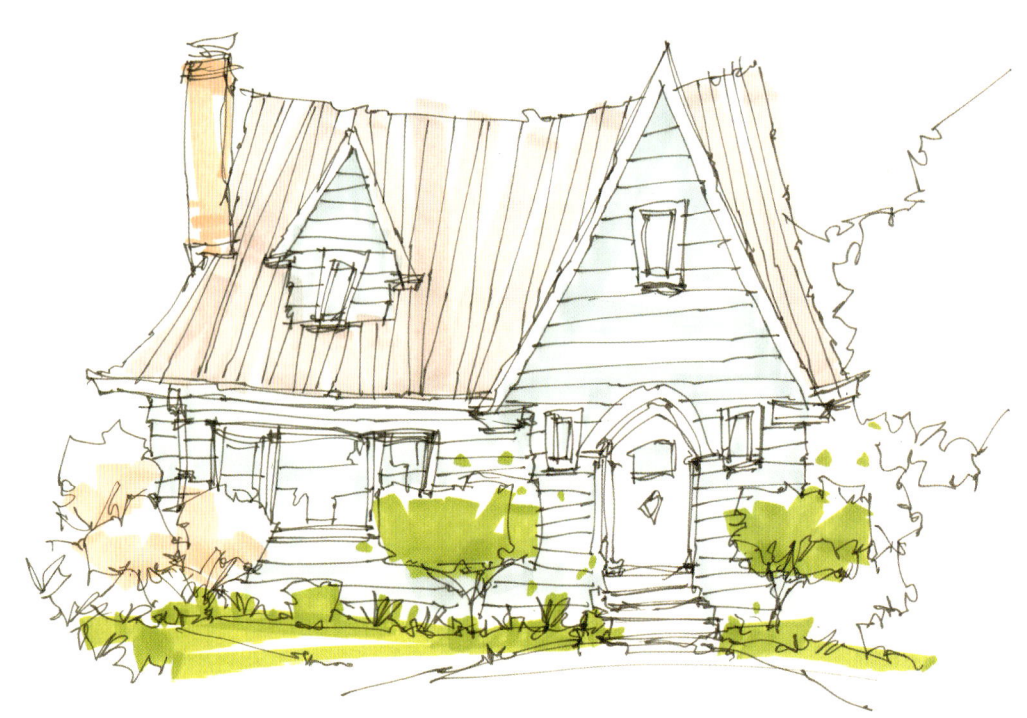

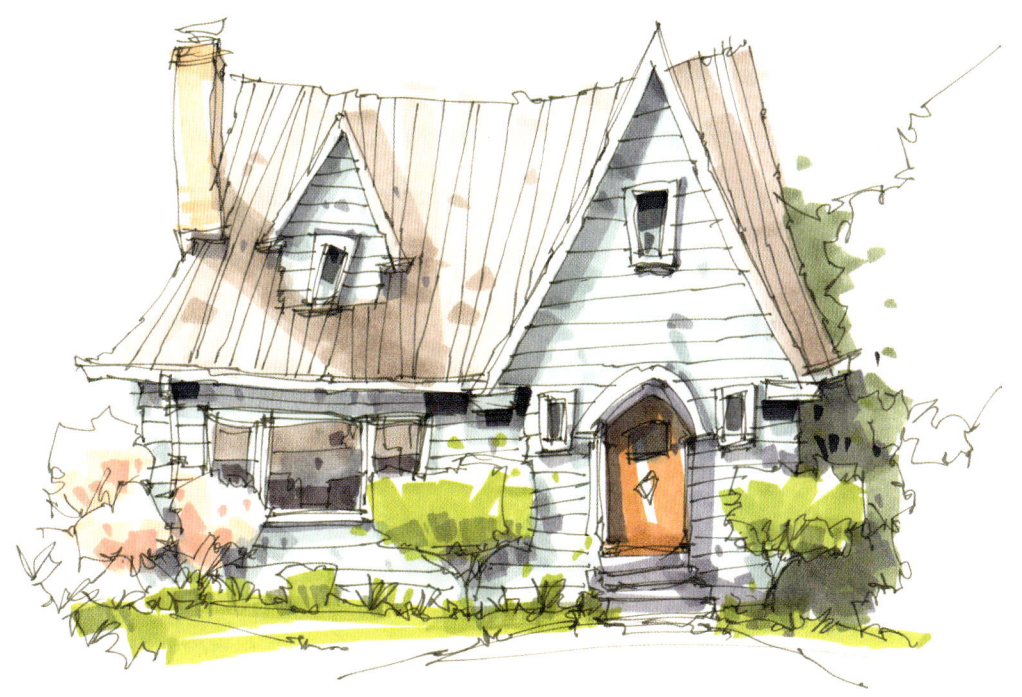

STAGE 4

I added darker values where the shadows would fall (under the roof sections and the bushes). This house quickly becomes very 3D. I deviated from the photo here as well to add that extra bit of punch to the house by not fully backlighting it.

Colors used: C217, C5, C7, BG96, E71, BV25, BV29

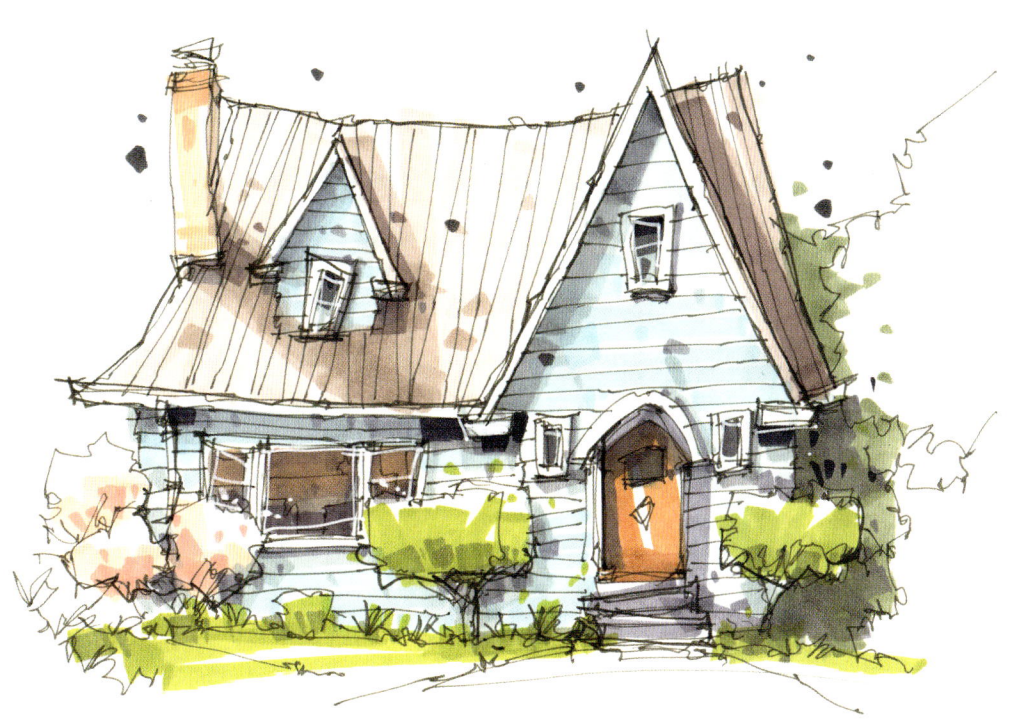

STAGE 5

Deepening shadows, adding some accentuating dots, and creating some line interest by adding white acrylic pen lines are all that's needed to finalize this sketch. By making the shapes more cartoony (sagging roof and off-balanced windows and door), I pushed this sketch to a more characteristic interpretation. And that was great fun to do!

Colors used: R215, R327, B119

Castle Gate House // Tegelen, Netherlands

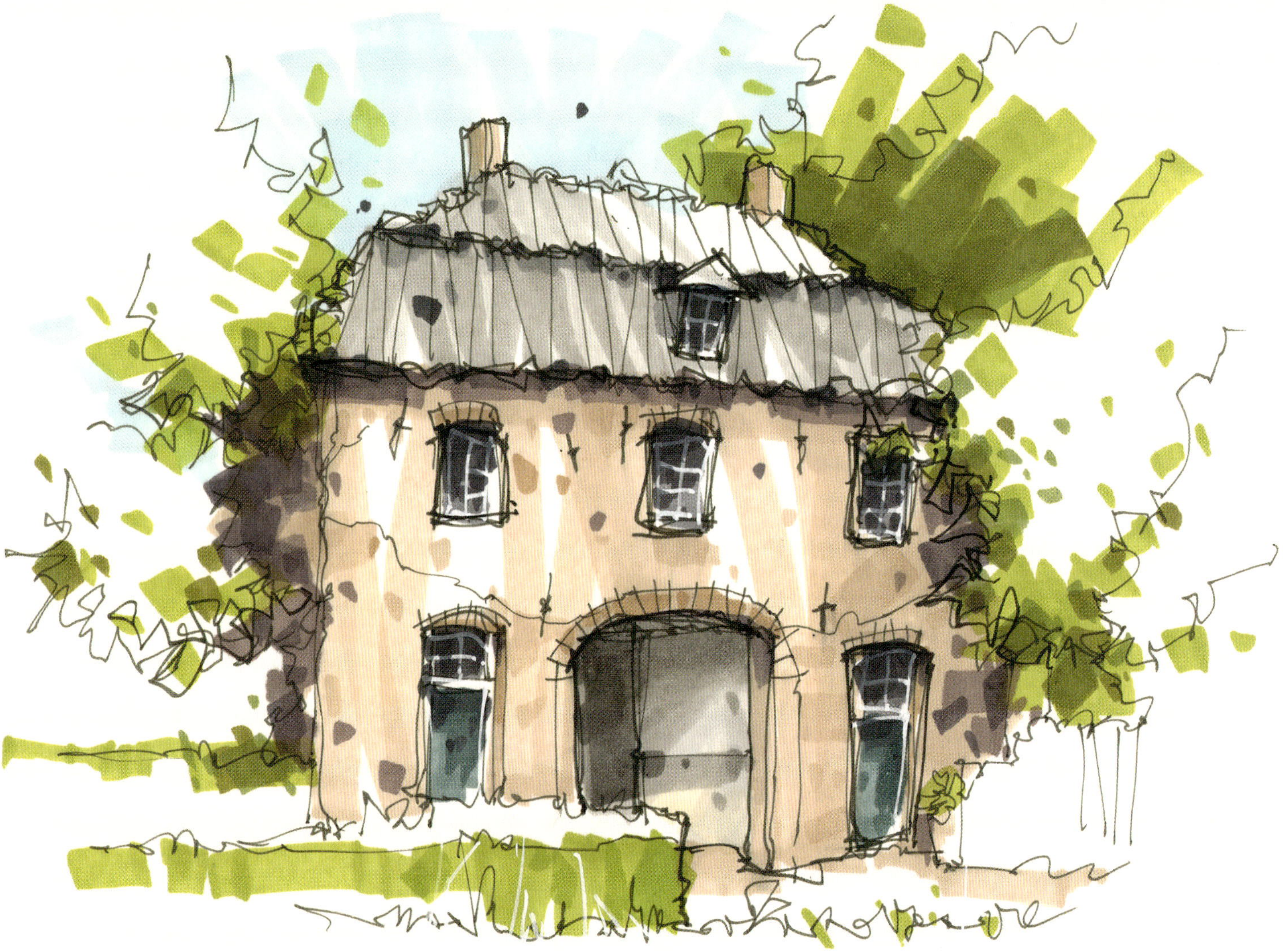

This gate house is part of a wonderful complex now owned by a hotel. As a kid I used to pass by this building every day on my way to school. My grandfather had the opportunity to live here; unfortunately, he ended up not doing it. But here's my capture of it.

MARKER COLORS

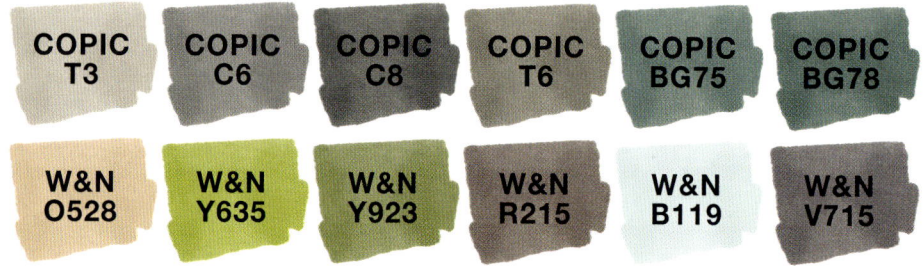

COPIC T3	COPIC C6	COPIC C8	COPIC T6	COPIC BG75	COPIC BG78
W&N O528	W&N Y635	W&N Y923	W&N R215	W&N B119	W&N V715

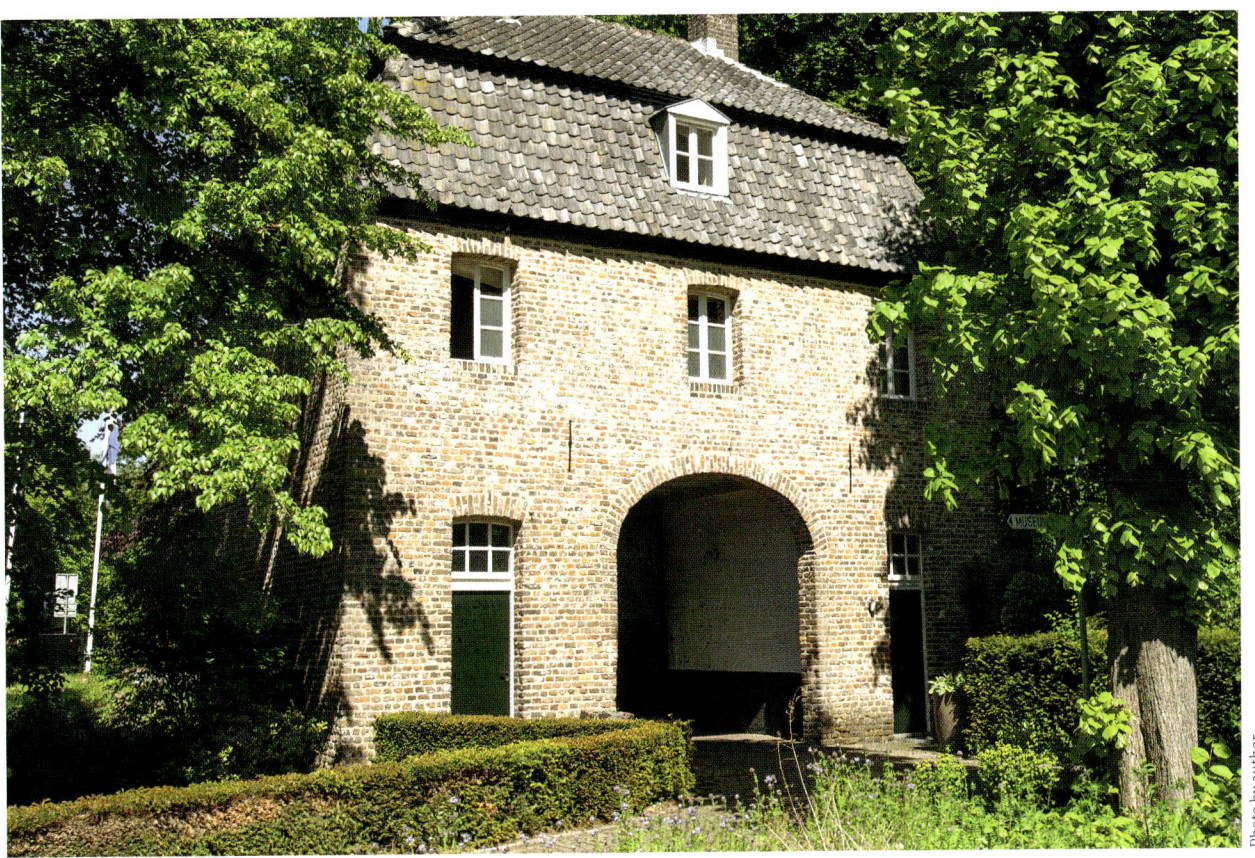

Photo by author

THE PROCESS

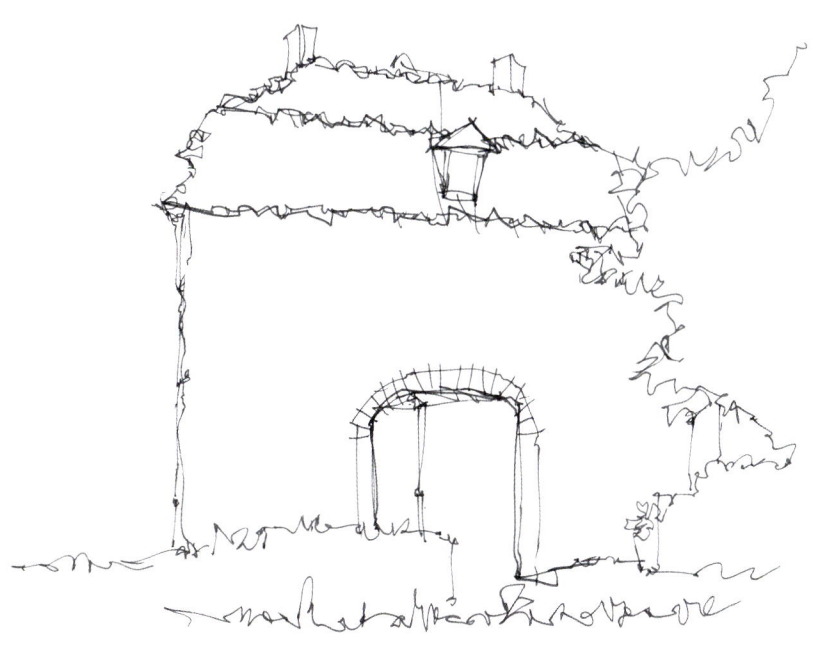

STAGE 1

I started this sketch with the main lines from the roof to the vanishing point (off paper) to the right. The left side is completely covered with foliage and shadow, so that second vanishing point is not necessary. This has the main features established quite quickly. I roughed in the foliage on the right to overlap the building.

STAGE 2

I sketched in the features like windows and doors. I indicated the roof tiles once again with irregular lines flowing down. This always gives a nice dynamic to the roof without feeling overworked. I indicated more foliage around the building, already knowing that I would leave extensive areas page-white.

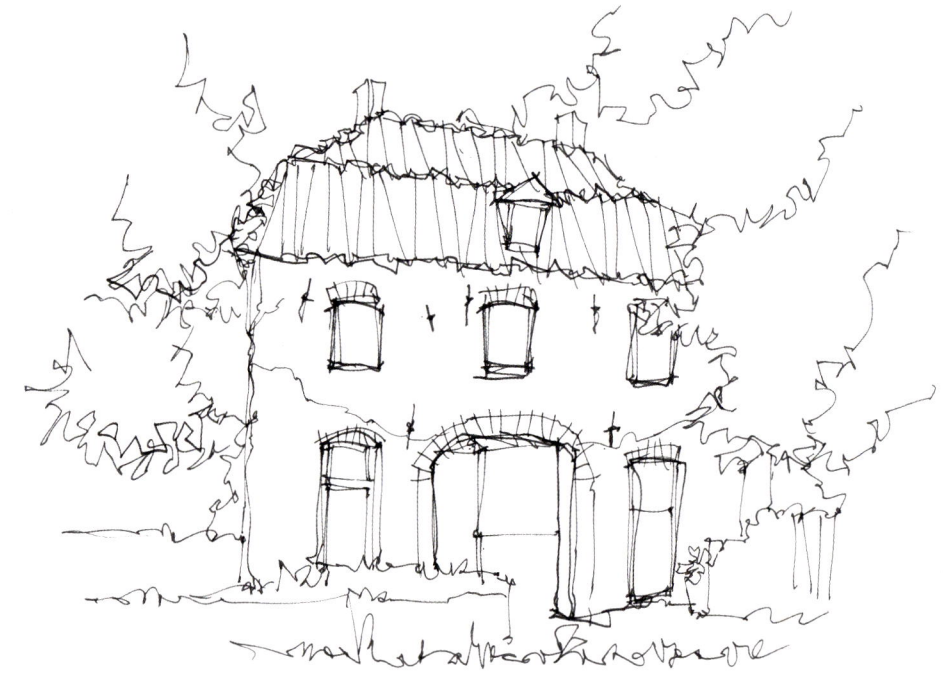

STAGE 3

This sketch shows that even with just two basic colors you can lay down a foundation. While I was doing this, I also saw that leaving the shrubbery mostly page-white would bring the attention more to the main building. Also notice once again the "sharding" of strokes and page-white.

Colors used: O528, T3

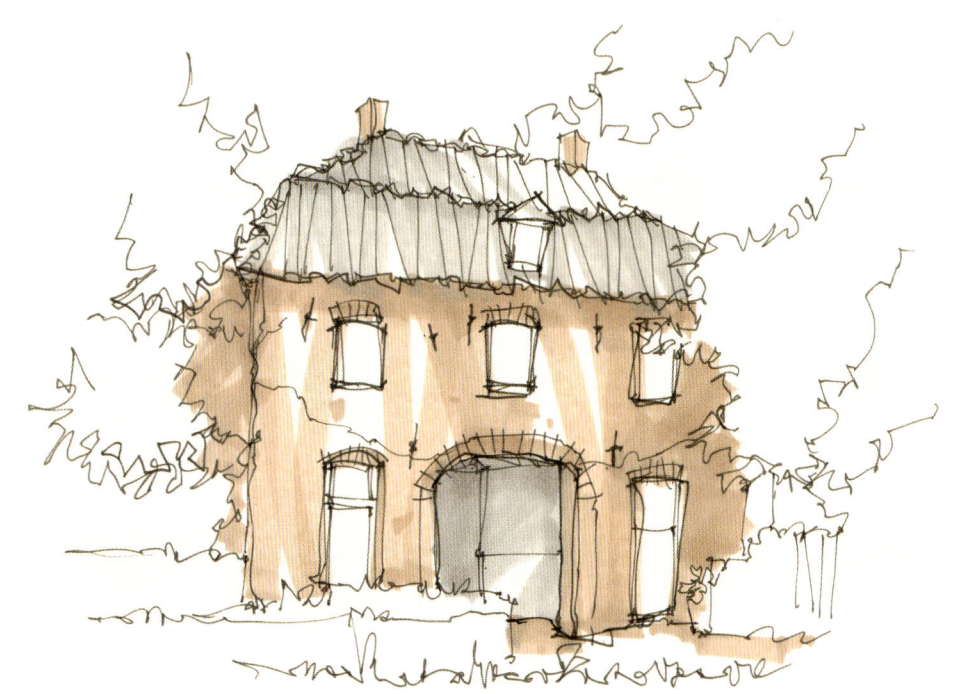

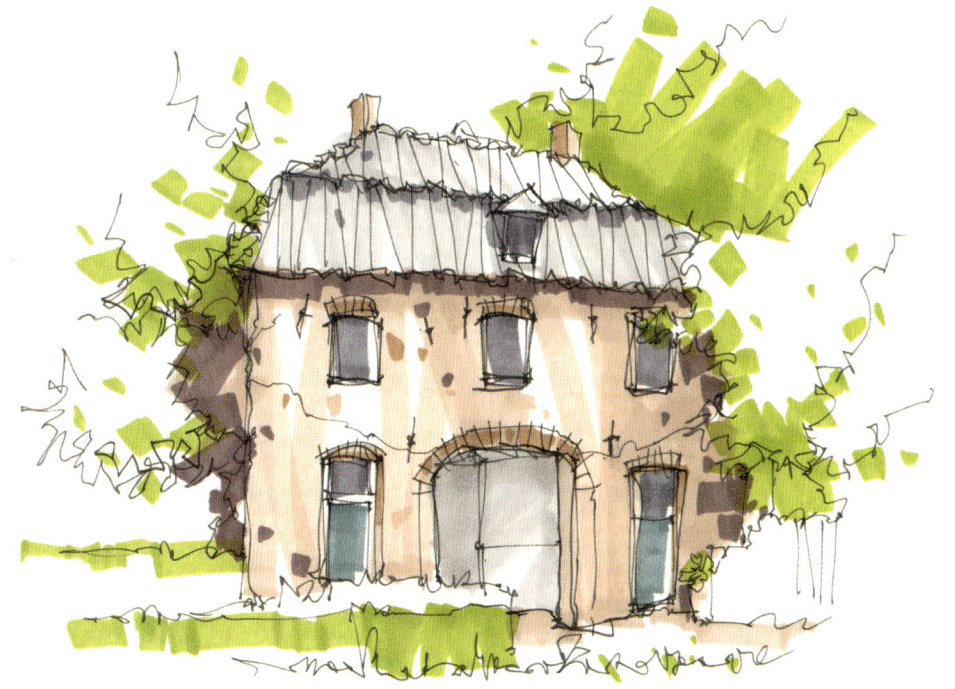

STAGE 4

Painting in the shadow areas with a darker gray value and with a purple immediately punches in the volume. You can observe that it doesn't need a lot of coloring to quickly get depth. Only a few well-placed colors can already give you a very promising direction. The next stage will punch in some necessary accents.

Colors used: C6, Y635, R215, BG75

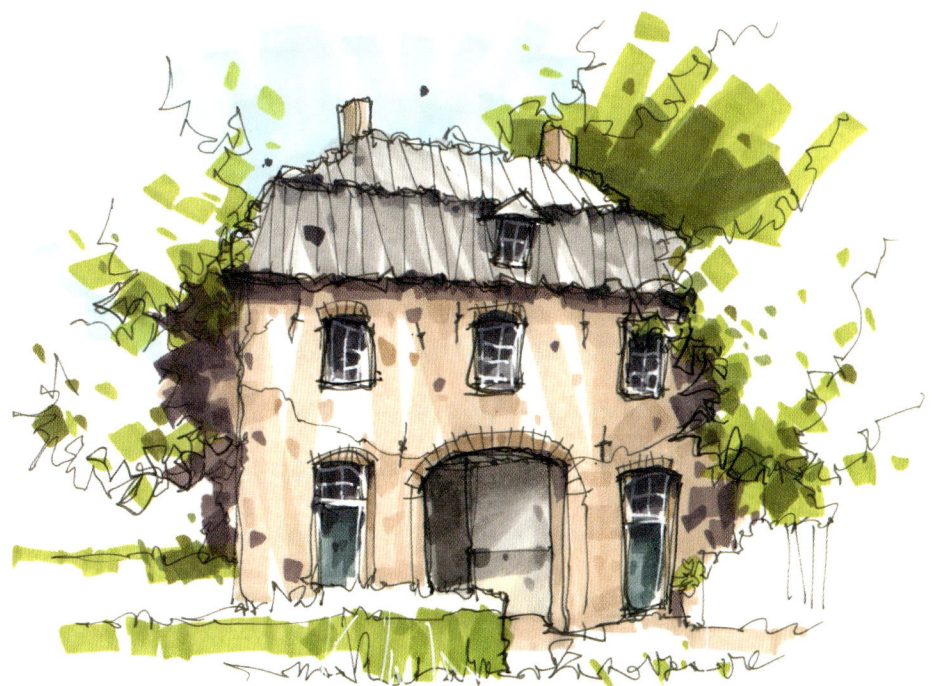

STAGE 5

I have deepened the shadow areas and the recesses of windows, the gateway, and foliage with deeper grays, greens, and purples. The finishing touch is the white trimmings for the windows and door frames that I then partially push back into shadow with a darker gray marker. I wish my granddad could have seen this one!

Colors used: C8, Y923, T6, B119, BG78, V715

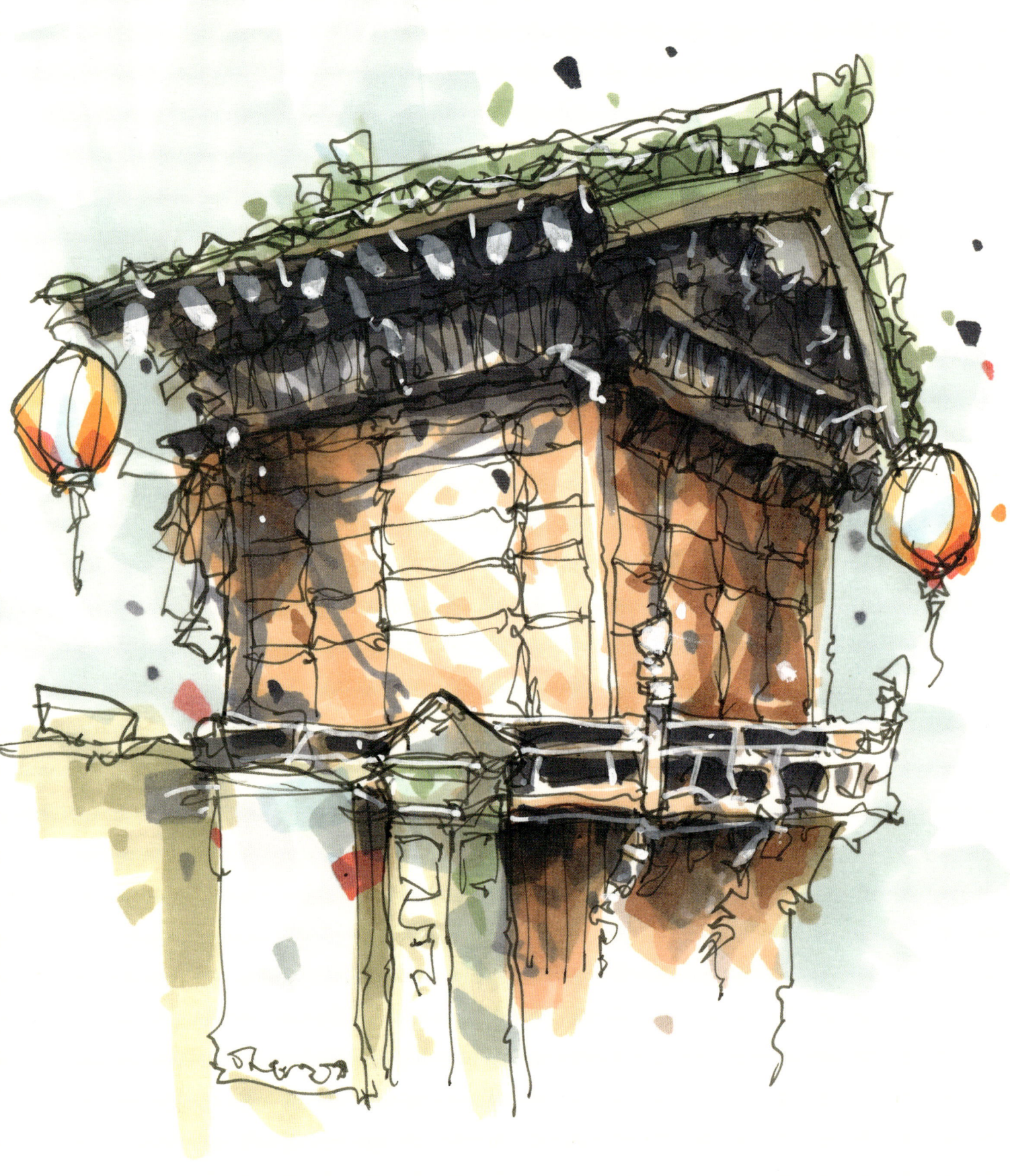

Shrine // Tokyo, Japan

Another very inspiring theme of Japanese architecture is its countless shrines. They look amazing, and when I saw this photo, I just had to sketch it. I love the way the sun plays on the sides of the building, and this one almost sketched itself!

MARKER COLORS

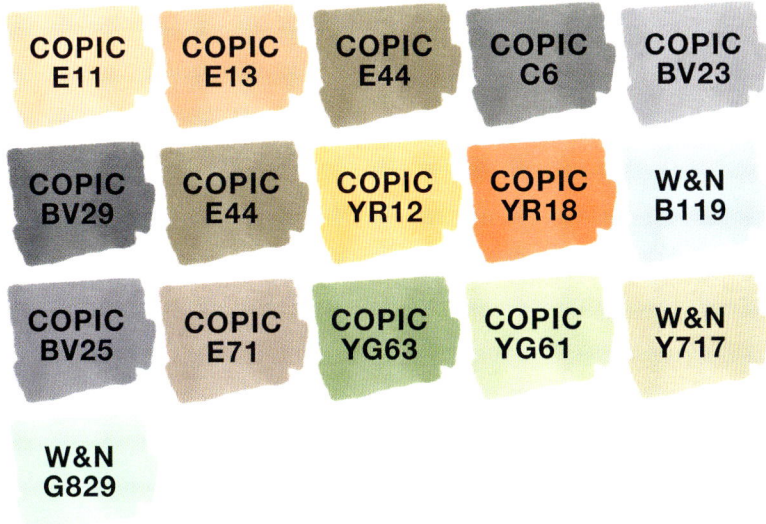

COPIC E11
COPIC E13
COPIC E44
COPIC C6
COPIC BV23

COPIC BV29
COPIC E44
COPIC YR12
COPIC YR18
W&N B119

COPIC BV25
COPIC E71
COPIC YG63
COPIC YG61
W&N Y717

W&N G829

REFERENCE PHOTO

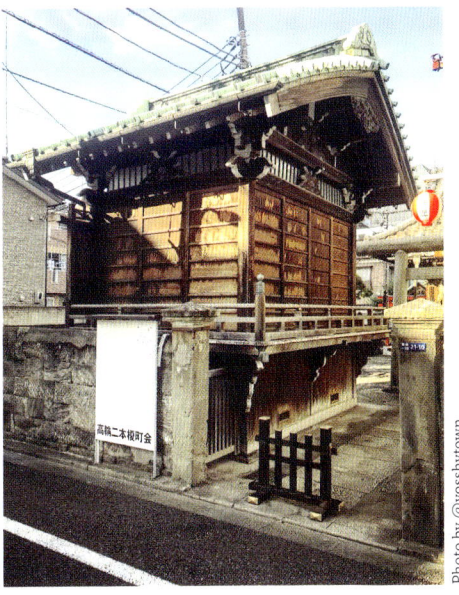

Photo by @yosshytown

THE PROCESS

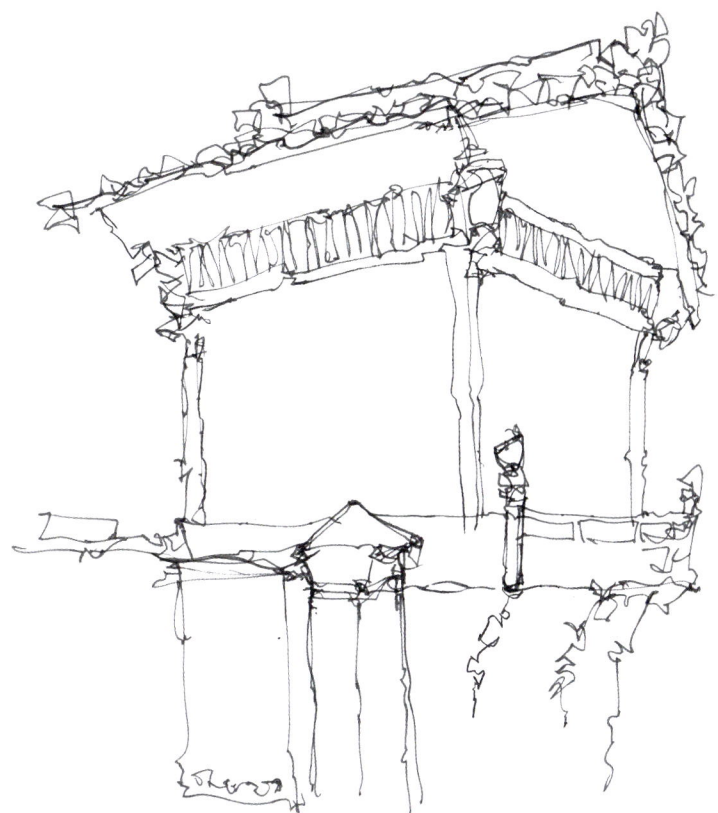

STAGE 1

Here is another typical two-point perspective case with two sides of the shrine clearly visible. After roughly establishing the directions to the vanishing points, I sketched in the main features (and got carried away a little with the smaller hatched band). The base makes sketching in the rest of this shrine easy.

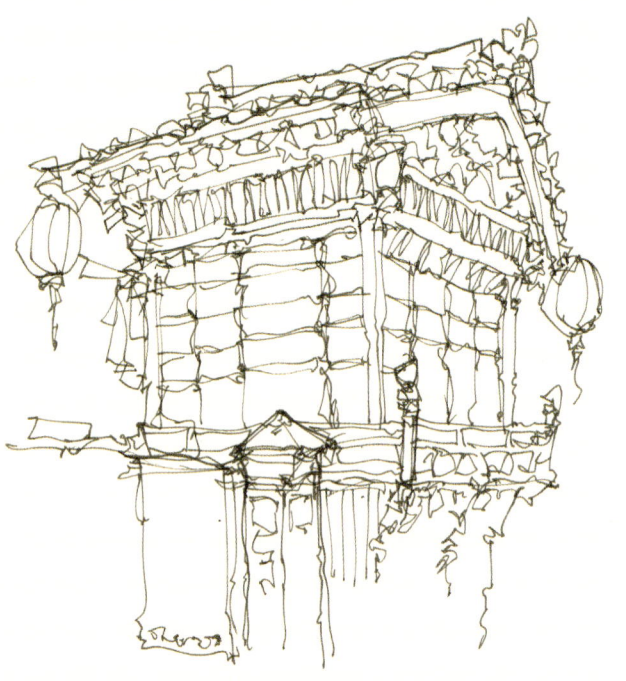

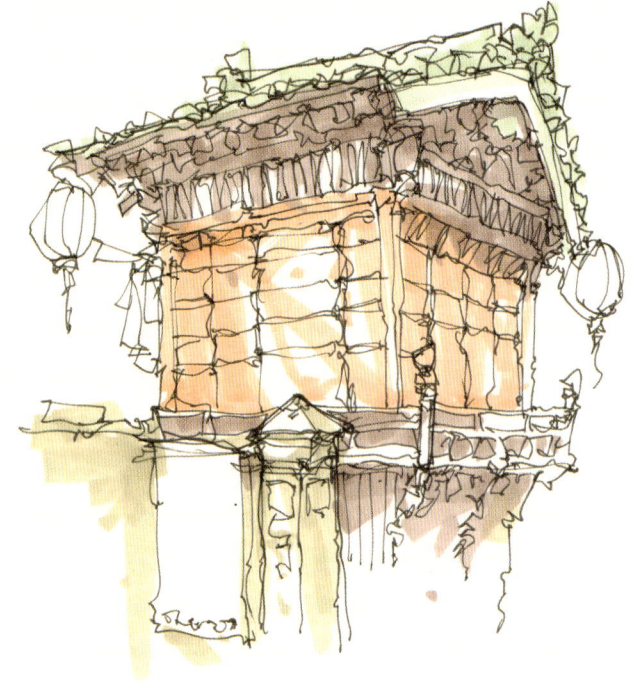

STAGE 2

I decided to add not one, but two chochin, or Japanese lanterns. This was a better balance for the left side of the sketch. Adding all the stacked planks was easy because I could follow the main directions of the two vanishing points. Because the ground was not interesting, I kept it undefined on purpose in the sketch.

STAGE 3

The main color drives for this shrine are warm browns and oranges. So, these were laid in very lightly as a first pass. For the shadow areas, I used a light purplish base color. I added some light blue green tints for the roof and some gray greens at the base.

Colors used: E11, G829, Y717, E71

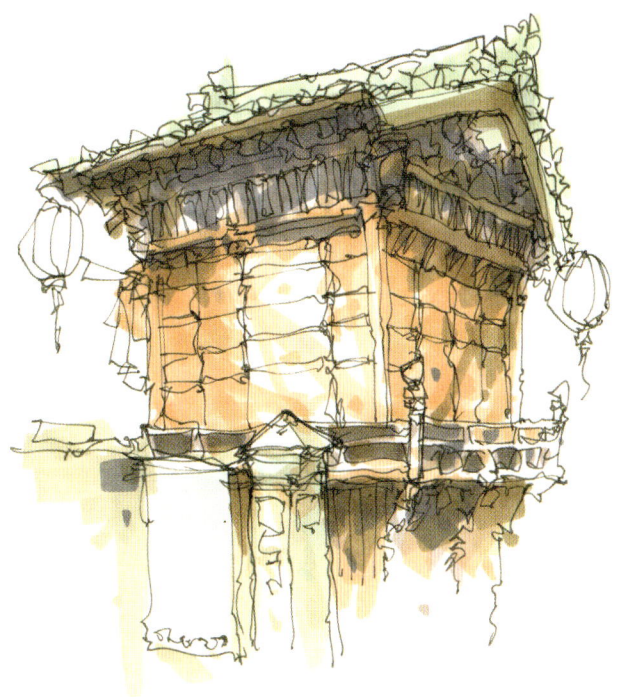

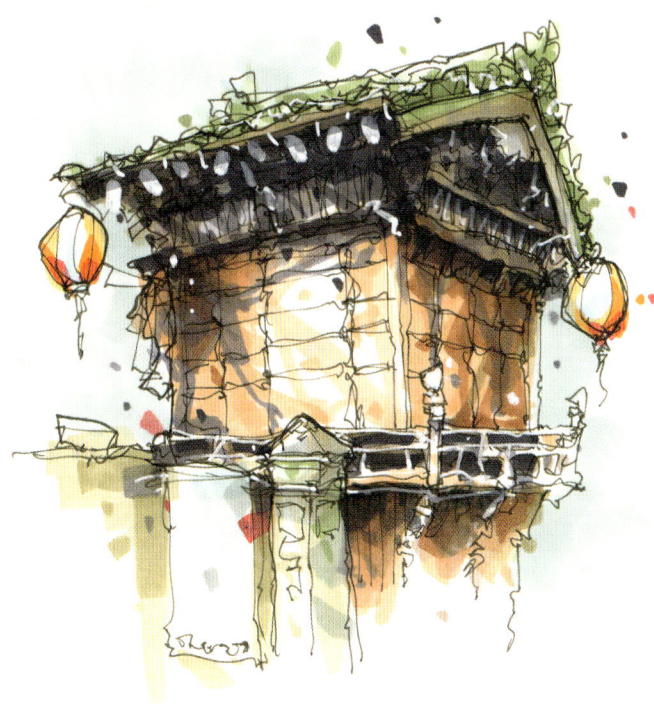

STAGE 4

Extending the warm browns with a slightly deeper pass, I start to emphasize the light areas even more. I also push down deeper values into the roof section. This will become quite dark in the end so that I can start to play a lot with suggestion using the white Uni Posca.

Colors used: E13, C6, E44

STAGE 5

In the final stage I placed some distinct Uni Posca marks (the white acrylic pen), and I deepen the shadows even more. I also place some darker blue greens on the roof and accentuate some of the linework with a heavier fineliner. The blue sky is indicated by some bold flowing strokes.

Colors used: BV23, YR12, YR18, YG61, YG63, BV25, B119, BV29

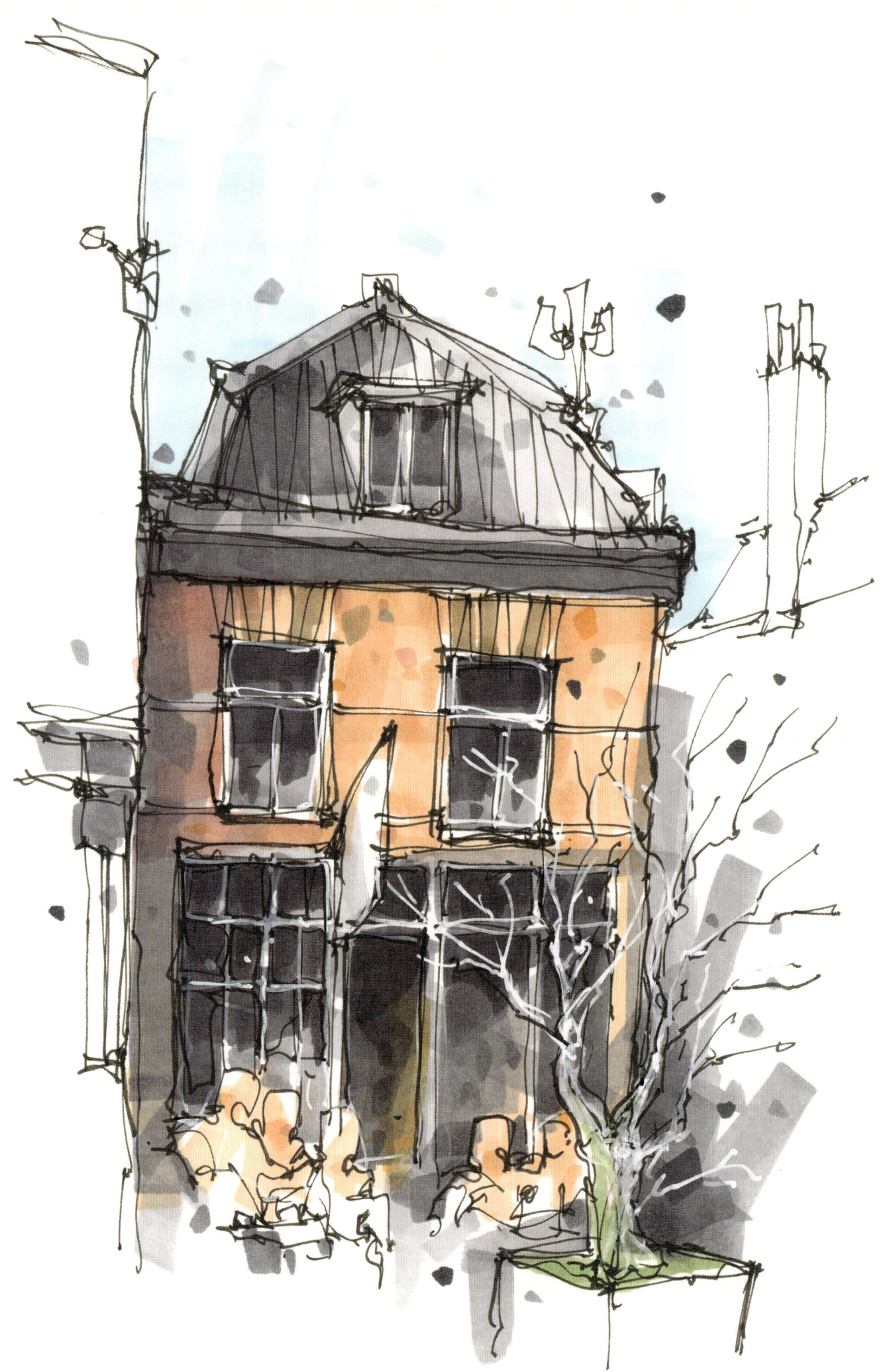

Coffeehouse // Utrecht, Netherlands

The sun was already setting and it produced some very nice stark contrasts in this coffee house in Utrecht. I added a hint of people in the foreground that created a nice offset against the deep darks of the interior with just a slight hint of warm inside.

MARKER COLORS

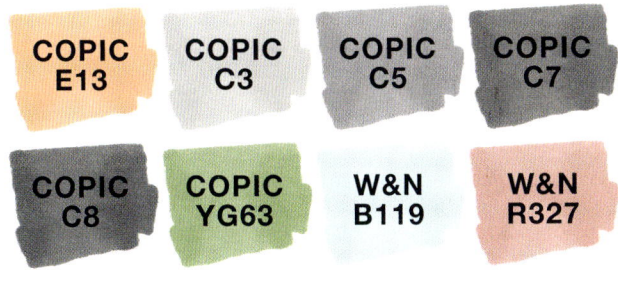

COPIC E13

COPIC C3

COPIC C5

COPIC C7

COPIC C8

COPIC YG63

W&N B119

W&N R327

REFERENCE PHOTO

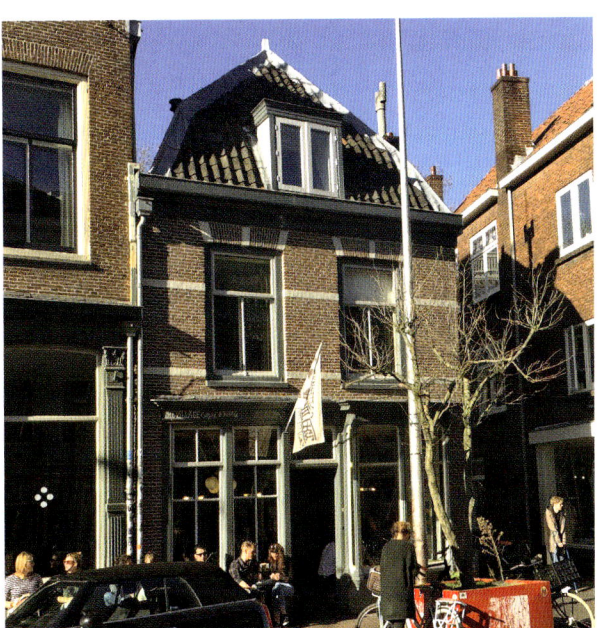

Photo by author

THE PROCESS

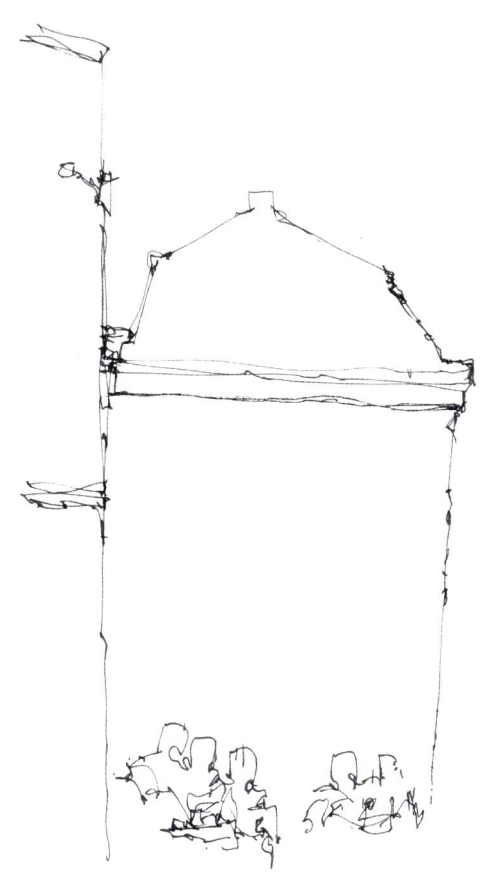

STAGE 1

I wanted to show this house in the street context it was in without adding overwhelming extra surroundings. So I chose to keep these neighboring buildings mostly linear. The structure is quite basic with a simple rectangle for the main façade, but with an interesting roof silhouette. Indication of the visitors delineates where I can close off the window shapes.

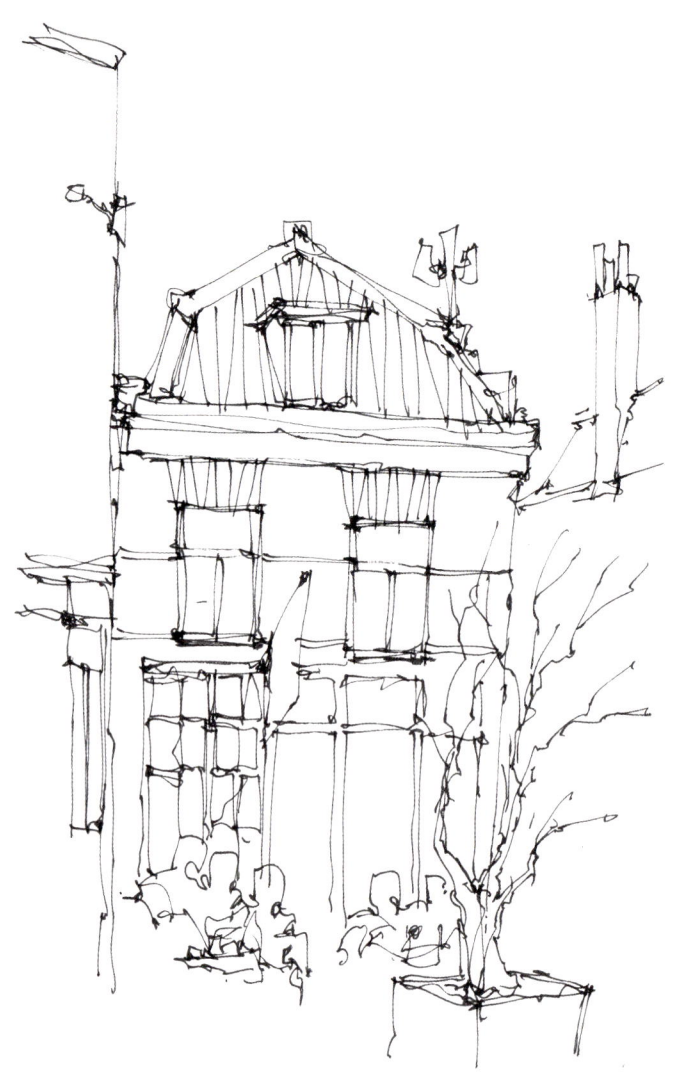

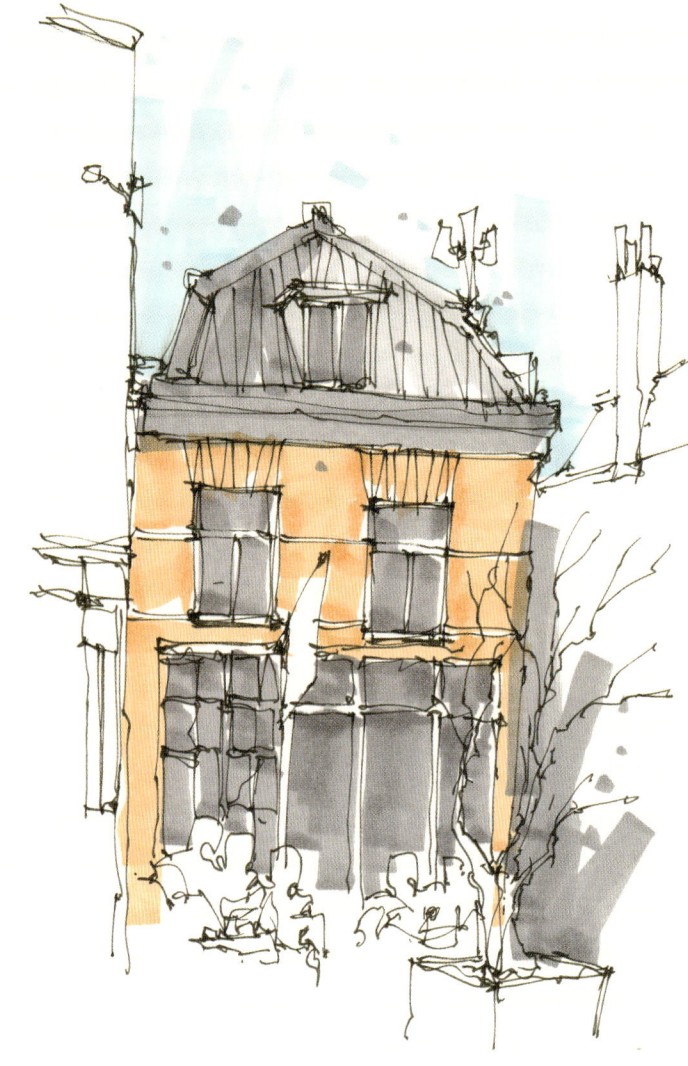

STAGE 2

I loved that tree being touched by light. It also presented a nice foreground element. Adding windows, door, and roof details completes the final stage of sketching. Note (once again) the irregular long flowing lines, suggesting roof tiles. Extra elements are also added in the form of chimneys and a side wall.

STAGE 3

A light wash of the pale colors is laid down to quickly get a sense of the sections that I'd like to work out further. I try to keep the broader framework page-white, but don't worry too much if it isn't. The more careful you are, the less spontaneous it will end up looking.

Colors used: B119, E13, C5, C3

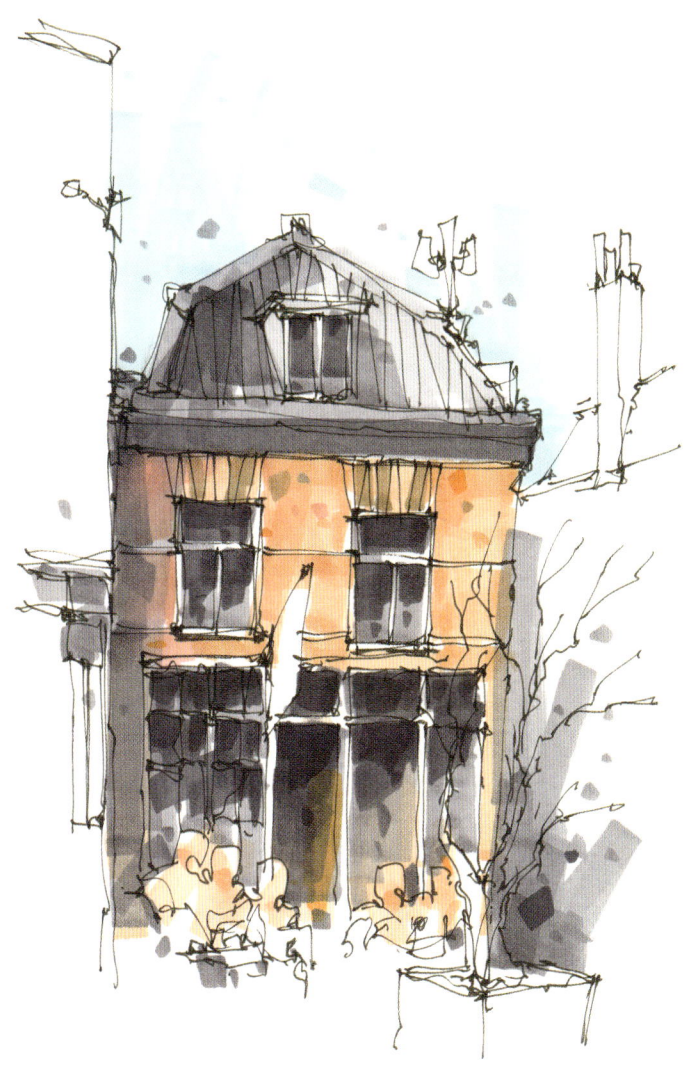

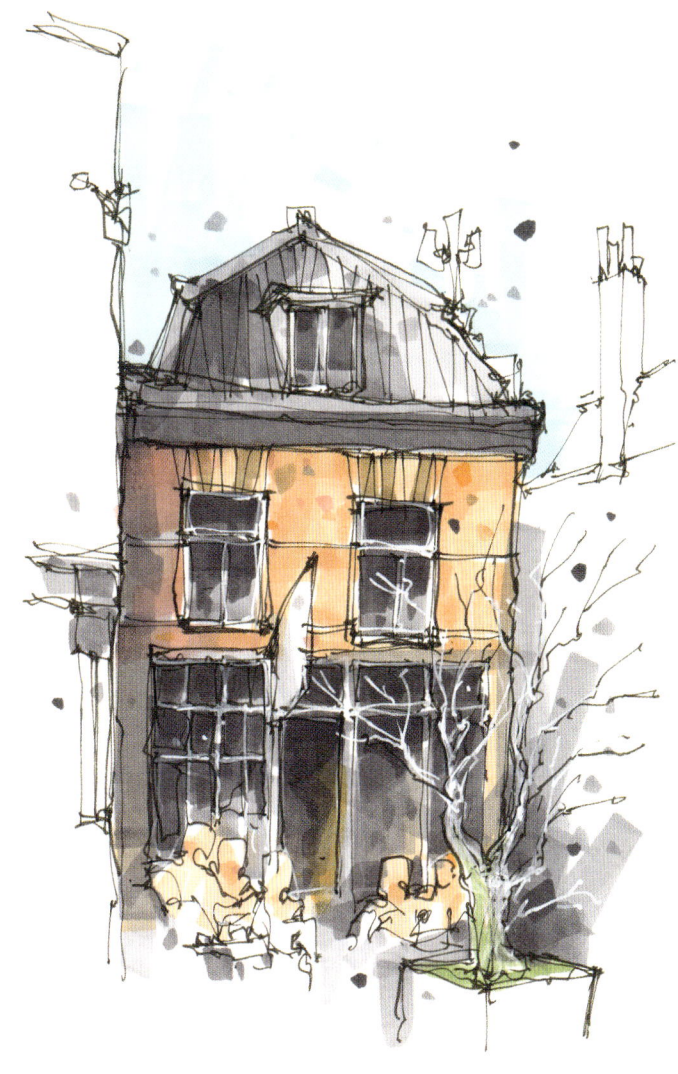

STAGE 4

Time to place dark accents in the form of shadows from the neighboring building onto this coffee bar. That gives nice depth to the roof area and also to the façade. This suggests that the building on the left protrudes a little. I punch in deep darks in the window areas as well.

Colors used: C7, C5, E13, R327

STAGE 5

As always, the final stage is adding white lines, as well as addressing where I brushed in too much dark on the ground level windows. Some extra spots of very dark gray and some warm dashes on the façade keep the surfaces and the surroundings more alive. Also note the white highlights on the tree.

Colors used: YG63, C8

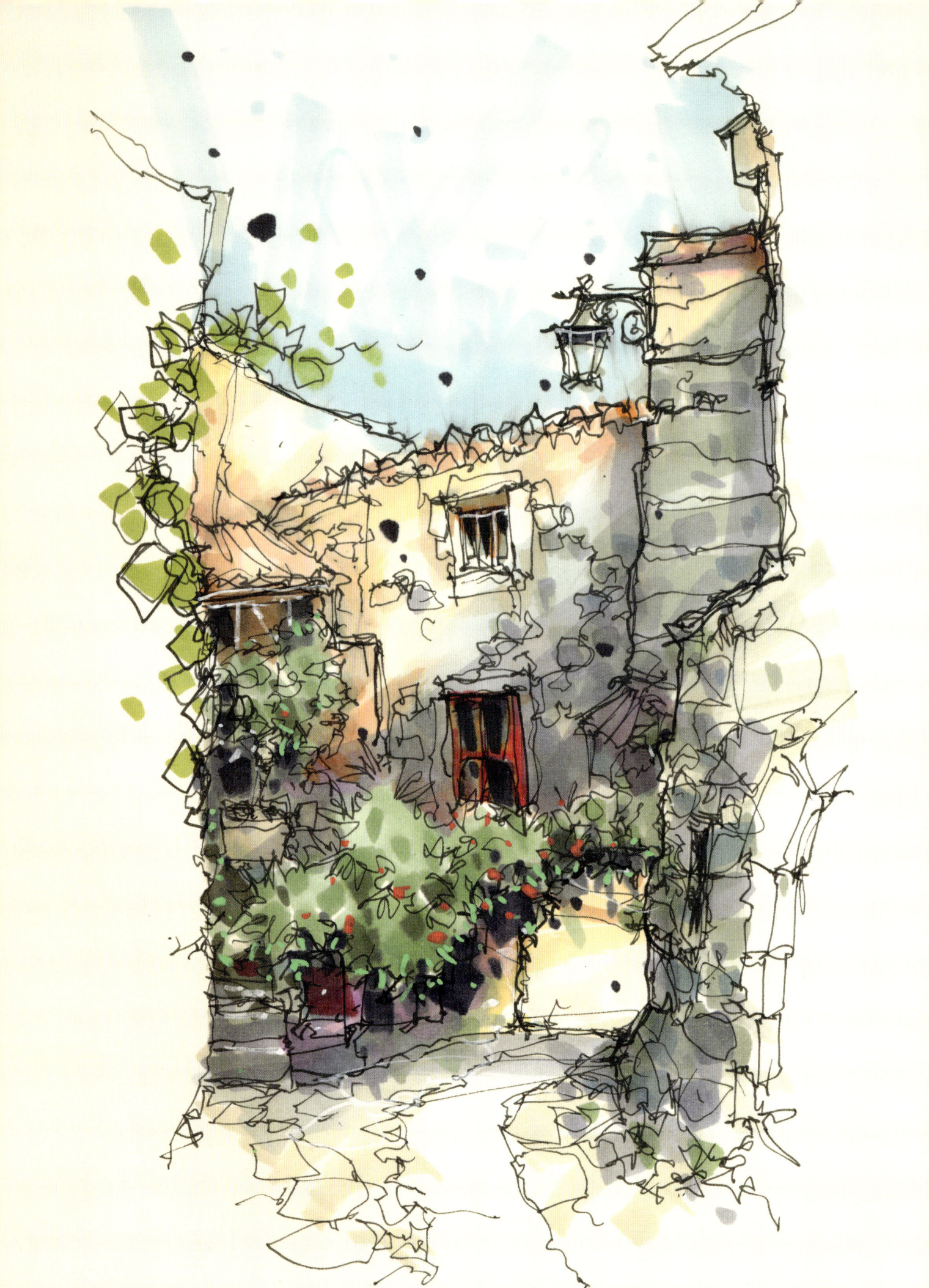

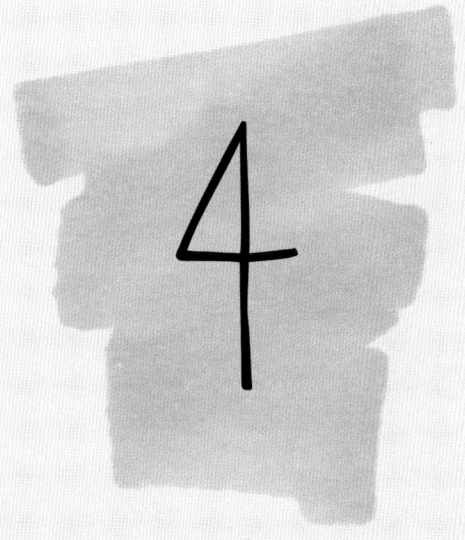

4

SHOWTIME

"You should share these sketches on Facebook," my wife,
Niek, said to me after I made my first sketch. One of the results?
Well, the book you are reading now is among the things that have
happened because of that advice. And this chapter shows you
steps you can take to get your own work seen.

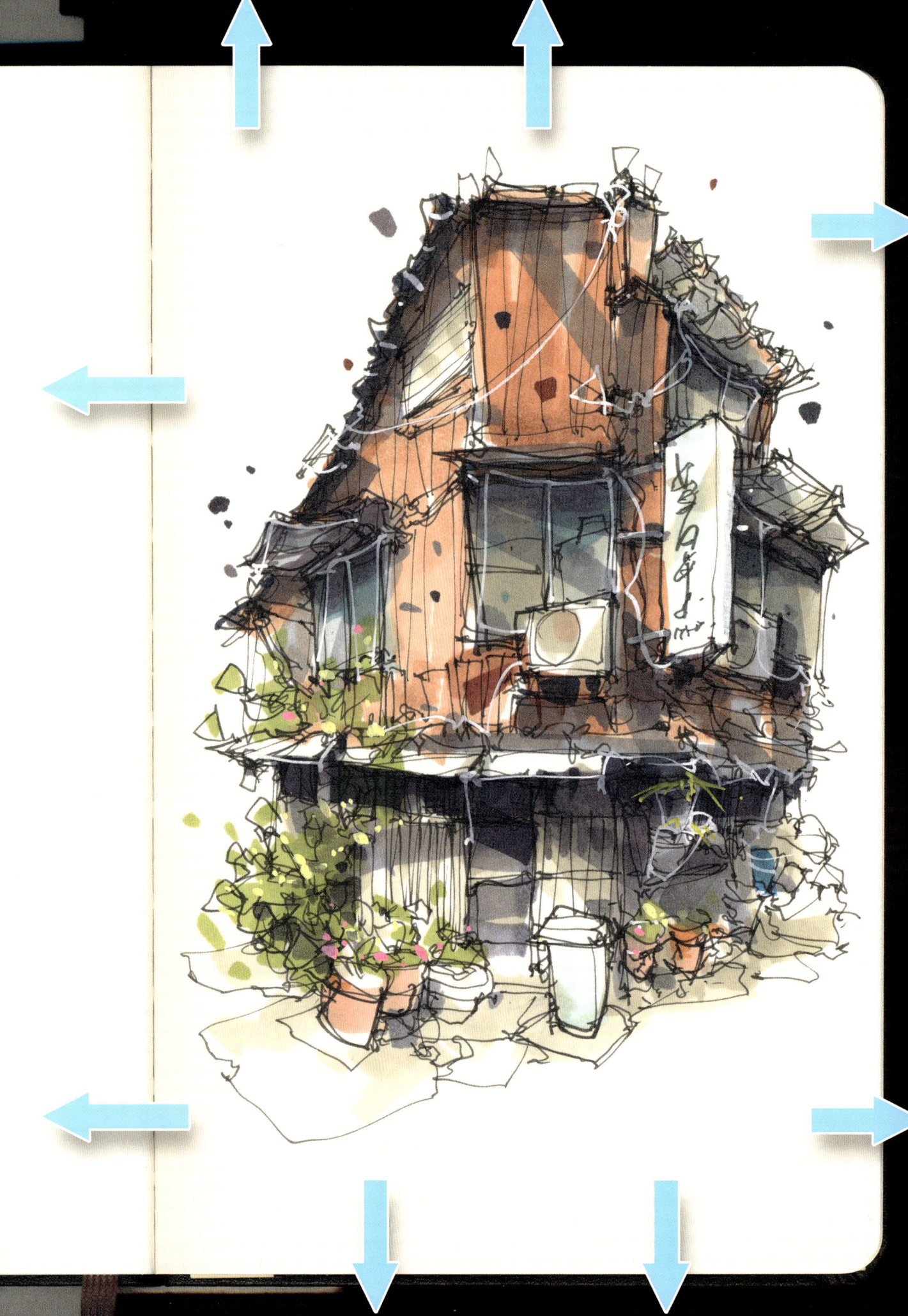

SCANNING

Before you share your work online, you're going to need to capture it in some digital form or another. The simplest method, of course, is to just shoot a picture of it with your smartphone or with a digital camera. It's very direct and easy to do and involves little effort. But this will not always give you a faithful reproduction of your work. Things might be distorted and colors can deviate from your real sketch. For a better solution you can scan your work in, or have it scanned by a service bureau. For me having a very good digital archive is very important. Maybe that's because of my background as a digital artist (and being a perfectionist!). I invested in a decent scanner and I scan everything I sketch. That means that I have a complete digital archive of all my work. Is it top-notch lithographic quality? No, but it is very adequate for posting work online and creating the book that you have in your hands right now.

There is, however, one aspect that I do before posting on social media. It is quite possible that my sketch has not landed exactly on the page the

TIP If you invest in a decent scanner and scan all of your sketches, you will have a complete digital archive of all your work ready for any use.

way I intended it to. In that case I open the scan in Photoshop (other software could do the same) and extend or crop the area around my sketch to place it exactly where I want it to be. In Photoshop there is a function called "Content aware fill" that I use for that. Its only function in my case is to add more "paper" to the sketch in case I need to extend my canvas. This is also a really helpful technique to add that extra space when you want to create printed artwork for cards and canvases. There, you often need some extra space to accommodate for edges being cropped off or different layouts and formats (square, portrait to landscape, or vice versa).

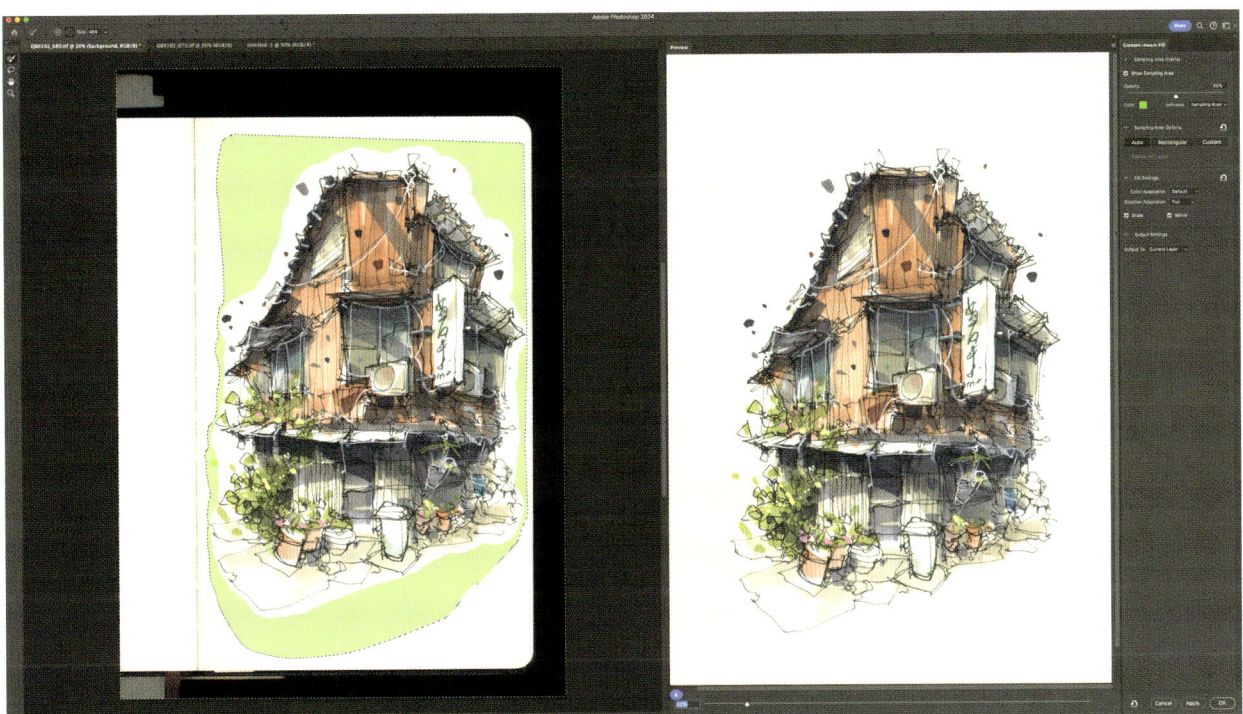

← A fictitious example of a sketch that's too large for the page. It needs extra "paper."

↑ Photoshop "Content aware fill" in action. Situation solved!

SHARING

At the beginning of my sketching adventure, I was not thinking about sharing my work. First, because I thought that nobody would be interested in seeing my house scribbles. Especially the very first ones. But there was a good reason why, in hindsight, it was a great idea to share my work (actually suggested by my wife). It helped me to consistently make a sketch every day, regardless of how it looked. This has resulted in a couple of things. First, it gave me an opportunity to share new work every day on platforms like Facebook and Instagram. And when I look at what I have achieved there, I can still not believe it. I remember looking on Instagram and seeing people with thousands of followers and thinking that was unattainable.

Well . . . I have an incredibly wonderful group of followers now. Some have been with me from the very beginning and new ones keep finding my work every day. So, speaking to you, it is really worthwhile to investigate this route of showing and sharing your work online. It's not all roses and moonshine, which I will share in the section Closing Thoughts. But I encourage you to share your work. I have had many students who have found commissioned work or that have been invited to exhibit in local galleries after they shared their work online. Give it a try!

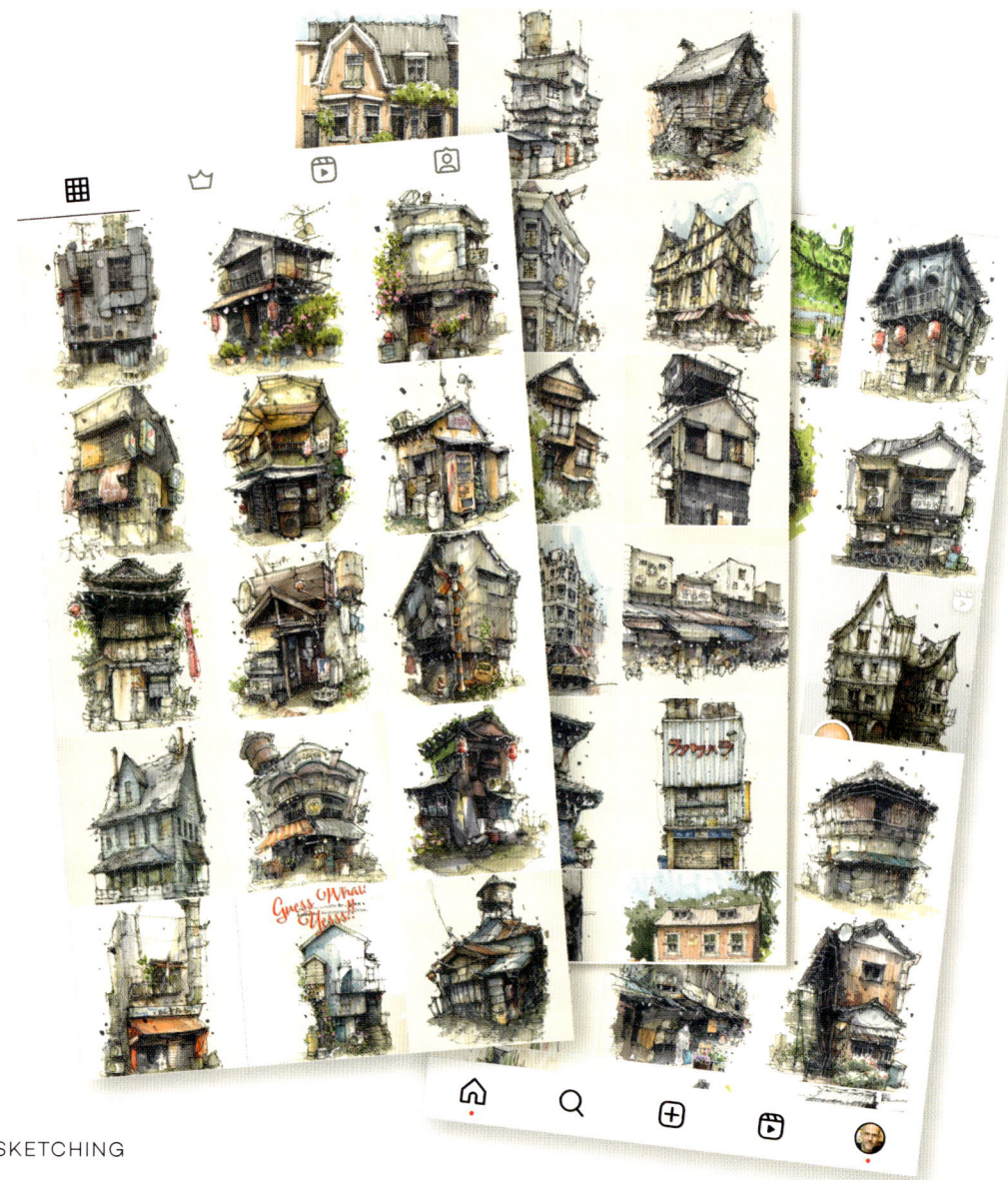

ARCHIVING

You are scribbling away and filling page after page with sketches, and suddenly you have a pile of work scattered around your place. Some work may be in sketchbooks, some on loose pages, and others are likely to end up gracing somebody's wall. So how can you keep track of it all? For me, my main body of work is contained in a series of over 40 sketchbooks (as of this writing in 2023). I can browse back to my very first sketch and see the development my "style" has undergone over the last seven years. The advantage of a sketchbook is firstly that it keeps everything in a nice chronological order, but it also prevents direct sunlight from fading your sketches.

But like I mentioned, the other part of keeping track of my work is a digital archive I created by scanning every work. So even if my sketchbooks might get lost, I still have every work in digital form on a hard disk. And not only that, I have a copy of that hard disk as a backup, just in case, stored elsewhere.

Now it is very possible that you don't need to have such an extensive archiving plan in place, but I still think it's a good idea to think about how you're going to handle work once it's finished.

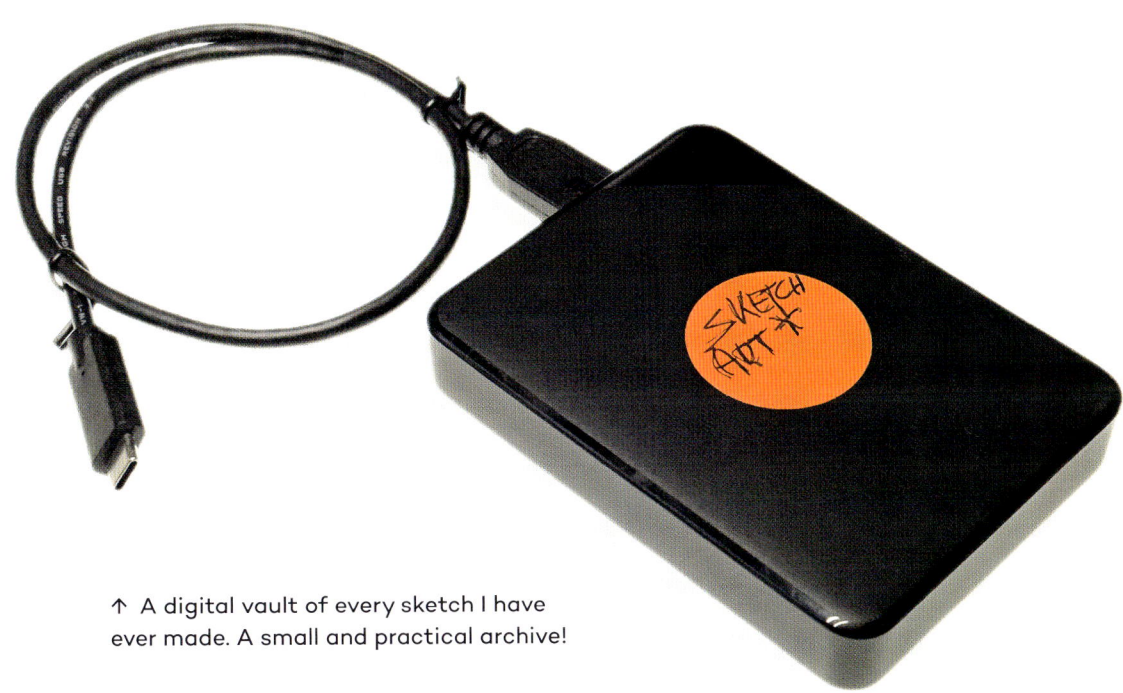

↑ A digital vault of every sketch I have ever made. A small and practical archive!

MONETIZING

You might not have considered making money from your sketches, but the possibility or opportunity might present itself. There are many online service providers that allow you to open up a store and sell your work as prints or printed on a plethora of objects (shower curtains, anyone?).

The most obvious ways to try to monetize your sketches are to have them turned into prints, either as postcards, posters, or canvas prints as room decoration. Another nice option is to turn your sketches into stickers. Since most of my houses are on plain backgrounds, they lend themselves very well to be turned into "character stickers." These can make for great series to sell.

Then, there are T-shirts. Again, depending on how you have sketched your subject, they might make for a great T-shirt design. For this, you could also use just the black-and-white version of your sketch (keep in mind you need to sketch your line art before starting your coloring stage).

The advantage of using online services is that they will take care of all the hassle of shipping and producing your artwork on the requested

TIP If you want to try selling products with your artwork but don't want the hassle and expense of producing and shipping them, try one of the many online services that will do it for you.

surfaces, without you having to invest in ordering a minimum amount of these materials. Basically I don't see any drawbacks from enlisting the services of such online companies. They print and produce on demand, so you're never bothered by having a surplus that doesn't sell. The only thing you need to do is set up a store on their website and upload material that you have prepared for the specific purposes. (Remember the paragraph I wrote about scanning, where I mentioned preparing your art in software like Photoshop?)

Of course, you could also do things your own way and enlist a local printshop for printing a certain amount of postcards. I have done that for subjects that I had a hunch would sell well. But it's still a risk because you invest money without really knowing if people are going to love that design.

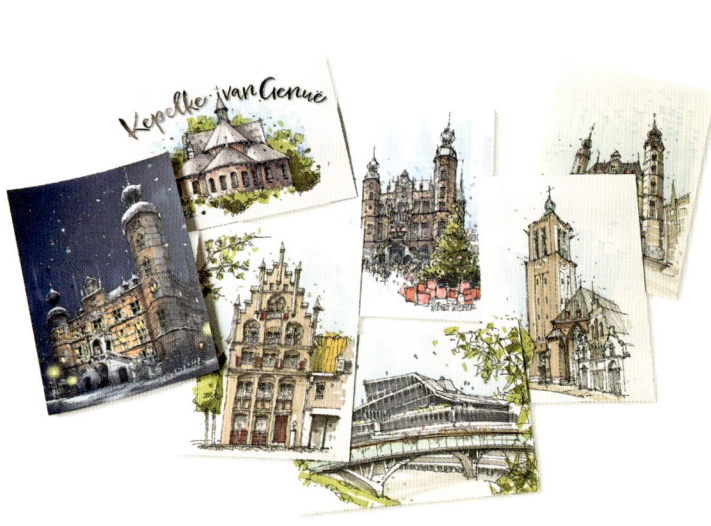

Just a few of the types of projects you can print your sketches on.

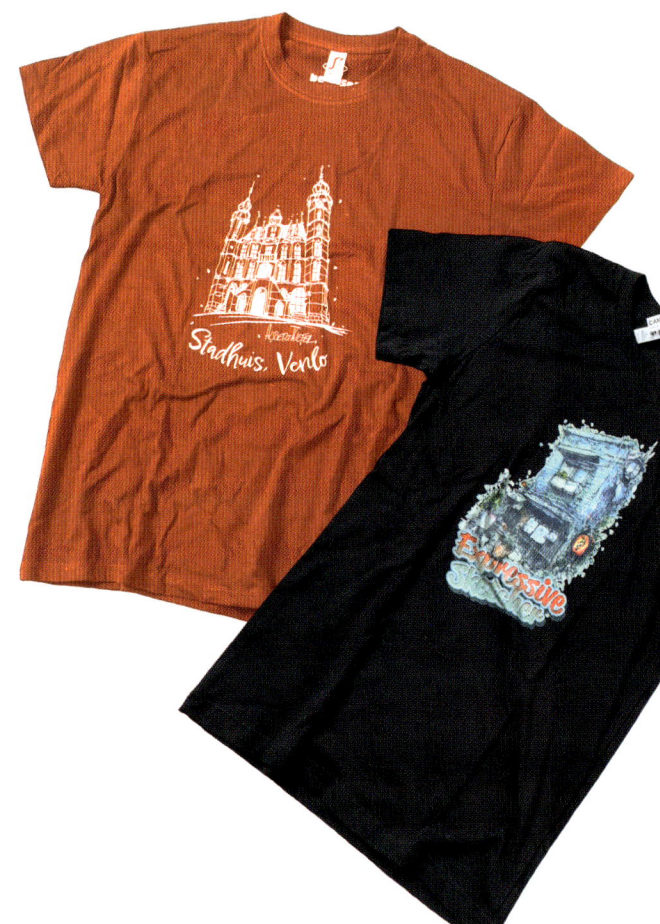

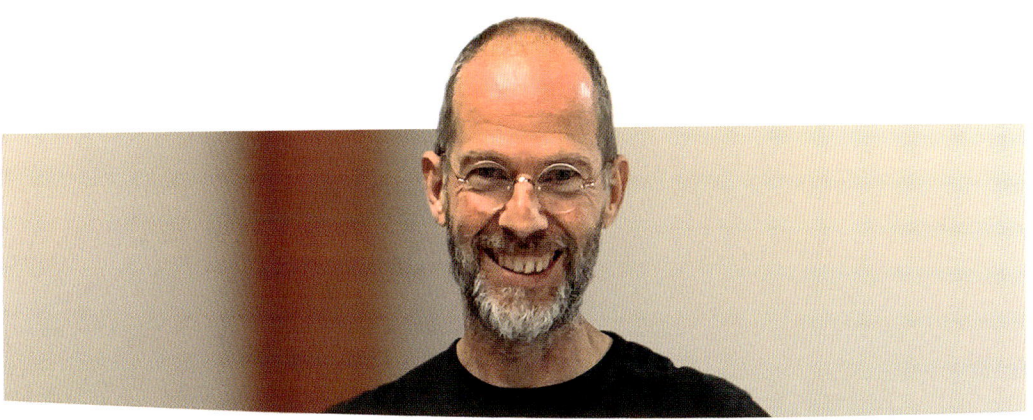
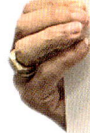
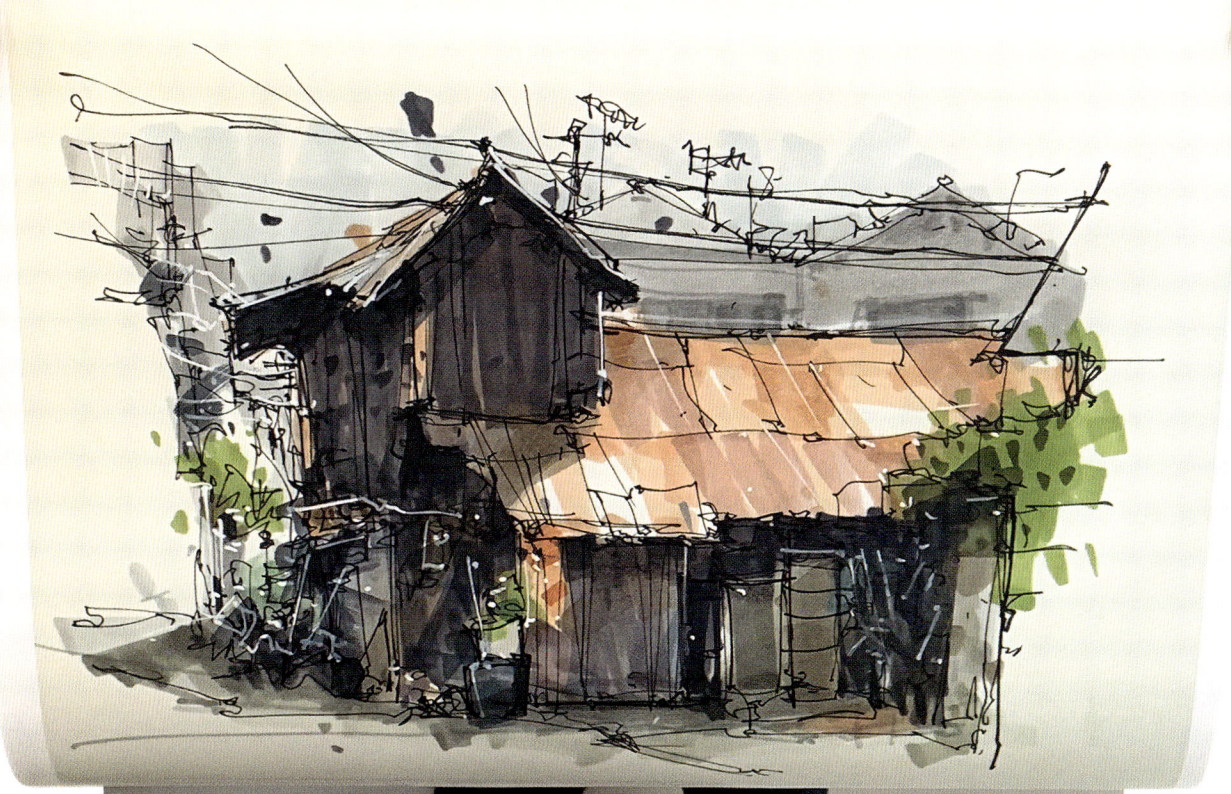
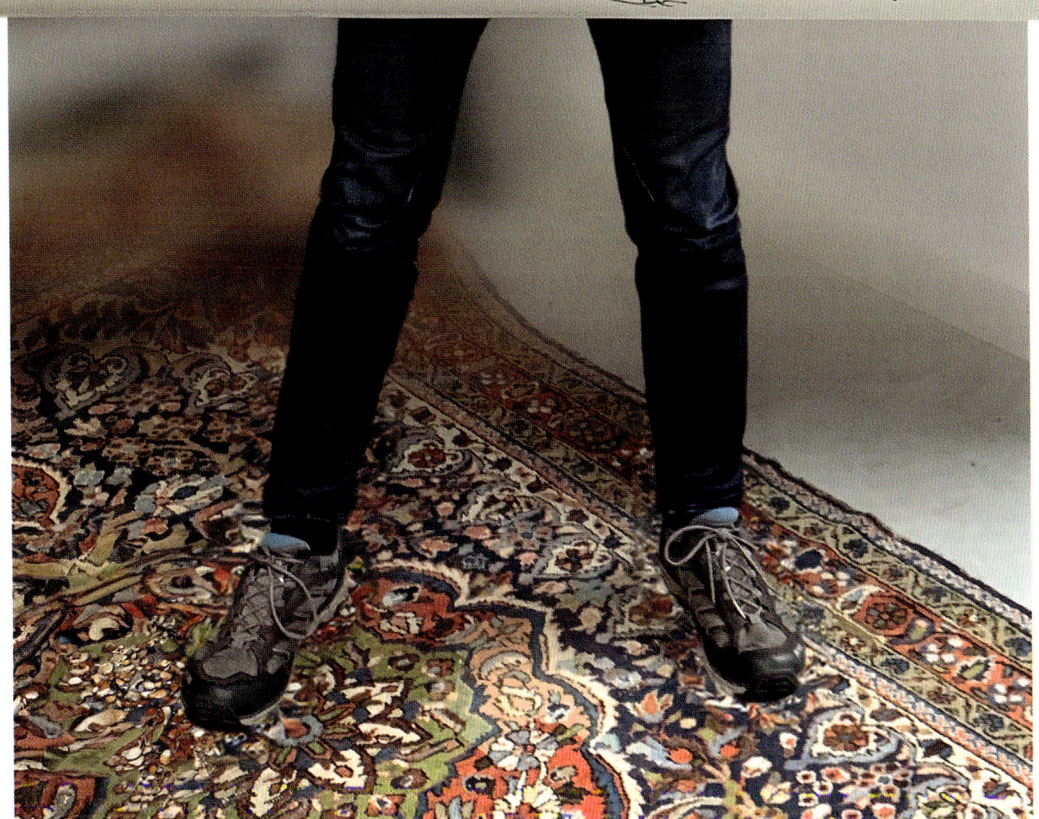

TIMELINE IN SKETCHES

Nobody just grabs a sheet of paper, immediately makes that perfect sketch, and on top of that, has a directly recognizable style. And of course, the same certainly applies to my work. Let me show you, in a series of sketches, how my style slowly evolved over the years.

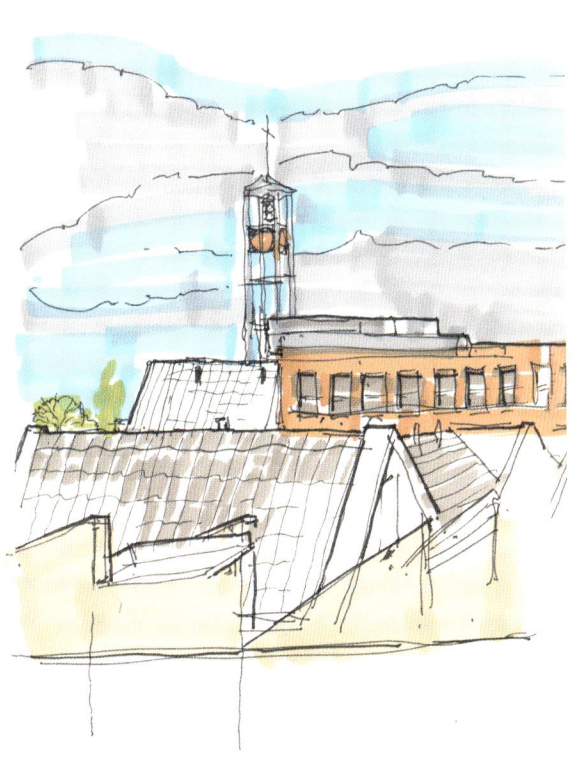

My very first sketch in a sketchbook in well over 30 years (2016).

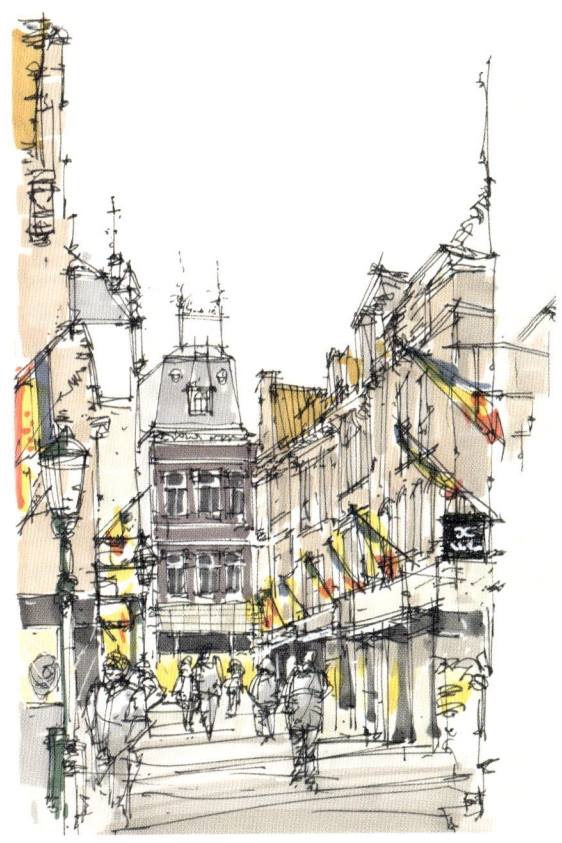

Working on perspective and rudimentary color treatment (2017).

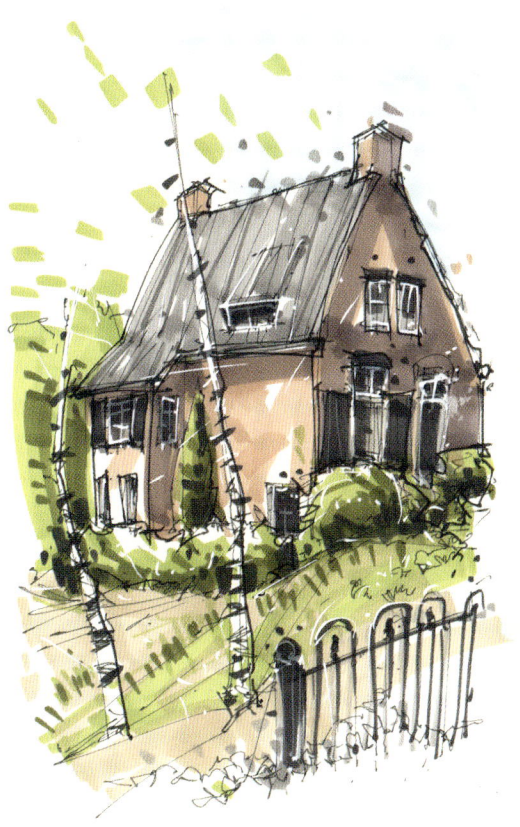

Very quick and dynamic sketching with even better color modulation (2019).

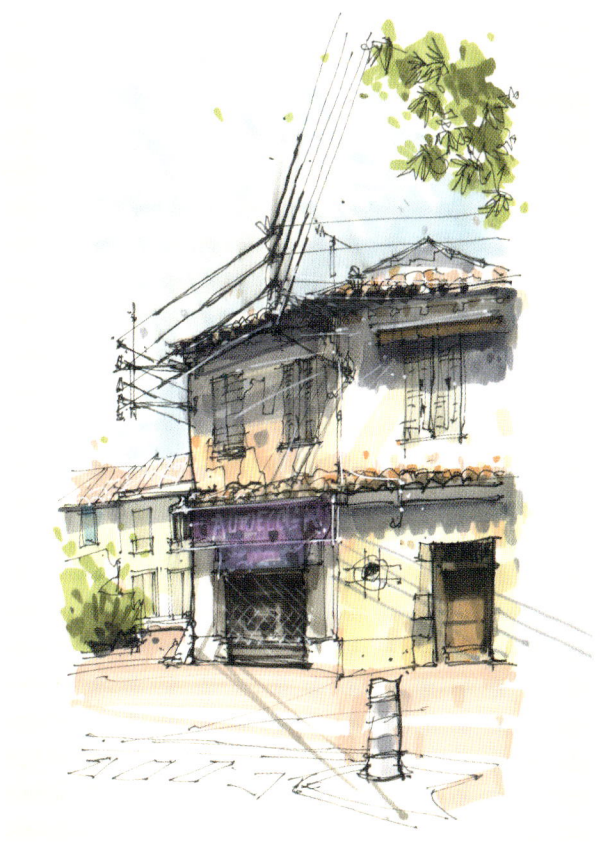

A holiday trip to France definitely changed my color palette (2019).

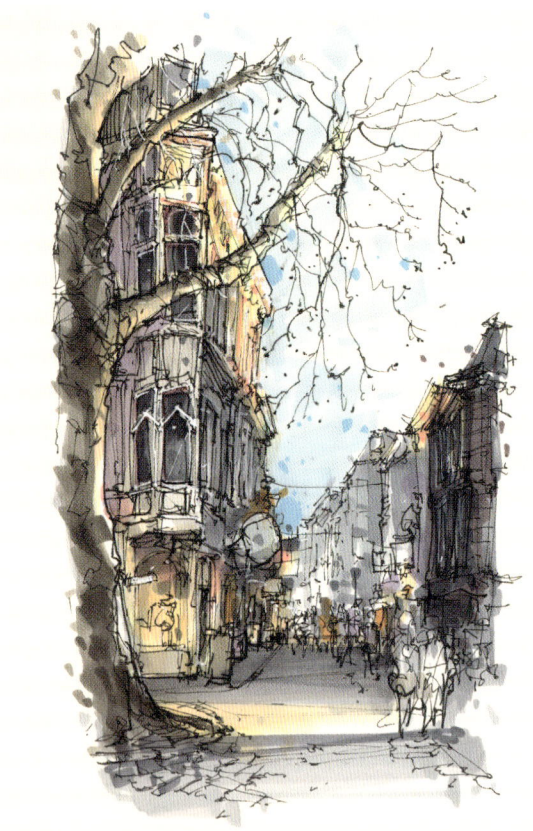

Using color to create atmospheric moods (2019).

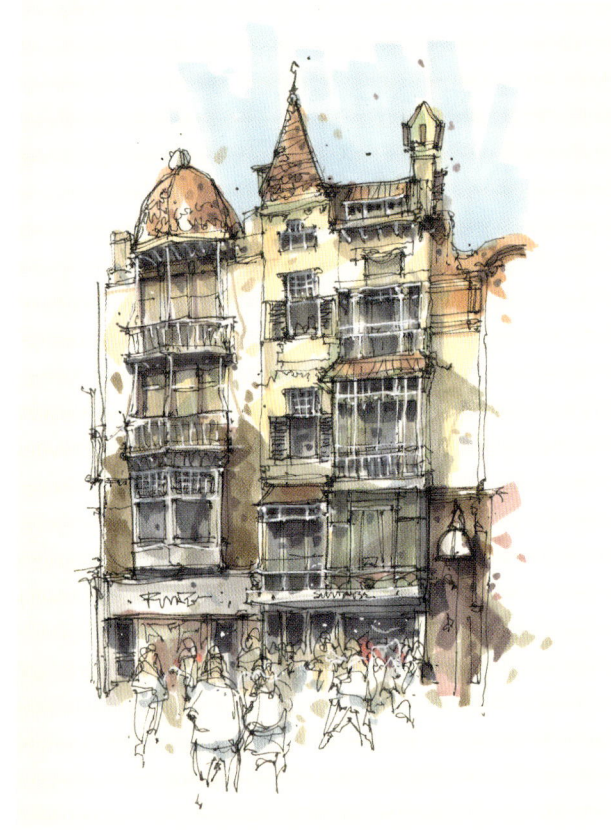

Trying to capture the grandeur of period buildings in local cities (2020).

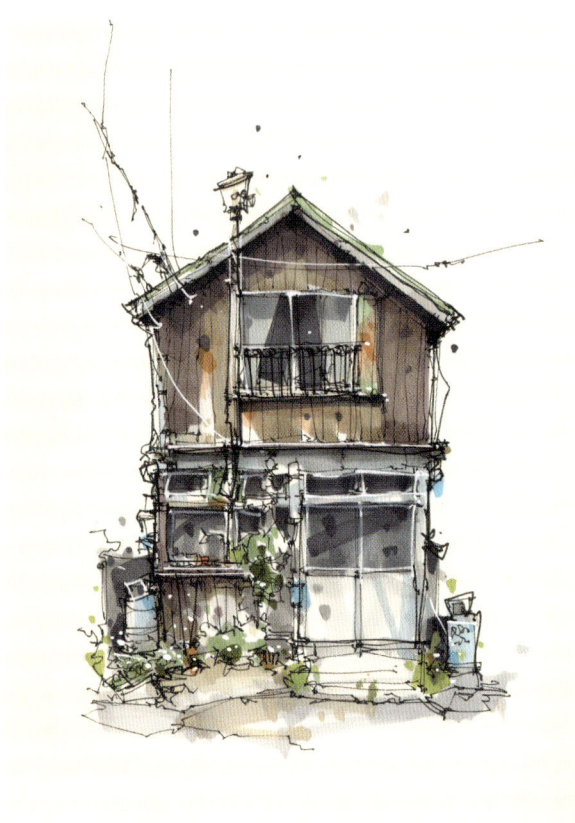

Turning point! My first Japanese house, due to COVID-19 lockdown (2020).

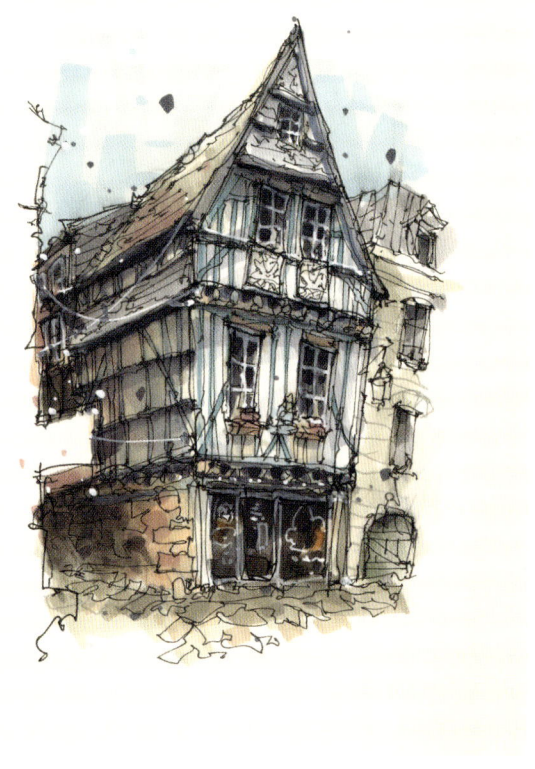

Varying the theme and sketching different types of houses, like half-timbered ones (2021).

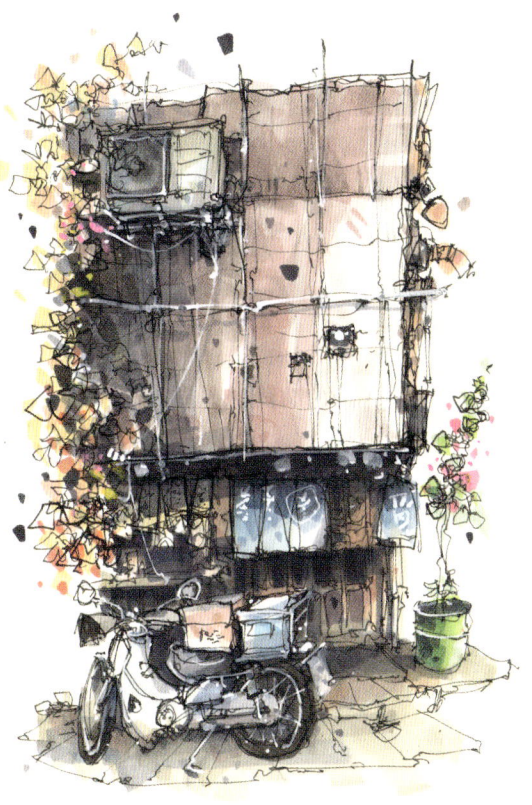

Using imagination to improvise on existing structures (2022).

Simple and powerful, this blue house is a personal favorite (2023).

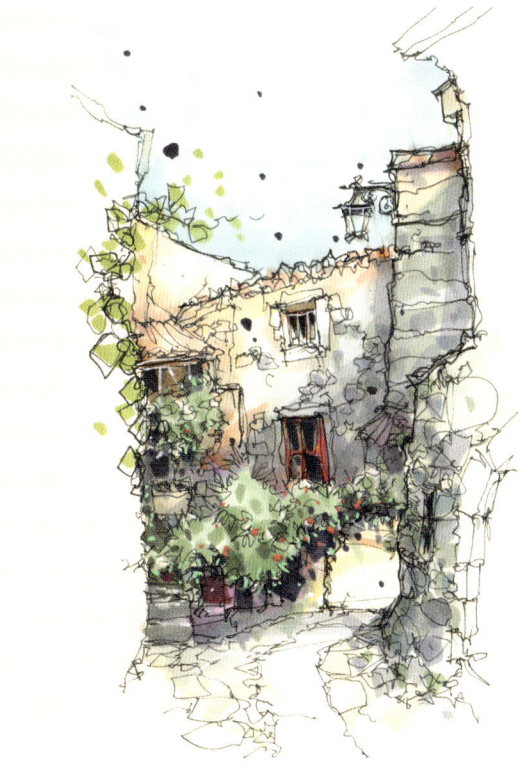

An Italian arched overpass. Always trying to vary the theme (2023).

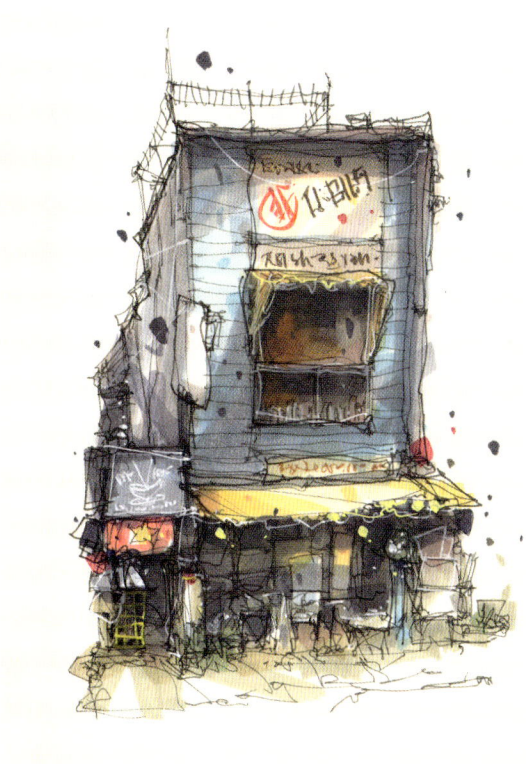

Experimenting with exaggeration and linework to keep developing my way of working (2024).

CLOSING THOUGHTS

Sketching houses is a wonderful and fulfilling activity. I hope that after reading and working through my book, it will give you as much pleasure as it has given me. I have described ways to approach sketching using some materials that you might not be familiar with. It's perfectly okay to find your own way and, very likely, tools to work with.

Sharing on social media can be very inspiring and even motivating to keep working. However, try not to fall into the trap of just sketching for likes. And, certainly, don't get discouraged if you don't get many likes. You are sketching for your own artistic expression and development in the first place. Keep that in mind, write it down, and never forget it.

I have quite a big following on Instagram, but sometimes I upload a sketch that I really have a good feeling about and it only gets a mild response. I have to admit that this sometimes affects my motivation. Thoughts of "why bother?" start popping up. But I still have that primary drive of regular sketching, because that is the only thing that will improve my work. Yes, there are also periods, even without the "likes" issue, that I feel I don't improve, or that older sketches were better than the work I make at the current moment. This is also normal! The key is, and always will be, to stay the course. Stopping at such a moment will solve nothing and will certainly not improve your work.

I wish to thank you for your trust in buying my book and I look forward to seeing your work online! Tag your sketches with #quartohousesketching.

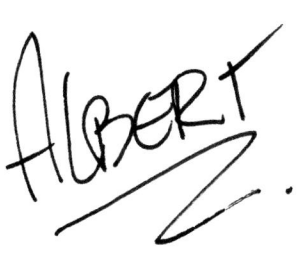

ACKNOWLEDGMENTS

Special thanks, first and foremost, to my wife, Niek, and our children, Bodi and Ivy. Without their inspiration, patience, and support, nothing would be possible!

A warm thank you to my mom, who has always supported me, no matter what crazy endeavor I wanted to engage in. Going to art school instead of finding a regular job? Sure . . . but maybe do an art teacher's training as well, just to be safe? Of course, so I did!

Thank you to my late brother, Ron. I miss you!

Thank you, Michelle Bredeson, for reaching out, being very patient with me, and keeping me on course whenever I sailed off in many different directions!

Thank you to the entire team at Quarto and Quarry Books: Marissa Mikolaities, David Martinell, Gabrielle Bethancourt-Hughes, Kerri Landis, Joy Aquilino, Anne Landa, and everyone from the editorial, art, production, and sales and marketing teams, for your part in making this book what it is.

PHOTOGRAPHERS

Thank you to the following photographers on Instagram who generously allowed me to use their wonderful images as references for my sketches.

bozlo
1chome_1banchi
alaingueranger
cittaaukoto_japan
cittaaukoto_se_asia
cristinaproietti_photo
doco_go
hacarchar_ken
hello.im.stefan
i_ba.118
japanpropertycentral
kozoan
manuuu_manuuu_manuuu
masktnak
moto_street_blues
non_sugar25
passionmontreal
quniko
retrog19
sparrowinlondon
storefronts.japan
themodernleper
tokyo.doorways
tokyo.doorways.by.day
tokyostorefronts
umitsubame0501
win022403
yosshytown
zigiottonadia

RESOURCES

I encourage you to try different types and brands of paper, markers, and other materials to see what works best for your sketches. These are some of the brands I use.

PAPER

Canson
Copic
Moleskine
OHUHU
Royal Talens
Strathmore
Winsor & Newton

MARKERS

Copic
Faber-Castell
OHUHU
Pantone
Sakura
Spectrum Noir
Staedtler
Tombow
Touch
Winsor & Newton

SKETCHBOOKS

Canson
Crescent
Etchr
Hahnemühle
Moleskine
Royal Talens
Sakura
Stillman & Birn
Strathmore

FINELINERS

Artline
Faber-Castell
Sakura
Staedtler
Uniball

ACRYLIC PENS

Molotow
Sakura
Tombow
Uniball (Posca)

STORAGE SYSTEMS

Spectrum Noir

ABOUT THE AUTHOR

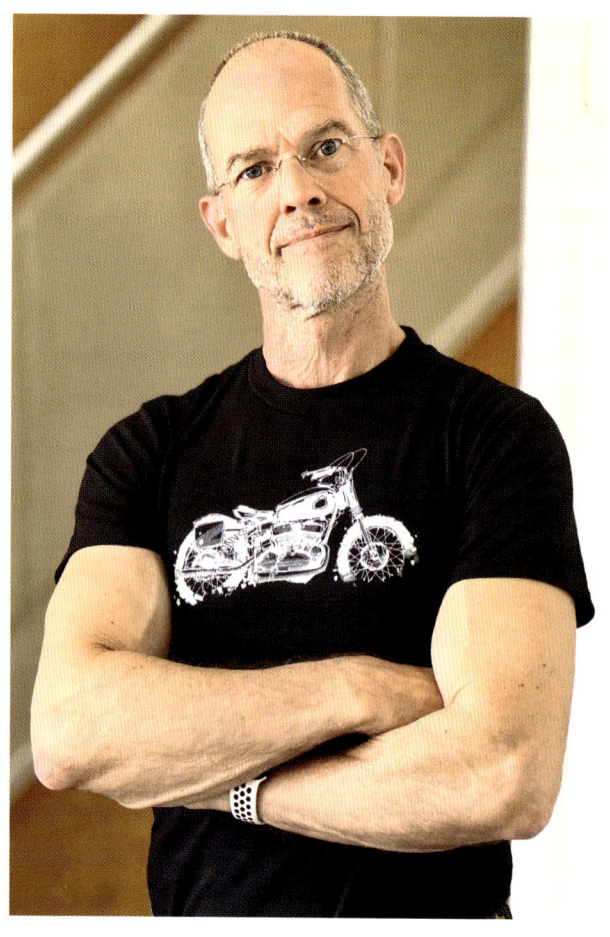

Artist **ALBERT KIEFER** studied drawing and art history at the Maastricht Institute of Arts in the Netherlands, then worked at a computer graphics firm, where he learned techniques like 3D modeling and rendering. He now works as a freelancer in the field of visualization, taking ideas and concepts and transforming them into pictures or animations. Albert later began to miss more traditional art forms and returned to his love for sketching. As he sketched every day, his style evolved into the expressive and colorful one that we see today. His wildly popular Domestika class, "Expressive Architectural Sketching with Colored Markers," has helped more than 70,000 students learn his approach to sketching. French publisher ELYTIS asked Albert to create two sketchbooks: *Au Japon!*, a collection of sketches of Japanese buildings, and *Harley-Davidson Sketchbook*. He also created a series of workshop videos for European art supply retailer Gerstaecker. Albert showcases his work on social media under the names Housesketcher and, recently, Ridesketcher.

HOUSESKETCHING ONLINE

Check out my various social media accounts to see more sketches and learn more about my sketching process.

Instagram
https://www.instagram.com/housesketcher

Threads
https://www.threads.net/@housesketcher

YouTube
https://www.youtube.com/@housesketcher

Domestika
https://www.domestika.org/en/courses/
3675-expressive-architectural-sketching-
with-colored-markers/housesketcher

Patreon
https://www.patreon.com/housesketcher

INDEX